Praise for *R*

"At age 17, Stokke was diagnosed wi the initial shock of diagnosis wore off, she was drawn to blogging as a way to document how she was living with disease. With a moving and honest voice, she takes readers along on her journey from diagnosis to despair to acceptance. . . . readers will find themselves rooting for Regine until the end." —*School Library Journal*

"'Face your fear. Accept your war.' [Regine's] writing is honest and raw, insightful and inspiring. While her moods swing with the course of her treatment and relapses, her outlook remains steadfastly positive throughout all but the most difficult days . . . an inspired read." —*Booklist*

" . . . Stokke's blog, a detailed account of her life before and after the diagnosis, drew many readers in her native Norway and became a bestseller in book form . . . Stokke's openness and honesty are the chief draw. . . . readers will feel as though they have truly come to know her . . . it's a rare, valuable window into life with a terminal illness." —*Publishers Weekly*

"*Regine's Book* is a haunting and inspiring and moving look at Regine's life, at the life of a young girl trying to be a teen when faced with the everyday possibility that this day may be your last good day. . . . A beautiful journey . . . Regine is the real deal, and teens will relate to what she thinks and feels. . . . Highly recommended for all collections." —Teen Librarian's Toolbox

"The heart of this book . . . lies in Regine's heartbreakingly honest and vivid emotions. . . . [Readers will] cheer with her when she makes it to music festivals, ache when she is in pain, and, most significantly, challenge themselves to understand what she is truly going through. *Regine's Book* is a simultaneously poignant and inspiring read, and the young woman's story is one that will have a lasting effect." —*ForeWord Reviews*

"An honest, gut-wrenching, raw, powerful and inspirational story told in Regine's own words. Although Regine only wanted to be ordinary, she was extraordinary . . . She urged people to register as blood and bone marrow donors. In those short 15 months, Regine accomplished a lifetime of work. . . . It is a book filled with so much love and grace." —Children's Books Heal

"This is unlike any other cancer book I've read. . . . It feels as if she is writing to you, and you get an inside look at her philosophies and opinions. The book is honest and painful. . . . Regine had an eloquent way of writing, and the comments she received and the posts her parents wrote were all very powerful. . . . I would recommend this book as one to take seriously and learn something from, because it is so meaningful." —YA Think, Burbank Library's Teen Blog

REGINE'S BOOK

REGINE'S BOOK

a teen girl's last words

Regine Stokke

35 Stillman Street, Suite 121
San Francisco, CA 94107
www.zestbooks.net

Norwegian edition published by Gyldendal Norsk Forlag AS, Oslo
© Gyldendal Norsk Forlag AS 2010
Published by agreement with Hagen Agency, Oslo, and Gyldendal Norsk Forlag AS, Oslo

This translation has been published with the financial support of NORLA.

Translated by Henriette Larsen

Medical consultant: Karen B. Larsen, MD

Library of Congress Control Number: 2013946665

ISBN: 978-1-936976-01-0

Manufactured in China
SCP 10 9 8 7 6 5 4 3 2 1
4500448575

Connect with Zest!
zestbooks.net/blog
zestbooks.net/contests
twitter.com/zestbooks
facebook.com/zestbook
facebook.com/BooksWithaTwist
pinterest.com/zestbooks

Foreword

Regine Stokke began to blog about her day-to-day life shortly after she was diagnosed with leukemia in 2008. Regine's stated purpose with her blog was to give people a sense of "what it's like to live with" such a serious illness, and in retrospect, her choice of words seems incredibly apt—because, up to the last, Regine was relentless in living every day to the fullest.

Regine writes openly about the emotional and physical aspects of her fifteen-month struggle to recover and explains how her disease impacts her life and her relationships. But that's only a part of her stunningly broad engagement with the world around her. She also takes painting lessons and shows her art at several shows. She goes to concerts and festivals whenever she can. She treasures every day she gets to spend with her friends and family. And, no matter how difficult things get, she remains a tireless advocate for cancer patients everywhere.

Regine's Book, as it appears here, is Regine's story as we encounter it on her blog—supplemented with diary entries, a selection of photos, comments from readers, and remembrances from those closest to her. The book became an almost instant classic in Norway, and we at Zest are proud to have brought this tragic but ultimately uplifting story to American audiences.

On the day she died, Regine's passing was mourned by family, friends, and thousands of other people who had come to know and love her through her blog. Regine's honesty and bravery are an inspiration, and through her eyes, readers will discover a more vivid world—and a new appreciation for art, life, and the power of the human spirit. We hope that you will gain as much from Regine's story as we have.

Hallie Warshaw, Publisher, Zest Books

Leukemia: An overview

To help understand Regine's disease and treatment, it may be helpful to have some general information about how blood cells are made, how different types of blood cells function, and how leukemia disrupts the body's ability to produce healthy blood cells. Blood cells are manufactured in the bone marrow (especially in the marrow cavities of the skull, breast bone, ribs, backbone, and pelvis) and can be divided into three main types, all of which play crucial physiological roles.

• Red blood cells (erythrocytes) carry oxygen to and remove waste products from the body's tissues.

• White blood cells (leukocytes) act as the backbone of the immune system and fight infections by destroying bacteria and foreign materials. There are five different types of white blood cells (neutrophils, basophils, eosinophils, lymphocytes, and monocytes), each with a particular function.

• Platelets (thrombocytes) control bleeding by helping to form blood clots.

All blood cells develop from "master cells" called stem cells. During their development, stem cells develop specific characteristics (in medical terms, they "differentiate") and ultimately mature into all of the peripheral blood cell types required for survival. Early on in their development, stem cells differentiate along two major branches and become either myeloid or lymphoid stem cells. These go on to develop into slightly more mature, but still primitive, "blasts." After many additional maturational events, the blasts become fully functional mature blood cells and find their way into the peripheral blood stream to perform the many important roles listed above.

Leukemia is a cancer of the blood-forming cells in the bone marrow. It is caused by mutations that occur early on in blood cell development, and it results in abnormal growth and differentiation of hematopoietic (i.e., blood-forming) cells. Leukemias can affect either the myeloid or lymphoid stem cells or both. So-called "acute" leukemias develop quickly and result in a proliferation of blasts—immature cells that are incapable of performing their normal functions. This results in many of the symptoms seen in leukemic patients.

Treatment

Chemotherapy is the main treatment for all forms of leukemia. Chemotherapy targets quickly dividing cells with powerful drugs. In the process, however, other quickly dividing cells (such as the blood-forming stem cells and hair-forming cells) are damaged as well. This results in the common side effects associated with chemotherapy: damaged immune system, damaged bone marrow, and hair loss.

A bone marrow (or stem cell) transplantation is a procedure that helps restore the blood-forming stem cells destroyed by high doses of chemotherapy. It involves "harvesting" healthy stem cells from a donor and transfusing the harvested cells intravenously into the patient's blood just like a blood transfusion. After entering the bloodstream, the stem cells travel to the patient's bone marrow where they start producing new blood cells. A bone marrow transplantation may be a harrowing experience due to complications, but for some patients it is the only option for a cure.

Some brief introductions

Julianne and Lasse: Regine's mother and father

Elise: Regine's younger sister

Josefine: Regine's cat

Eli Ann: Regine's best friend

Martin: Regine's closest male friend

Anne Marthe, Silje, Karina, and Marthe: Regine's girlfriends

Svein Kåre: blogger and lymphoma patient at Riksen hospital

Anne Marie: Svein Kåre's wife

Bengt Eidem: Norwegian politician and author diagnosed with AML (Acute Myeloid Leukemia) in 2005

Sofsen (Sofia Frøysaa): blogger and Regine's friend

Morten Krogvald: photographer and artistic director of Nordic Light International Festival of Photography

Ann Olaug Slatlem: *Nordic Light* volunteer who helps Regine exhibit and sell her photos

Maren-Sofie: blogger diagnosed with ALL (acute lymphoid leukemia) in 2006

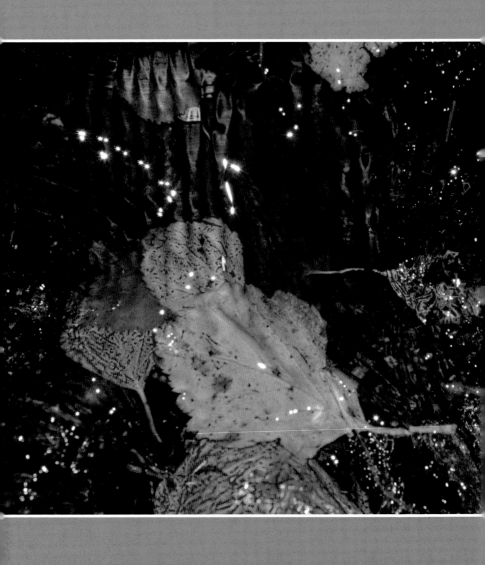

Autumn, 2008

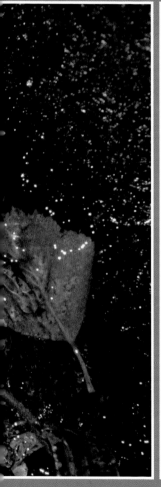

Autumn, 2008

On being diagnosed with a serious disease

Tuesday, November 4, 2008

Disclaimer: I've decided to start a blog about what it's like to get a life-threatening disease. Some of the content will therefore be too heavy for some people.

The whole thing started on Friday, August 22

I had just come home from school and didn't have a care in the world. Then Mom walked in, and right away I realized something was wrong. She had tears in her eyes. The doctor had called, and they suspected leukemia. I had to go to the hospital as soon as possible for a bone marrow biopsy.[1]

Right away I felt like my life had been shattered. I was crying my eyes out. I had a million conflicting emotions, but more than anything else, I was scared.

At the hospital in Kristiansund they started right out with the tests. The biopsy wasn't pleasant at all—I was shocked at how painful it was. And then I had to wait three hours for the results. I sat around at the hospital with Mom and Dad until the doctor came in. We were nervous and scared. He had tears in his eyes: I had leukemia, more specifically AML (acute myelogenous leukemia[2]). I could feel the fear spreading

---

1 In a bone marrow biopsy, small hollow needles are used to remove solid or liquid bone marrow tissue from the posterior pelvic bone for diagnostic purposes.

2 Acute myelogenous leukemia (AML) is a rapidly progressing bone marrow cancer in which abnormal, immature blood cells proliferate in the bone marrow and negatively impact the development of healthy blood cells. More information about AML is provided at the end of this chapter.

all through my body when he said that. Cancer. The whole family was crushed. I couldn't stop asking myself: Is this a death sentence? On Monday, August 25, we drove to Trondheim. That's where I had to go for treatment.

I was referred to the adult unit, where I had to take another bone marrow biopsy. This time it was going to be even more extensive than what they'd done before. In this kind of a biopsy, they have to drill out a bit of bone, and it's incredibly painful. I could feel my whole body jerk when the doctor yanked the piece out.

After that they showed us around the unit. It was like going down into hell. There was a small narrow hallway, old people, and one nineteen-year old. The first thing I thought when I saw him was "poor guy." The doctor told me I might not get a single room. Damn it. I started crying. In the end though, I got my own room, but it was small and run-down. How would I manage to stay there for so long? I wondered. We asked the doctor if I could be placed in the children's unit. At first, he said no, but we kept at it, and the third time he said he'd try to arrange it. It worked. Third time's a charm.

After a while I was moved to the children's unit. They told us the cutoff age was eighteen. So then why the hell was I put in the adult unit in the first place? I get irritated just thinking about it. I'm glad I'm not eighteen.

The children's unit was much better—renovated and a lot larger. The rooms were big and had flat-screen TVs. There was even space for my family. My mood got way better, even though I still felt really sick.

On Friday, August 29, Regine's mother, Julianne, wrote in her diary:

We're now at Day 5 in the Trondheim hospital, and it's been exactly one week since we found out that Regine had acute leukemia. Who could have possibly seen this coming? In the blink of an eye we went

from being blissfully unaware to being devastated by desperation, pain, and a sense of injustice. Why would this happen to our dearest possession—our lovely, intelligent daughter, who's never hurt anyone? Everything I've ever seen from her shows that she's a good person through and through. Still, it's happening; it seems unreal. Can this actually be happening? It's unbearable.

Our life was turned upside down in the course of a few minutes. Life isn't a given anymore (and that thought makes my head spin). It seems like I'm losing my grip on reality, like the world is slipping away from me, and it's driving me crazy.

The day before we traveled to St. Olav's Hospital, Regine and I went to the movies to see *Mamma Mia,* just to do something nice together so that we would be able to focus on something else for a bit. It wasn't easy to concentrate, and I cried during the wedding scene.

The bride was wearing such a beautiful wedding dress, and I imagined what Regine would look like in a dress like that. I want more than anything to see Regine in a dress like that one day. There were so many tears and it was so hard to sleep during the weekend before we traveled to St. Olav's. I was frightened of what lay in store for us, and worried about what Regine would have to go through—not to mention the emotional toll that this was taking on her.

When we arrived at the hospital on Monday, August 25, they took a bone marrow biopsy from Regine. It was brutal and painful, but she clenched her teeth and didn't make a sound. The doctors told us that there was no doubt that Regine had AML. After telling us what to expect and what could potentially go wrong, she was admitted to Children-4 (the children's unit for cancer and blood diseases) at 11:30 pm. They took great care of us there. The next step is to have another conversation with the new doctors.

Yesterday, they took another biopsy, and then inserted a Hickman line. A Hickman line is a long intravenous tube inserted under the skin on your chest, and it's what they use to administer chemo and take blood tests. Here at the children's hospital, the procedure is always done under general anesthesia, and everything went well. When Regine woke up, she was still under the influence of the anesthesia, and we got to hear quite a few interesting bits of information. Among other things, she admitted that she and Silje had raided our liquor cabinet and tried a bit of everything, and that they almost broke a cognac bottle. The way she said it, in a slurred whisper, was so funny that Lasse and I had to laugh. She also said that Elise should move here and take dance classes at Trondheim . . . so that she could try out for *So You Think You Can Dance*. But eventually the laughter had to stop. After a while, Regine said she wanted an assisted suicide.

Regine has highs and lows emotionally. Sometimes she feels like she wants to die right away to avoid all the pain. But other times (most of the time), she's optimistic, and says she's going to get through this, and that she feels comforted at the thought of all the people who love her. As she put it recently, "You won't get rid of me so easily."

I'm so impressed by Regine. She's so calm and strong and sensible—and talks very openly with doctors, nurses, and the other patients and their families. I'm proud of you, Regine: You're unique, and you're special, and I love you so much!

After a day of chemo, she's in pretty good shape and has a good appetite. Eli Ann and Anne Marthe visited this evening, and the three of them sat in her room and had a little pizza party together. The girls brought pictures and decorated the room with them, and Anne Marthe's parents gave Regine a basket of goodies too. Regine's good mood (partly the result of all the drugs) has been rubbing off on us, too.

On Sunday, September 7, Regine writes in her mother's diary:

I can't sleep, so I thought I would write something here. This is my first night alone at the hospital. I guess things are going pretty well so far, but I'm still really scared and afraid I might even have a panic attack. But they're taking good care of me here. I'm crying right now, but there are a few different reasons why. I read what Mom wrote and I was totally overwhelmed. And I'm thinking of all the great people who are supporting me through this tough time—both friends and family. Martin sent flowers twice. He really cares. Not many guys would do that.

Everyone tells me I'll get better, but I'm having a hard time believing them. I'm just so afraid of dying. What if I don't make it? What if

I die . . . ? I'm scared of death. I have so much planned for the future. No one should die when they're seventeen.

I've been sick for the last two days. Fever. Have started taking antibiotics and am getting better, but visually, things seem to shift around a lot. I'm told the entire family is really upset and feeling pretty down about all of this. It's unsettling. They wouldn't be so scared if they knew I'd survive. And if I die, what then? It will destroy them.

Why did I take things for granted before? Why did this have to happen before I had a chance to realize how valuable life is? I'm only seventeen. It's so unfair.

A bit about what I've been through

Wednesday, November 5, 2008

As a lot of people probably know, chemo can have some complications. I had to have the strongest chemo cycle that they can give—at least as far as I know. The cycle lasted six days. It actually went okay, all things considered. You have to be prepared for blood poisoning (which I got), and E. coli in the blood is a pretty big deal, but they gave me antibiotics, and things eventually got better. With a temperature of 105.8 (and chills), there still wasn't anything to do but just wait for my blood count to recover. Unfortunately, my platelet count was so low that my spleen started to bleed. It hurt so much I couldn't get out of bed.

About the same time, I got some unexpected and shocking news. The whole time that all this was going on, the doctors had been trying to determine what subclass of AML I had. Apparently it was really hard to figure out, and they thought it had to be something pretty unusual. The answer came three weeks after I had my first bone marrow biopsy. I had something called myelodysplastic syndrome ("MDS").[3]

MDS causes cells to function incorrectly; it makes the cells defective. I also have a defect in chromosome 7,[4] which just developed randomly. No one knows why it happened. Technically speaking, it's not leukemia, but it's just as serious, and it creates the same symptoms and often gets treated the same way. Without treatment, the disease will eventually evolve into AML. MDS is a very rare disease, especially among younger people.

The doctors didn't think I needed more chemo because the disease wasn't progressing that quickly, but then one day, a doctor came in with a serious look on his face. The white blood cell count had gone up in a short period, so a new chemo cycle was urgent.

I was totally shocked.

To function, the body needs physical activity, and that was pretty much impossible considering how much pain I was in. I was lying down for so long that fluid collected in my lungs. The doctors thought antibiotics would help, but after a while, it just got worse. My lungs filled up with even more fluid and I had a lot of intense pain, and it became really hard to breathe. Things just got worse and worse, and pretty soon I had to be moved to the main intensive care unit. The

---

3 Myelodysplastic syndromes (MDS) are a group of diseases in which bone marrow stem cells have genetic defects that prevent normal maturation into healthy new circulating blood cells. Patients may have similar symptoms to those seen in AML. Aggressive forms of MDS may evolve into AML and some patients may have intermediate features that are somewhat in between.

4 Chromosome abnormalities, or genetic defects, in bone marrow cells are the initiating event which may result in the development of leukemia or MDS. No one knows for sure why these mutations happen, but some of the possible causes include toxic exposures, infections, and radiation. Chromosome 7 abnormalities often correlate with a more aggressive disease course and may prompt earlier consideration of bone marrow transplantation.

nurses there were competent and easygoing, but I had such severe pain that I had to take morphine and a type of sleep medicine. A drain was put through my chest wall to remove the fluid. But finally it became so difficult to breathe that I was put on a respirator. I lay there for four days. It was horrible when I finally had to wake up, since it felt like I was suffocating. The first thing I did was try to remove the tube from my throat. I couldn't speak. So frustrating. I tried writing but it didn't go well because of all the medication.

Because I had intestinal inflammation, they had to feed me intravenously. But then my stomach kept getting bigger and bigger, so they had to stop the intravenous food. I couldn't eat or drink anything.

Eventually I was put into the children's intensive care unit. I don't know quite what to say about that, but it was really bad. I couldn't move for about two to three weeks, and I couldn't eat any food at first either. Eventually I was able to start on some real foods, but I didn't really want anything, and only ate about two pretzels a day. My stomach couldn't handle any more. I was also shown to have E. coli in my blood *again*. I was so cold that I shook. Thankfully, the antibiotics helped a lot. Someone gave me ten times more sleeping medicine than I should have had—just by mistake—which is pretty shocking, and makes me worried. Luckily they figured it out in time. A lot of what happened in the unit could have been avoided—but I won't go into that too much.

When I was well enough, I was moved back to the children's unit for cancer and blood diseases. Finally, I thought, a better environment. I stayed there for a week before I could go home. It came as a shock that it was even a possibility. I hadn't been home for ten weeks. My doctor and nurse were really happy for me. So was I (to say the least!). It wasn't that easy to get home though, because my body was dependent on morphine. I had some serious withdrawal symptoms but managed to travel home anyway without too many problems.

Tomorrow I'm traveling to Oslo for an informational meeting in advance of the upcoming bone marrow transplant. A donor hasn't been found yet, but they're saying it won't be a problem to find one; it just takes a while. Meanwhile, I'll probably need to stay in Trondheim for chemo.

The meeting in Oslo
Saturday, November 8, 2008

My first impression was good. We sat in the waiting room and were greeted by a woman with a big friendly smile on her face. She was to accompany us throughout the program. The schedule they gave us was packed: Among other things, I was going to have my heart checked, get X-rays taken, have my teeth checked, talk to a doctor and a nurse, have my lungs tested, talk to a previous transplant patient, and then do some other stuff too. This would all take place over just two days.

My first impression of the doctor was pretty good too—at least at first. But then, during the discussion about the transplant, he was really negative. He named all the possible infections and complications, and listed off everything you could die from. He also said it wasn't certain my hair would ever grow back, but I know it will. Most patients survive, but there are tons of obstacles along the way. Anyway, my first impression didn't last long—I can't wait to get out of here now.

In the afternoon I was scheduled for a bone marrow biopsy. I thought that I'd be drugged, and wouldn't actually feel anything. My doctor in Trondheim had even written a letter about that point exactly. Well, that's not how it turned out. I only got one shot of pain medication, and it didn't calm me down at all. I was still trembling and crying on the table when he inserted the huge needle into my pelvic bone to remove the bone marrow fluid. It was so painful.

It always hurts, but right now I'm even more aware of the pain because of everything I've already gone through. I'm so fed up with insensitive doctors.

At the meeting the next day, they told me that there were leukemia cells in my bone marrow. So now I'm confused. Which disease do I actually have? MDS or AML? The doctor said they still don't have control over my disease, and that I need another round of chemo. Damn it. In any case, the plan is for me to have another treatment, and they don't think I'll get as sick this time. I don't think I could take that. So that means maybe I'll get to be home for Christmas if I'm well enough, and then have the transplant right after New Year's. They've actually found a potential bone marrow donor, and several blood donors are available, too. Finally.

The next few months will be scary and really nerve-wracking, but I'm focused on only one thing: just getting through this.

The doctors and nurses say that I should not set my goals too high for the period right after the transplant. But I'm sticking with my plans, no matter what they say. On my eighteenth birthday, Martin and I are going out to dinner, and I plan to start school again in August. And when my hair grows back, I know exactly what I want to do with it.

Fortunately, I was allowed to go home again after the trip to Oslo—but I'm already due to start traveling back to Trondheim on Sunday evening. Every day I get to spend at home is as precious as gold.

The eleventh hour
Sunday, November 9, 2008

It's Sunday. I've been dreading it, but it's here. I have another hospital stay coming up. I'll be there tonight. How long will I stay this time, and more importantly, how sick will I be? I wonder if I'm ready for another tough treatment.

I've finally improved enough so that I feel okay about the upcoming treatment. I can walk normally and go for longer distances without collapsing—but now they're going to break me again, apparently. That's just how it is.

Since I'll probably be infertile after all of this, I've been asked if I want to freeze one of my ovaries.[5] I honestly don't know what to do. I'm not sure what I want to do in the future, but it's good to have options. And I think it's better to regret something you *have* done rather than something you haven't. Freezing eggs is still in the research stages, and so far no one has tried getting pregnant using this method. It would require in vitro fertilization, and they can't guarantee there won't be leukemia cells in the eggs, so it's possible that you would get the cancer back this way. But in ten to fifteen years, they'll definitely know more about all of this. In any case, it won't be possible before then no matter what, if it becomes possible at all. So what should I do?

Call me vain, but sometimes I sit in my bed and think about how I used to look. I miss the way I looked—especially my hair. I'm so worried it won't grow back, even though I know that only rarely happens. I want it just like it was before. Don't know if I could handle a drastic change. Of course it's pretty stupid to think like this, because first I need to get through the transplant itself. I want my whole self back.

---

5 Ovarian tissue freezing is an experimental option for preserving fertility in chemotherapy patients. Other options for preserving fertility include embryo freezing and egg banking.

Preparing for war

Monday, November 10, 2008

11:30 am

I'm sitting in my room in Trondheim right now. I haven't started the treatment yet, but I feel nauseous already. It makes me wonder if on this cycle I'll be really sick and have to throw up a lot. I hope not. At 9:00 pm the hell begins. I'm scared to death.

I just heard that some people rented out a movie theater for me this coming Thursday. That is so nice, but I honestly don't know if I'll be in any shape to go. I'll try at least.

So far today I've gone in for a bone marrow biopsy and for a chemo injection in my spinal fluid (but don't bother asking me why).[6] Well, at least it was done under anesthesia. I woke up with an intense headache that still hasn't gone away. I feel really horrible today. But right now I'm just waiting to speak with the doctors.

8:30 pm

It's half an hour before I start the chemo. It will go better this time. I'm much healthier now than I was before. Last time they gave me chemo while I had a fever, a spleen infarction,[7] and fluid in my lungs. I don't have any of that now. I have every reason to believe it will go better.

---

6 Leukemic cells can infiltrate the central nervous system (particularly the lining of the brain and spinal cord), which is less accessible to intravenous or oral chemotherapy than the rest of the body. Therefore, chemotherapy drugs must be infused directly into the cerebrospinal fluid, which circulates around the brain and spinal cord. This type of treatment is most likely to be required in acute leukemias.

7 An infarct is an area of tissue death that is caused by a lack of oxygen due to obstruction of the tissue's blood supply.

My mom, my dad, and I all had a lot of questions for the doctor. We found out that I have an aggressive type of AML due to my chromosome changes. I'm missing a chromosome 7, and one of my 3 chromosomes is also defective. Because this is aggressive stuff, they don't want to let anything go for too long, and they have to give me a powerful cycle to keep the disease at bay, so that I'm ready for the transplant and the chemo that comes with it. I have to trust that the doctors are doing the right thing. If the disease suddenly takes off, and too many cancer cells develop in my bone marrow, the disease would be very difficult to knock out. The doctor in Oslo is the best in the country, so I have no doubt that if anyone can get me healthy again, he can.

His plan is for me to have the transplant over the New Year. He wouldn't have done that if he didn't believe it was the right thing, because it's a serious procedure.

I was terrified when the doctor said that this was an aggressive type of cancer, but I have to believe that they're still the ones who are in control. So we now have a plan A, but we have a fallback plan too.

Tomorrow the whole Rosenborg soccer team[8] is visiting the unit. Rosenborg is my favorite team, so this is great news! I just hope I won't be too sick by the time they arrive. I don't think I will. And even though it's going to be embarrassing to meet them like this, it will be pretty cool too. We're going to eat pizza with them, and we've been told to bring our cameras and autograph books. So I guess every cloud has a silver lining—at least sometimes, anyway.

---

8 Soccer team from the city of Trondheim.

Riding the emotional roller coaster
Wednesday, November 12, 2008

This cycle of chemo has been pretty rough. I was right to be worried about nausea and vomiting this time around, but luckily there have at least been some periods where I haven't felt that bad. I found out that tomorrow could be the last day of treatment. It usually lasts for six days, so hopefully they know what they're doing. Anyway, after feeling so bad for so long, I'm at a better stage now. I've eaten more, and even been able to socialize a bit. I visited a boy named Patrick in his room. He's super nice.

I found out today that someone from the unit completed his transplant. He came back yesterday, I think. I'm so glad that everything worked out for him! His disease is pretty similar to mine, but there are a few key differences. He's in pretty good shape and was there only five weeks. It gives me a bit of hope, even though every patient is different.

Today I talked to the hospital pastor (which was kind of a surprise, at least for me). I felt like talking with someone, and even though the previous psychologist was a bust, I thought it was worth trying someone else. The nurses told me that he was really easy to talk to, and that he didn't force anything religious on you while he was here. He didn't say a word about Christianity. And of course that's not why I wanted to talk to him. I had just heard rumors that he was good at having actual conversations with young people. We had a deep and really thoughtful discussion. He brought out some thoughts in me that I didn't even know I had. I managed to put words to my fears about death and about everything that's about to happen. We talked about what death is, and how we imagine it, and that it's scary because we don't know what it means to not exist. And before he left, he told me that I was very unusual. He said it several times. He said I was good at putting feelings into words. That felt good to hear. I was deep in thought after that talk.

And so in other news, yesterday I actually talked to someone from Rosenborg! I wasn't in any shape to go downstairs, so I didn't think I would get to meet them (and I was disappointed because I'd been looking forward to it so much). But then a nurse came in and said that they could come to my room! That was so, so awesome. I actually felt better right before they walked in. The ones who visited were Per Ciljan Skjelbred, Roar Strand, Steffen Iversen, and Marek Sapara—so pretty much everyone I wanted to meet. I was scared that it would be awkward, but it wasn't. They were down to earth and easy to talk to. They asked me how I was, and I talked a bit about what I had been going through and what I still had coming up. I also gave them a hard time about Kristiansund BK beating them in the playoffs. Apparently they'd forgotten about that. ☺

Regine in her room at Trondheim Hospital on November 12, 2008 with Rosenborg soccer team players (from left) Roar Strand, Per Ciljan Skjelbred, Steffen Iversen, and Marek Sapara

A moment of reflection

Thursday, November 13, 2008

I t's strange, but the last few days might have been some of the best I've ever had. I've learned to appreciate the small things in life. I've felt joy, in spite of my situation. I asked Knut, the pastor I spoke with yesterday, why I sometimes feel happy when I don't really have any reason to. But do you always have to have a reason?

You get a new outlook on life in a situation like this. I wish there was another way to get this kind of a wake-up call. Maybe there is, but I just don't know about it.

I wish everyone could learn to appreciate life, even when it seems cruel. We have to stop demanding so much from life. You can't get everything you want. What if you end up with a mediocre existence? I definitely didn't want that before, but now it wouldn't bother me so much. After this, if my life becomes normal again, I think I'll appreciate it more, and be better. I won't complain anymore. (Of course, everyone complains sometimes—that's totally normal—but I won't complain like I did before.) I'm going to appreciate every day I'm here. Life is suddenly very important to me.

It's a bit of an art to teach yourself to appreciate the little things in life. At least, that's how it was for me before the illness. I took everything for granted. Now I've finally learned that lesson. I got to go to the movies today, and even that was huge for me. I actually started crying today when I was thinking about the last few days, but they were tears of happiness. I mean, I met some players from the Rosenborg team, I had the best conversation of my life with a very special man, and I went to the movies. I haven't felt this happy for a long time. Today I even found out that I might get to go home tomorrow. I wasn't expecting that. It depends on the blood tests tomorrow. It doesn't matter how long I get to stay there; each and every day I get there is priceless.

I finished the chemo today—finally. It's actually gone surprisingly well, and today I wasn't sick at all. But I'm curious about what will happen when my immune system is depleted.[9] That's when the problems start. I'm scared. The fear of death is always at the back of my mind, and even though those thoughts have been hard to fight today, this has still been a good day.

The same day, Regine's grandfather (on her mom's side) wrote this letter to his grandchild. In the text, he posted a framed wedding picture of her mother and father that Regine took right before she got sick.

To Regine:

Do you remember August 4, Regine?

When you took that picture of your parents, everything was perfect.

None of us knew what was about to happen. You were going on vacation and were looking forward to wonderful days in the south.

Resting at home, before the new semester at school, you got sick, and on August 22 everything suddenly went black.

The world fell apart and time stood still.

What happened?

Is it possible?

Yes, it is.

Like lightning from a clear sky, the disease struck. And since then we've lived in hell. You, Elise, your mom and dad, your grandparents,

---

9 Chemotherapy drugs are capable of killing rapidly dividing cancer cells, but they also suppress the production of the normal white blood cells needed for an intact immune system. After chemotherapy, the immune system gradually recovers as the bone marrow produces new white blood cells. Drugs (so-called "growth factors") can be given to speed up this process.

and all of your dearest ones. Your entire family is affected by your misfortune.

But there's a light at the end of the tunnel. That's where we're going: out into freedom. All the trials you've been through are now bearing fruit, and we're looking forward to life returning to what it was like when that picture was taken.

In difficult hours: Look at how happy your mom and dad were.

Life will be like that again, because love and happiness can move mountains.

In the future, what you've been through will just be a bad memory.

This picture is a reminder of how precious life is.

Take good care of it!

I want it all

Monday, November 17, 2008

So I actually got to take a trip home—who would have thought that would happen? Didn't know that you were allowed to take a trip home after such intense chemo. In any case, tomorrow the holiday is over. Then I'll have to get up early and get to the hospital at a reasonable hour. My immune system is almost gone now. Apparently that's when it starts to get really bad. Of course it won't necessarily be terrible, but it will definitely be challenging—that much I know. It's pretty rare for someone to go through a treatment like this and not get some kind of an infection when the immune system is gone. The uncertainty is the worst. You can be worried for no reason, or you can be unprepared if it gets really bad. I wasn't at all prepared for the last round. Didn't think it could get so bad. Of course I had to be the one to get this rare disease. I won't ever think, "It will never happen to me" again. I've realized that anything is possible; anything can happen to anyone.

I had hoped for visits from girlfriends when I was at home, but no one came. Everyone who could have come had a cold. And unfortunately, I can't be around anyone who's sick right now. It's a strict rule. If I catch a cold from someone, I can get really sick, and I'm extra susceptible to contagion. You have to avoid what you can avoid. I miss everyone here at home when I'm away. It's sad that I can't meet some of them while I'm actually at home. Fortunately I have lots of good friends who drop by Trondheim once in a while.

It's hard to hear about friends who are going to parties and having fun. I just get so jealous. I can't help it. I also want to party, dress up, and have fun. I miss that so much. Just to do my hair. Why did I complain about my hair before? My hair was nice. Now it's gone.

I don't mean that my friends shouldn't tell me about the parties they go to—after all, it's fun to hear about them. And we can't just talk about me. That would be too depressing. But I would do anything to be in their situation. I just want to say to everyone that's reading this, that you have to enjoy life—you have to live.

My mood swings annoy me: positive, negative, positive, negative. Why can't I just hit a switch that makes me positive all the time? I hate wasting energy on sadness. But that's probably impossible. In any case, I've made huge progress in that area. In the beginning I was almost always pessimistic. Whenever we talked about the disease, I could only say that I was going to die, that I wouldn't manage to get through this. But I've worked on myself a lot, to try to be more productive with my thoughts. The fear of dying is always there, but I've taught myself to push that fear to the back of my mind—so I manage to have better days with better moods. Sometimes.

The transplant is coming up fast. Six to seven weeks isn't very long at all. Not when it comes to things like this. I'm both dreading it and looking forward to it. It can be a beginning or it can be an end.

It has to be a beginning. I'm not going to be one of the unlucky ones this time. I just can't be.

The thrill is gone

Monday, November 17, 2008

I'm at home, looking through some old pictures on my computer. I miss the old days! I miss the laughter, the fun, the concerts, and all my friends. Someday I'm going to get my life back like it was before. Someday.

Regine's entries soon started to draw even more comments and responses. Her best friend Eli Ann's encouragement is representative of the 27 other people who commented on this entry:

Hi, Regine. Even though I talk to you every other day, I still feel that a small comment is in order. I think it's so great that you've started to blog, and found a way to channel your feelings. I hope people's eyes are opened to how fast things can turn upside down (something you know all about). Three months ago we sat at a café planning "drink night," and six hours later we were sobbing at the hospital. Life is full of surprises. You've been so strong, and I don't think anyone could imagine the hell you've been through over these last few months. When you get well, we're going to live life to the fullest, and restart all the trips, concerts, parties, and other everyday things we used to take for granted. Now you just have one thing to do: Beat the shit out of the cancer so we can all get you back. Love you. ☺

—Eli.

Home sweet hell
Friday, November 21, 2008

My immune system is gone. I'm in hell. It started yesterday. I could feel it in my body. *It's starting now*, I thought, but it took a while before the infection really kicked in. It finally happened tonight, right before I was going to bed. At first it was a fever, then chills. Some people might think it's just like shivering when it's cold out, but it's way worse. You have to just lie there while you go on shaking uncontrollably. I had trouble breathing and talking because of all the trembling. Finally I threw up, and that went on for a pretty long time before it finally stopped. That happened twice during the night. So it's pretty safe to say I didn't sleep at all. It's probably blood poisoning. They took blood samples and sent them to the lab for cultivation to try to find out what kind of bacteria might be in my blood. In the meantime, I think the antibiotics have worked—I've been in good shape since eight o'clock this morning. I hope it lasts.

I spent the night in the intensive care unit. I didn't want to go, but my blood pressure was so low that they felt like they had to send me there. Some of the doctors tried to force me to insert a urine catheter and a tube in my chest for draining fluid, but I refused. Why should I have a urine catheter if I can manage to go to the bathroom myself? It makes me so angry. For one thing, it's incredibly painful, and for another I can't get out of bed when it's in. Do they want that? I'm not supposed to be here for very long anyway, so why start messing with something?

I was right, and now I'm actually sitting back in the Children-4 unit again. Luckily the nurses down in intensive care were easygoing and helpful. But for all that, I don't want to be there. I hope there won't be any trouble tonight.

Daring

Sunday, November 23, 2008

Maybe I'm being a little too aggressive, but I think it sort of helps me accept things somehow. Up until now only my parents, sister, and nurses have seen me like this.

This post resulted in 220 comments. Regine's closest family, as well as strangers, wrote in to offer their support. Many also thanked Regine for her openness and for the way she put life in perspective. Here is a small selection:

We think you're beautiful like this too, Regine. (You have such a nice head.)
  —*Grandma and Grandpa*

Agree with Grandma and Grandpa. ☺
  —*Elise*

Can imagine that was a difficult decision but a step in the right direction. Still more proof that you are tougher than most folks. And as cute as always.

And it won't be like this forever.

—*Martin*

You've lost your hair for now, but what's important is that you haven't lost your clear head. No one can take that from you. Hope you have a good day. Many good thoughts from us in Kokkolav.

—*Grandmother and Grandfather*

Hi Regine, You got the same Christmas haircut that I did. No one knows how much this haircut costs, emotionally, until they've had to experience it themselves. I've also struggled through losing my hair, and after fourteen days I finally just cut it all off. But it resulted in lots and lots of tears. (I also had long, thick hair.) So now I suppose we're both skinheads—you and me! I think you're tough—and you have a gorgeous head!! I'm running around wearing hats and emergency wigs. It's good to have the hat at night—because it's cold when you're bald! Hope you have some good days now!

—*Leva*

You're totally tough! And do you know what? I've decided that when I have a baby girl, her name will be Regine! Just wanted to say that, since that's your name. ☺ Hang in there. You're gorgeous just the way you are! Hug from me. ☺

—*Marita Petrine*

I totally understand that you miss your beautiful hair, but luckily it will grow back. You're beautiful now, too! When you start to get better after a while, I thought it would be nice for you to try expressing yourself on a canvas.

I am sure it would be an interesting painting: expressive and full of feeling. Do you remember when you took a painting class with me?

You already knew that you had talent. One day when you feel like it, you can visit my home studio and paint (maybe bring a CD that you'd like to listen to at the same time). It is so liberating and it will definitely be an exceptional painting!!

> —*Best wishes from Else, who currently has a painting exhibition at the beautiful Water Tower in Nesodden.*

Waiting time

Tuesday, December 2, 2008

The reason why I haven't written in a few days is just because I don't have anything new to report. The last few days have all been spent waiting. Waiting to go home again. The only thing I needed in order for that to happen was for my blood count to go up again after the bone marrow biopsy—and it did! Thank goodness! I had crazy butterflies in my stomach before I got the answer. I was scared to death that the results would be bad, but it's actually never been better than it is now. I was so incredibly relieved. But there's one more thing the doctors have to decide on: Do I need a new cycle?

It's a month until the transplant and it seems unlikely that I can go a month without chemotherapy. Even if my bone marrow is fine and almost free of cancer cells, it doesn't mean that the cancer is gone. It will flare up again, but no one knows when. My doctor absolutely doesn't want me to do another cycle, so she's doing everything she can to reschedule the transplant for an earlier date. She didn't think it would work, and the doctor in Oslo is difficult to persuade. Maybe they don't have room for me yet, or maybe they don't want to have too many patients in the hospital over Christmas. Still, I have trouble understanding why it has to be so difficult to go down there now. I want to get started right away. Just to get it over with.

The upcoming plan is, as I said, a bit unclear, but we received a call from a nurse a while ago who said we should go to Oslo in a week to switch out my catheter (the one sitting in my chest, which is used to take blood tests and administer medicine) and to do the laparoscopic surgery[10] to take out part of my ovary. They'll also take a bone marrow biopsy to check if the number of cancer cells has increased at all. Then they'll revisit the question of when I'll have the transplant. There can still be changes. It will be interesting to see.

In the meantime, I'm going to enjoy myself at home!

A wasted journey

Tuesday, December 9, 2008

So we drove to Oslo, as planned. The first thing I had to do when we got to the hospital was to have a blood test and a bone marrow biopsy. We had to do it without anesthesia this time too, but I still didn't dread it as much as last time. The doctor gave me some pills to relax. I really wonder what kind of pills those were, since I got a laughing cramp from them, even though I didn't have any real reason to laugh. I want more of those pills.

The bone marrow biopsy was taken from my chest bone this time. It was painful, but it was definitely better than before. Everything is better when the doctor is nice.

Afterward we talked a bit to the unit nurses. I was going to get to see an isolation room. It actually looked pretty good (for a hospital room, that is). The room was pretty big—it had a DVD player, a TV, and a big bathtub. It was even possible to walk outside in the fresh air.

---

10 In laparoscopic surgery (also known as keyhole surgery) operations in the abdomen are performed by inserting a camera through a small incision.

On the other hand, it's not so exciting to know that I'll have to be here for up to six weeks.

Later in the day, we were supposed to speak with the gynecologist. This turned out to be a pretty unpleasant meeting. I got the unexpected news that I was infertile. The way she said it ("the case is hopeless") wasn't very nice either. It turned out that they knew from when I was there before that I was infertile! You have to start wondering what they're up to. They'd dragged me down to Oslo for no reason at all. They clearly knew from last time that I was infertile. I got seriously annoyed and frustrated. I wasn't ready to hear that I was infertile. I had been going around thinking I had the option of removing some eggs. How could they be so careless!? Even worse, I had a bone marrow biopsy when I didn't even need one. The reason for the Oslo trip was clearly just for the operation. Nothing else was going to be done. Well, at least the bone marrow biopsy turned out fine.

I've cried a lot. I'm so sad, so frustrated by everything. It's incredibly tough to experience defeat after defeat. When will all this stop? Just when I think everything is as bad as it can be, it gets even worse. The transplant—I'm dreading it so much. What else is coming?

I imagine the pains I'll have to go through, and I'm scared. The plan is for me to be admitted to Oslo on January 5. It will be a long and anxious wait. In the meantime, I'm at home, and I hardly know anything about what lies ahead.

Chemotherapy again . . .

Friday, December 12, 2008

Today I learned that I need a new cycle. I actually knew that this was coming. Still, it's not good news. Luckily, this cycle will be

Regine and Eli Ann, before Regine's diagnosis

milder. The goal, for me, is to just not get any sicker, but you never know. Have to start tomorrow or Saturday.

The question is: Will I get to go home for Christmas?

When I get well, I won't be able to stop smiling.

No one knows

Saturday, December 20, 2008

You've probably started wondering if everything was okay, since I haven't written for so long, and so I just wanted to let you know that everything is going fine with me! I've been at home since Monday now, and things have been pretty good. Cross all my fingers that I get to be at home right until January 5. I can't handle another blood poisoning. I want to stay healthy. I've received the treatment schedule from Riksen[11] now. That's when you become aware that it's really approaching. I feel a little reassured when I read the letters and brochures from Riksen. It says you should take things with you—things like cards, board games, etc., to occupy yourself while you're there. It gives me a tiny hope that the stay will be pretty easy—that it will only be kind of boring—but inside I still know it will be really tough.

I'm so incredibly tired and feeble lately. But I hear that it's normal to feel that way after everything I've been through. I wonder if you know what I mean by the word "feeble"? When I say that I mean seriously incapacitated by fatigue. I can't even do the most basic tasks—like buttering a piece of bread—without having to sit down after a few seconds. Luckily it's not so bad all the time.

Over the last few days, I've been able to go to the physical therapist, get home schooling (I took a history test), visit with friends who stopped by, and even paint a bit. Good to do some "normal" things, even though everything here is pretty far from normal. So while everyone else was at the Christmas dance, and going to parties and having fun, I sat at home and studied for a history test.

My blood values are sinking (totally normal), and as of yesterday we found out that I need some more blood. And that's not an easy task here in the city. I have to have irradiated blood because of the transplant, and they don't have that here. So they have to order it from Trondheim. In fact, my blood is going to come with the Hurtigruten,[12] but I won't get it before tomorrow. I'm a little worried that it will take too long, but I'm still counting on it going well overall.

---

11 The National Hospital located in Oslo, Norway.

12 A passenger, freight, and tourist line with ships sailing along the coast every day.

Yesterday I read online that bone marrow transplants don't help with MDS. Got so irritated with both the internet and myself. I shouldn't read anything about it, since this isn't relevant anyway. All the doctors say I'll get well, and I trust them more than the internet.

Old branches are the hardest to break
Thursday, December 25, 2008

Christmas Eve was much better than expected. I wasn't actually looking forward to it very much. Was thinking the whole time that I didn't need gifts, and this year I hadn't bought any either. But Christmas Eve is about more than gifts, of course. The nicest thing is being able to spend time with family. Grandma and Grandpa visited and so did my cousin. It was super nice and everyone gave super nice gifts. Among other things I got a flatscreen TV (I'm so spoiled!), a dress, CDs, DVDs, makeup, and lots of other stuff too. The best gift I got was from my two best friends. They made a photo album with a lot of pictures in it. The pictures were of us for as long as we've known each other. In other words: a successful evening all around.

My thoughts go out to everyone who had to spend Christmas Eve at the hospital. I hope you had an okay time, all things considered, even if it wasn't the same as being at home. Luckily Christmas comes around every year. ☺

Losing sight of the goal
Sunday, December 28, 2008

It's a little more than a week until I go to Oslo. (Help.) And I have a cold. (Bad timing.) Hope I get well before I travel. I'm thinking about the transplant a lot lately—probably way too much. Hardly five minutes go by without me thinking about it. I wish I was going into

"Sorrow's Chamber"
Tuesday, December 23, 2008

The echoes of silence set the hour.

Choked by the chains of depression, I fall away.

I won't be trapped behind the wall of sadness.

I'll finally do what I want—I'll leave.

Did I drink too much from the cup of life?

Did I take happiness for granted? Was I vain?

My fight against this emptiness, this drunken sense of death,

Is all that I have left . . . It's all that's mine.

In my loneliness I still know

That I have none to thank but myself.

This is why I remain calm,

As the rope pulls tight around my neck.

—*Dimmu Borgir**

Norwegian black metal band that derives its name from an area in Iceland called Dimmuborgir, which has unusual volcanic rock formations. Dimmuborgir means "dark cities" or "dark castles" in Icelandic, Faroese, and Old Norse.

this without any ideas or knowledge of what was about to happen. Ignorant about all the painful things that can happen. Now I know way too much. I've read a lot about the transplant. Read about the pain. Read about the relapses. I've never dreaded anything as much as this. I'm scared. More accurately, I'm terrified. Thinking of death. Death is sinister. That's what I fear most of all right now. I don't want to die and be separated from my friends and my family. Don't want to leave them behind, depressed. I want to live more, experience more. Will I ever get out of here, out of this prison?

Eighty-seven bloggers commented on Regine's entry, among them her good friend Martin, and Anne Marie, a relative of cancer patient Svein Kåre:

As I've said before (the last time being earlier today), you have nothing to fear. This is a war, but the resistance movement on your side is effective. ☺ In a while, and probably sooner than you think, you'll be able to look back on what's going on now as a finished chapter—and then you can start a new one.

Because with every day that passes, you're one day closer to getting well—or getting free, to borrow your metaphor.

—*Martin*

Hi, my dear Regine. I know you've visited and read about us. I hope we'll get to meet you when you come here—we'll probably be here until you come. It's a fight . . . it's tough . . . but if you fight to survive, you can do so much!!! You find strength you had no idea you had, and the bad/sucky days all end eventually. There are better days ahead, I know it. You've had bad experiences already because of the disease, and that helps you, even if it doesn't always feel that way. Knowledge is both good and painful. Use what you've learned to make yourself strong and prop yourself up. The fact that you're able to read about others shows how incredibly tough you are—most people aren't brave enough! Hang in there! We're rooting for you!!! Over here we've celebrated Christmas Eve today and had a great time!!! SK has gotten much better and we're doing well!! I wish you a speedy recovery from your cold!!!

—*Big hug from Anne Marie*

What's MDS/AML and what's it mean to get a bone marrow transplant?

Tuesday, December 30, 2008

First of all I want to say thank you so much for all the great comments on my previous post (and on all my other posts). You all are just amazing!

A lot of you ask and a lot of you probably wonder what both of my conditions are, and what a bone marrow transplant is. So I thought I could write a separate entry about that. It's not always easy to understand what all of this is about and I'm not sure if I totally understand it myself.

You can find all kinds of strange and varied information about these things on the internet. (I've been told by my doctors not to read about this stuff online. They say I should only refer to the information they give me.) Some internet sites say that you can't recover from MDS, but that's not true—not anymore. Still, some other web pages have some good general information about this disease.

A lot of people also think that a bone marrow transplant is an operation. That's not true either.

Giving bone marrow is totally safe, and I encourage everyone to become blood and bone marrow donors.

MDS—Myelodysplastic syndromes

Myelodysplastic syndromes encompass a variety of conditions related to damaged stem cells in the bone marrow. Stem cells give rise to all other blood cells, so in other words, all blood cells develop from stem cells. Both the number and function of the cells can be affected by this syndrome. The classification of MDS is based on which type of blood cell is affected.

Patients may be asymptomatic for long periods of time. Symptoms arise due to loss of the normal function of peripheral blood cells.

Fewer red blood cells (anemia) can lead to fatigue, shortness of breath, increased heart rate.

Fewer white blood cells can result in recurring infections.

Fewer platelets can cause bleeding into mucous membranes and skin.

The disease can become so serious that, among other things, it can turn into acute myeloid leukemia.

AML—Acute myeloid leukemia[13]

This is a form of cancer in which immature blood cells in the bone marrow, so-called myeloid progenitor cells, grow and divide uncontrollably. Myeloid cells are the precursors of other blood cells, including red blood cells. The uncontrolled growth of myeloid cancer cells results in fewer normal blood cells, i.e., fewer red blood cells, white blood cells, and platelets.

_____

13 The following medical information comes from online health website www.pasienthandboka.no.

AML can be sub-classified into different types based on the appearance of the cells and their biochemical properties. The malignant cells can be seen in both the bone marrow and peripheral blood. Symptoms usually develop over a relatively short period of time. Symptoms include:

- Fatigue and tiredness due to fewer red blood cells (anemia);
- Frequent infections due to decreased immune function (fewer white blood cells); and
- Bleeding in the skin and mucous membranes due to fewer blood platelets.

Other symptoms can include blurry or double vision, rashes, headaches, nausea, and vomiting (due to irritation of the meninges or lining of the brain). Some individuals complain of bone and joint pain. Up to 50 percent of patients have had symptoms for three months before being diagnosed.

Bone marrow transplant (stem cell transplant)[14]
This is a type of treatment only offered to patients with diseases with a very bad prognosis—diseases for which life expectancy would be limited with any other treatment. An allogeneic stem cell transplant means that the patient receives cytotoxic drugs to destroy the diseased bone marrow, which is then replaced with healthy bone marrow from another individual. The treatment is so toxic that there are many potential complications, including death. Before being offered this treatment, the patient's condition is carefully reviewed by a health care team.

At the time of bone marrow donation, a healthy donor is admitted to the hospital. The bone marrow is aspirated from the pelvic bone.

---

14 From the Riksen Hospital.

The donor is under full anesthesia. Donating bone marrow is completely safe.

The bone marrow from the donor is given to the patient through a catheter eight days after the chemotherapy. It is similar to a long lasting blood transfusion. The stem cells find their way to the bone marrow, settle themselves in, and begin to form blood cells. No one can explain exactly how this happens. It takes about two weeks for new stem cells to start producing blood cells. The day the patient receives the bone marrow is called day zero, and is the beginning of a waiting period, which can be a significant ordeal for the patient and their family. From now on, it's the supportive care that is most important. This includes receiving blood products and antibiotics until the new bone marrow starts functioning.

A look back—Part 1

Wednesday, December 31, 2008

I can clearly remember the day I was at my primary care physician, and she told me I might have to have a bone marrow biopsy. I had gone to the doctor so many times since May, and now it was August. My doctor did a physical, but didn't find signs of anything serious. She listened to my heart, and it beat rapidly. That wasn't so strange, I thought, but I was still in tears. My doctor told me it was nothing to be worried about. If they were going to take a bone marrow biopsy, it was only to rule out anything serious. This was definitely nothing serious. It was strange leaving her office with the thought that it might be leukemia. I knew something was wrong with me, and even suspected leukemia. But I didn't really think it would be.

I'd just started the second year of high school, and I'd been looking forward to it. I thought this year would be better. Things were finally falling into place. But it didn't turn out that way. I'd been going for three days when the terrible news came. I remember one particular day around then, in class, when we were supposed to write about our plans for the future. Ironic, I thought. I wrote and wrote, barely managing to hold back the tears. I really wanted to live and get to experience what I was writing about. I was thinking I might not have a future if it was leukemia. But I managed to convince myself that of course it couldn't possibly be anything so serious. That same day I found out that it had really happened: I had it. My world collapsed. Strange to think that I was supposed to go to a party that day. Everything happened so fast. My freedom was ripped away from me.

I often think about how things could have gone if they hadn't discovered the leukemia that early. What if I hadn't gotten such rapid heart palpitations while I was on vacation in Rome?[15] There wouldn't have been a reason to contact my uncle, who's a heart specialist. If I hadn't gone to him, they wouldn't have discovered it when they did. Then I would have had to go to my own normal doctor—definitely without making any progress there either. It could have had deadly consequences. But it didn't seem like she really thought it was leukemia. Don't misunderstand me. I'm not blaming my doctor. Who really thinks that a seventeen-year-old could have leukemia?

A look back—Part 2

Thursday, January 1, 2009

Once in a while I think that this is a kind of test I've been made to take. A trial I have to go through. Inside I know I can get through it. I'm not dissatisfied with my life anymore. I want to fully

---

15 Palpitations can be due to anemia (decreased hemoglobin), which decreases the circulatory system's ability to deliver enough oxygen throughout the body. An increased heart rate is one way to compensate for decreased oxygen carrying capacity.

experience it. To be confident that it won't suddenly vanish. I can't lose it. Sometimes I also feel so guilty, as if I deserve this somehow. Because I was so dissatisfied before. Of course, I wasn't dissatisfied all the time—don't misunderstand me. I actually did like my life. But lots of times I was. And I regret that. I regret it so much. Why couldn't I just enjoy it? The only thing I did was wait, wait for it to get better. To get better than it was.

Ever since elementary school, I've waited. Back then I looked forward to middle school, when I thought everything would get better. But then I started middle school, and things didn't change very much. I can understand why I was dissatisfied in 8th grade. A lot of people weren't very nice. People were mean because I was smart. And they were mean because I was thin. Their reactions really affected me, and I felt insecure, and that insecurity never really disappeared. I cried a lot and was always in a bad mood. I hated how I looked.

Luckily, things changed. In 9th grade things got much better. I had more friends and there were fewer mean comments. I cut and colored my hair, which made me prettier. I became more self-confident. But I still wanted something more from life—and meanwhile the insecurity was still there, just to a lesser extent. In 10th grade my friends and I spent our time looking forward to high school.[16] That's when things would get better, even though the middle school was excellent. When I think back on middle school now, at least the last part of it, it was actually the best time of my life. Things were great.

Finally I started high school. Things weren't as expected. I was hoping for so much. Because of my insecurities, I held back, and didn't get to know many new people. I guess I wasn't really open to getting to know them either. Now I regret not getting to know them.

---

16 Norwegian schooling generally breaks down into three parts: elementary school (grades 1–7 for ages 6–13), middle school (grades 8–10 for ages 13–16), and high school (grades VG1–VG3 for age 16–19).

They seem like a great group! They sent me a great card and gift when I got sick. I hope I get to know them because I really want to. Definitely.

I spent my first year at high school complaining a lot. I'd done things I wasn't proud of and I really regretted them. I guess I never managed to get over that regret. After a few months, I got a boyfriend, and I was happy. I'd wanted a boyfriend for a long time. But my love life wasn't quite what I expected either. It ended, and when it did I was crushed and hurt, and it took a while for me to get over it.

My girlfriends and I hung out a lot, and whenever we got together, we sat around and complained. Things were never good enough for us. We wanted to have fun all the time. We'd been on a language trip and to a concert that year and we were happy about that, but we weren't as satisfied as we should have been. We wanted to go to concerts all the time, and go to crazy parties. But it wasn't like that, and so we had to whine about it. We didn't know much about life back then. And little did I know that my life would soon be turned completely upside down.

This summer I had so much fun. I went to the Hove music festival, and to Metallica and Iron Maiden concerts, and I went to Rome. I did lots of great things and got to know lots of new people. But the whole time, I felt sure that something was wrong with me. I almost fainted a bunch of different times. I found blue spots on my feet, and bled from my gums. I was scared too. I knew these were signs of leukemia. I also had lots of infections: a sore throat, a urinary tract infection, a sinus infection, etc. When school was about to start, I felt better, and things seemed to be working themselves out. *Seemed* to be. I was wrong.

I just want to say this: You shouldn't wait for life to get better. You have to realize you can't have it all, and every once in a while, you're sure to experience a setback. I was always focusing on the future. Try instead to look at what you have in the here and now, and enjoy it. Be satisfied, and if you aren't, do something about it. I can't do anything about my life right now. I'm not in control anymore. If this hadn't happened, I would probably still just be sitting around waiting for college to start, because just like before, I would think that only then would things start to get better. Maybe this had to happen for me to open my eyes to reality? In any case I've gotten a new perspective on life. I just hope I get another chance.

Hanging out with friends.

A look back—Part 3
Sunday, January 4, 2009

I remember the chaotic weekend before I traveled to Trondheim. All I did was sit around anxiously waiting to leave. I spent the entire weekend with my mind spinning around in circles. I was so scared. The only certainty in my mind was that I was going to die. While I was waiting, I looked through old diaries. Somewhere I'd written, "Who knows what could happen in two years?" I was pretty freaked out, because I wrote that almost two years ago.

Today I took the diary out again, and read what I'd written. I get sad and angry when I read some of it, but some of it's well written, and makes me happy. It's almost as if it's written to me today. I might as well share some of it with you.

"Just thoughts"

(1/20/2006)

A lot of times I wonder why I'm here. What's the reason? I feel empty even though I'm full of feelings and thoughts. I'm drowning in loneliness. I have people around me who I enjoy, but do they really care about me? I sometimes think that if I died, no one would really care. Nothing would really change if I were gone. I'm just one life among many.

But even if you feel alone, there's always someone to help you get up when you fall. Loneliness is an interior pain that people always have to try to hide. No one can see the hurt. It's a superficial world we live in, too focused on exteriors. One should look at a person's inner beauty before anything else. Never judge anyone before you get to know him.

We're all searching for answers to the same questions. Is there anyone who has the answers? Does something exist outside this world that we can't sense and don't have the ability to know? In this endless universe everything is possible. Think of the possibilities and forget the doubt. Trust yourself, be yourself. I think that everyone should be able to think independently without being pressured by others. It's your own perspective that makes you who you are.

We're all hoping that there's something better, but focus instead on what you have now. Take care of your happiness and forget the sorrow. It's said that "it's better to be lucky than good," that there's nothing better than being lucky. But what does it mean to be lucky? Infinity never ends.

All in all, 235 readers commented on Regine's three "look back" entries, among them several people with their own experience of illness. Here's a small selection.

You have nothing to fear (even though I understand that you are totally scared and frightened)! My mother had a heart transplant in 2007. I was terrified about what would happen, even though the procedure was pretty safe then and I knew that everything would go well. I was depressed the whole day, had to stay overnight with the neighbors (who I didn't really like), and I also had a math exam scheduled while she was gone. Maybe it's a bit presumptuous of me to write this, but I'm doing it so that you'll have a good precedent in mind: I took the math test for my mom's sake, because she wanted me to get a good grade, and I got my first A in math. Now she's in great shape, everything's going well, and she's happy with life. She was so happy to get a transplant! Imagine if you didn't get a transplant at all . . .

—*Anonymous*

Be strong! I went through the same thing that you're going through now when I was twelve. I was diagnosed with bone cancer. My life changed abruptly, but promise me that you'll never give up. That was the only thing I said to myself. I'm never going to give up and lose courage, no matter how horrible things get. Continue writing and talking about it; I think that can help you work through the hard times. You're a good writer. It's moving to read your writing. There are so many people who haven't encountered setbacks in life, and who have no idea what pain is, but I'll tell you one thing, that when I was sick, I felt everything was so unfair. I never understood why I had to be one of the unlucky ones. But I was, and that's the way it is. Something I just had to deal with and accept. But promise me that you'll never give up. I know this will make you stronger.

Take care of yourself and do things that make you happy, really.
—*Henriette, eighteen*

Amazingly good writing. I recognize so much about myself when I read about how you were in school. I always looked forward to middle school in elementary school, but I continued going to school and now I'm looking forward to moving away and studying. I have no idea what I'll do or what I'm going to do with my life, but after reading your blog, I've decided to focus. I'm going to be grateful that I'm well, that I'm happy, and I'll try and live life for the now. I hope you totally recover again—you really deserve it! You are so incredibly strong!!
—*Kamilla*

I am so looking forward to when you get better, Regine. We're going to live in the present, party more, kiss boys, stand in front of the mirror and say how totally gorgeous we are, and dream about a fabulous and 100 percent realistic future! It's going to be great!
—*Karina*

Hi, Regine. Some words from one of your old teachers at Nordlandet Middle School. ☺

You were a girl who made an impression on me: You were strong, and a wonderful and talented writer even then. Remember in 10th grade how eager you were when you had an oral presentation on the book you were reading—I think it was *Beatles* or was it *A Doll's House*? In any case you were so enthusiastic, and you could have talked forever without losing our interest. You seemed to be a girl full of thoughts and reflections about both the book and life in general. ☺

Then I heard that you'd gotten sick. It was so incredibly sad to find out. Today I've been reading your blog: your entries and all the comments. You have my total admiration. As do all the youth who give you comments along the way.

Somewhere you wrote: "Life is very important to me." I want to say that you, Regine, are very important to life. Important to all of us who get to read your thoughts and to everyone who is close to you. Your blog shines with hope and love for life. And that's what I wish for you for the New Year.

—*Hug, Berit R.*

P.S.: It's so delightful to see pictures of you, Eli Ann, and Marthe and the others. I wish you lots of good times together. ☺

Baking, camping, and hanging out—good times and good memories.

Winter, 2009

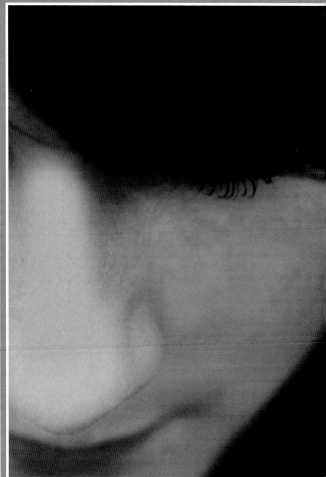

Winter, 2009

New surroundings
Tuesday, January 6, 2009

I'm in Oslo! I arrived yesterday, and so far the setup seems pretty good. The nurses are nice, and they all said that everything was going to be okay—that I'd come to the right place. I had a bone marrow biopsy yesterday, and it actually wasn't that bad! I liked the doctor who did it. Today I started the chemo cycle. I had to take twenty-four pills today in four doses. Still, I haven't had much of a reaction yet. Am just a bit dizzy from the pills (which are supposed to work against the chemo-induced cramping). The food here is good, too—luckily. I've already put up some pictures and some other things to make the room feel a little bit cozier.

Spoke with both a teacher and physiotherapist today. Will have classes as long as I'm able to, and will have physiotherapy during the isolation period.

Just keeping my head down
Saturday, January 10, 2009

Just wanted to post a quick update. Things are still going well, given the circumstances. Yesterday I took the last chemo pills—and all in all I've taken 384 of them (which is a lot). I've got two days of intravenous chemo left. It starts tonight. I'll probably have to take a kind morphine-ish drug to deal with the facial pains.[1] But the thing I'm most worried about is the nausea. Hopefully it won't be too bad.

---

1   Facial pains can be caused by a number of things, including infections or nerve damage from chemotherapy.

I'm still managing to eat, and hopefully I can keep that up a while longer. It's a little scary how sore my throat can get, but at least it isn't dangerous.

The isolation period is approaching, and that's going to be really intense. I'm obviously scared about it, and really anxious, but hopefully it won't be as rough as we're expecting. What worries me the most is the possibility of lung complications or organ bleeding—that would be really serious.

Days go slowly. They're sad and boring. There's nothing to do. I'm just sitting around and waiting. Hours drag on and on, and days seem to take weeks. I wish I could just sleep through all of this.

The road ahead

Wednesday, January 14, 2009

I finally had the transplant! The bone marrow was transferred to my blood yesterday morning, and there weren't any complications! The doctor thinks everything is going really well, and that I received a lot of cells. Now we just have to get through steps three and four. Step three is the isolation period;[2] step four is recovery. The doctor said the isolation period usually isn't that bad, but we just have to take it one step at a time. He understands that at this point I just need a break, that I've been through enough. The isolation starts on Sunday, so they've already made a room ready for me. Like I said, it's all going to be pretty intense.

The chemo I had over the weekend, the intravenous one, made me really sick. One day I had intense facial pain, and I threw up a

---

2   Until the donated cells start making new blood cells, patients have few healthy white blood cells with which to fight infections. To protect patients during this period, they may live in isolation rooms that receive clean, filtered air free of potentially hazardous particles.

lot. It was horrible. I got painkillers, but they didn't do anything. The next day was better, but I still threw up a lot. And on Monday I just lay in bed, not doing anything; I could only manage to get up to go to the bathroom. I couldn't even watch TV—and that says a lot. Luckily things are going better now. I'm kind of struggling with eating because I've thrown up so many times over the past few days, but it doesn't matter anyway. My stomach hurts and it doesn't want any food. The nausea hasn't gone away completely yet, but it's getting better. This was definitely the worst chemo experience I've had so far.

It feels amazing to know the new bone marrow is in my body. Finally it's here, safe inside me. You're always scared something will happen while it's being transported. (Imagine if someone dropped it on the ground and it had all spilled out!) But it went well! Now I just have to wait for it to start working . . . .

Ninety-four readers commented on the good news, among them Regine's grandparents, and fellow cancer patient Svein Kåre:

Today is truly the first day of the rest of your life, Regine. The days ahead will certainly have some highs and lows, but you can handle it for sure. You're strong both in mind and body. It will be spring soon, and we can't wait to go picnicking with you!
—*Grandmother and Grandfather*

Congratulations on the fantastic milestone!!
I'm impressed that you managed to eat as much as you did during the chemo cycle. (I struggled a lot with eating, even though my chemo was way less intense than yours.)
Johanne, Anne Marie, and I hope to get to see you before we leave Riksen!

And I hope things turn out well. No more drama! We all think you've had enough now!

We're so impressed by your strength and your ability to handle all of this!

Go girl!

—*Svein Kåre*

Stomachaches, intravenous nutrition, and other stuff like that

Friday, January 16, 2009

My stomachaches are starting to really get on my nerves. It hurts so much! It's the worst at night, when they stop giving me the Sandimmune.[3] My appetite isn't good either; I hardly eat anything. Half a slice of bread, some ice cream, and a little bit of chocolate and pretzels is all I've eaten today. Drinking is also hard. So now they've started feeding me intravenously. It's a bit of a relief, actually. It's so frustrating when it's a struggle just to eat.

I had a good morning today. I was able to take a shower, and had physiotherapy and tutoring. Not bad! During the evenings I've just been staying in bed, watching TV. And that's how the days go. On Sunday I'll switch into the isolation room, where the drudgery continues . . .

---

3   This drug restrains the body's immune system and prevents it from attacking the new transplanted stem cells.

Isolation
Monday, January 19, 2009

Things are totally fine. Not very different from earlier, except for the fact that I can't walk out the door. Today we're just waiting for the fever to start (because of another bout of blood poisoning). They want to start me on Meronem this time, an antibiotic that actually works. I'm really worried that I've become resistant to it though. I hope the symptoms are limited to fever, tender mucous membranes, and stomachaches. I can't handle anything more than that. But I know other complications could come up. These are going to be some tough days ahead.

Life is just way too hard. Why am I the one, out of everyone, who has to experience this? I'm sorry but that's all I can think about. The whole time. It's impossible to accept. Life is just so unfair.

I think about this year and how much I'm missing out on. This is the year everyone turns eighteen and celebrates. Meanwhile I'm left to wonder if I'll even make it to eighteen.

I watch people who jog or walk by my window. They just have no idea how lucky they are.

A total of 128 people wished to express their support after Regine's entry:

Hey . . . words seem so weak . . . so I want to give you lots of encouragement and hugs . . . Even though I hardly know you . . . it still feels like we're so close, with Svein Kåre in the same unit . . . Sometimes, especially after we've gone through something so hard, I also can't help feeling that this is all just so unfair . . . Someone I know said that sometimes you have to go down into the cellar and just sit in the dark and pay attention to what you feel before you're ready to embark on the road ahead . . . There's probably something to that . . . You can't always manage to think positively and be optimistic . . . But as someone wrote on our blog, "If you're forced to walk through hell, don't look back: just keep walking." You do what you have to do, and better times will come. Stay courageous! Reach for the good things that lie ahead of you, big or small. We're rooting for you with everything we've got!!!

—*Hug from Anne Marie*

I have tears in my eyes, because you're totally right. The things we take for granted mean everything when you think about actually losing them.

I hope you don't have to go through any more of this, and that the light at the end of the tunnel is just around the bend. You're strong, and you're giving us a ton of insights into this whole process. Maybe you don't realize it, but your words will have an effect on a lot of people's lives by helping them realize what they have, and teaching them to appreciate that.

And for that you deserve the utmost respect.

—*Dora*

The coming time could definitely be tough, yes, but you've been tested before, and you fought your way through it. The staff said that the worst is definitely behind you now. You don't have much time left at the hospital. Soon you'll be free and healthy again! And of course you'll turn eighteen. I'm supposed to take you out that night! ☺

—*Martin*

I have to say it: You're incredible.

I'm pretty sure I would never be able to handle what you're going through right now. It's sickening how life can change so quickly. I've been reading your blog for a while now. ☺ But tonight I've been staying up and looking through some of your entries, and now I'm sitting here with eyes wide open, and tears pouring down my face.

It's sad, and it shouldn't happen to anyone. Cancer shouldn't exist, but unfortunately it does. And it's so unfair that someone has to get it.

Like so many others, I just want to tell you to get well, and good luck on the road to health. ♥

The day when I read your blog and see the words "I'm cured" at the top of the page, I'll be so happy.

—*Girl, fourteen* ☺

Possessed

Thursday, January 22, 2009

I've come down with a fever. Incredibly enough, I didn't have any chills, but that was probably just because the nurses gave me antibiotics right away. Otherwise, not much is new. I can't manage to write very much anyway, since I'm too spacey. I've been given a so-called pain-pump. I don't think it works that well, but the doctors say my pain would be way worse without it. The way it works is pretty simple: I just push a button whenever I experience pain. Naturally there's a limit to how much painkiller I can get though. It's convenient, but the downside is that I become really, really tired. I don't do anything but lie in bed and doze. Am too tired to manage anything at all—can't even watch TV.

But everything is moving along smoothly, according to the doctor.

Better prospects

Wednesday, January 28, 2009

Things are starting to get better (I think). The bone marrow has started functioning, so I get to leave the isolation room tomorrow! So in the end, I did it: I made it through the isolation period—the part I was most scared of; the part I've been so afraid of the whole time. It was definitely bad, but not as bad as I thought it would be. I think maybe the period right before I went into isolation was worse. Now I'm really wondering what's going to happen next. First of all, I have to start eating and drinking normally on my own, and I have to be able to swallow pills. It can take time, but I think it will go well. A nutritionist was here today, and he gave me some tips. Apparently, small, frequent meals are the way to go. I got started on that yesterday, but I haven't eaten anything today. I can't honestly say that I want food, but I have to try. I hope I won't get any GVHD[4]—or at least none that requires treatment at the hospital. That would be another bad break, but I'm prepared for the possibility, especially since so many people do have them.

Maybe I'll get to go to the patient hotel soon? That would be great—because at that point people tend to suddenly get much healthier. Just getting released from the hospital does something to you. I still have a ways to go before I can go home and live normally, but I feel like I'm definitely on the right track. If I can just keep improving, it won't be long before I'll take off on the last phase of this long journey—and start coming back to life.

I know that it will be five years before I'm considered truly cured, and that I could have a relapse during that time, but it's important not to focus on that. This treatment is going to make me well.

---

4   Graft-versus-host disease. This condition can occur when newly transplanted cells perceive the host's body as foreign and attack the tissues and/or organs of the host's body. ("Graft" refers to the donated cells and "host" to the patient.) The skin, liver, and gastrointestinal tract are especially susceptible to GVHD.

Hollowed out

Friday, January 30, 2009

The isolation period ended yesterday. I can't really say I feel any freer though, since I'm just sitting here in my room anyway.

It's just as boring and just as lonely as before. I'm incredibly fed up with all of this. I know things have been even tougher for other patients, and that they've spent more time here than I have. But I just want to go home. I could still be here a while. I was actually supposed to go to the patient hotel on Monday, but there aren't any free rooms, and now it could be a week before I get there. But what would the difference be? Maybe there's not even internet at the hotel. It's definitely not luxurious over there. But then again, what else do I have to look forward to?

Today I haven't done much except sit in front of the computer and listen to music. That's definitely something I hadn't done in a while—which is strange, because music is one of my big passions. Mom and Dad are in town, and hopefully they'll bring back the Wardruna[5] CD for me. (They said they'd look for it.) But either way, I've already listened to some great bands, like Sigur Rós, Enslaved, Ulver, and Queens of the Stone Age.

I'm looking forward to going to concerts again when I'm healthier. Today I've dared to look that far ahead at least. My mood has swung pretty violently between highs and lows today. I've looked back on the past and forward to the future. And I've thought a lot. It's not always that easy to look ahead. Everything seems so endless. I've been in this so long that it's difficult to see a life outside "the walls." When I look at pictures of myself before I got sick, I can hardly recognize myself. The illness has left its mark on me, both outside and inside. I

---

5   Norwegian musical group focused on ancient Nordic traditions, instruments, and techniques. *Wardruna* means "the guardian of secrets," or "she who whispers."

know that my life will never be 100 percent normal again, but I hope I can do well when school starts again (along with everything else). It's almost as if I'm afraid to plan for school in the fall. I'm scared of disappointment. The nurses and doctors are happy that I'm thinking so far ahead, and that I want to start school again, but still they always tell me that I might not be able to handle it. That's hard to hear (even though I know they're saying it so that my expectations will be realistic, and so that I won't get too disappointed if it doesn't work out that way).

By the way, eating is going much better. I've been able to take all of my pills. The doctors say that I've come a long way already, and that I should be happy about how quickly things have progressed. But they also made sure to say that I still have a long way to go.

On another note, I just want to say that I think it's tragic that they've started "developing" the forest behind my house. They're going to build roads and new houses there. I almost started crying when my sister told me about it. How could they ruin something so beautiful? That forest is one of my favorite places in the world. I have so many great memories there, and it was such a big part of my childhood. In bad times, I've looked for comfort and inspiration there, and even when things are good I love taking photos there. What's going to happen to all the wildlife that lives there?

"Taken by the Mountain"

Saturday, January 31, 2009

The Mountain welcomed her,

Embraced her hard and harshly

And then the world was Night,

And She was lost forever.

Her dying breath, a scream,

From a Time that's gone, but not forgotten;

From a body, once living, now Stone

— *"Bergtatt," a song by Norwegian band Ulver**

*Ulver (which means "wolves" in Norwegian) started out as a death metal band, but their musical style has evolved to incorporate diverse genres. The title of their first album, Bergtatt, means "taken by the mountains" and is a reference to people in Norwegian folklore who are lured into the mountains by trolls and other creatures.

Fifty-three readers commented on this entry, among them Regine's maternal grandparents:

Regine,

We didn't get to read your first entry before now. "Taken by the Mountain" is a really dark, depressing song; it doesn't reflect the person we know you really are. It's probably everything that you've gone through that makes you seem different to us now. (And that's understandable.) But it's over now.

You've made so much progress; the song's sad thoughts can't be allowed to win out.

Think of your mom and dad and how happy they were when you took photos of them in Sweden. It will be like that again, even though it's going to take some time. We can't wait for you to come home again. Be patient. Everything will work out in the end. Also, remember: All of Norway is rooting for you.

—*Grandma and Grandpa*

Remember tomorrow
Sunday, February 1, 2009

Well, the days keep rolling on, and things still stay the same. Everyone tells me that I should be thankful that everything has gone so well, and not to be so fed up. I'm thankful for that. I really am.

I talked to a nurse about my release and about following up at the outpatient clinic. It made me feel like this was really going to happen: I was really going back home. We even talked about that, about what it would be like to go home to Kristiansund. It's not a matter of going home and just living normally again. There will have to be a ton of follow-ups at the hospital. So this thing with hospital appointments won't end right away. But oh my god I'm looking forward to it so much. I plan on spending a lot of time outside, in nature—I won't need to wear a face mask there.

But then there's also the issue of GVHD reactions. I haven't had any yet, but they can happen really suddenly. I got a whole brochure about it. It was like three pages long. Insanely frightening. And I'm really scared I could have powerful reactions. I'm scared I could develop *chronic* GVHD. The brochure said you could lose lung capacity, and that it can affect the hair follicles so that your hair doesn't grow back, and that your pelvic area can narrow, which could make sex difficult (this is pretty rare, but still). And there are a bunch of other things, too. (Help!)

I'm having a hard time getting out of bed lately. I don't like walking around the hospital; it's boring. And I have to wear a face mask. That's what I hate the most. Everyone stares at me, and I feel like a freak. I have to wear it for the next three months. I know that it doesn't really matter, and that I probably shouldn't think about it, but still. And besides, it seriously bothers me not to have hair. If it doesn't grow back, I won't be able to handle it. (Just call me vain if you want to.)

I keep telling myself that I'm lucky. I hear about a lot of other people for whom this period has been much worse. I feel guilty when I get depressed and fed up. After all, I've almost made it.

In the silence you learn to sing

Friday, February 6, 2009

The latest update is that they finally moved me to the patient hotel! I've been here since Monday. Have taken daily blood tests and they've been totally fine, so now I don't have to go back to the hospital until Monday. So it's true: I've actually been released! It feels so good to be able to say that: *I've been released*. Feels strange. Fingers crossed that I get to stay here.

I'm going to have a bone marrow biopsy on Monday. It's always hard to wait for the results. I hate bone marrow biopsies, not just because they hurt so much, but also because the results scare me. Well, no matter what, I guess you can't really avoid reality.

There's not much to do during the day. It's freezing outside, so I don't take walks. And if I leave my room, I still need the face mask. So today I just walked up and down the stairs for a bit instead, which is still a major workout since I'm so out of shape. It totally exhausts me. Mom is in town shopping, so maybe she'll get something for me today, too? She was in town yesterday and brought me back a bunch of clothes. So now I'll have a lot to wear when I get home.

Some good news

Tuesday, February 10, 2009

The bone marrow biopsy I took yesterday was fine! I'm overjoyed. Since the bone marrow hasn't been good for over six months, this is really special. I just cried I was so happy. Hope things continue moving in the same direction.

There were some tense hours and a lot of nerves while my family and I sat waiting for the test results. It took six hours. I was nauseous and could not get it together.

Finally at home

Friday, February 13, 2009

Believe it or not, yesterday I finally got back to my house in Kristiansund again. So incredibly fantastic.

So unbelievably wonderful to see familiar surroundings: the house, the woods, and of course my sister and the animals. Some family jokers had put balloons, wine, and a nice card at the front door, which made it even better to come home.

Interview in today's newspaper

Thursday, February 19, 2009

You can read about me in today's edition of the *Kristiansund Daily*!

Less than ideal

Wednesday, February 25, 2009

I haven't posted many updates lately, mainly because there's no real news to speak of. Things are going okay. My blood tests are fine, and I still haven't gotten GVHD or any other infections—at least so far. My overall physical condition is fair. It varies from day to day, but I don't really have much to brag about on that front. However, it does feel like I'm improving—albeit very slowly. Maybe the people around me are noticing some differences though. I go see the physiotherapist a few times a week. Sometimes I'm totally exhausted afterward; other times it's just fine. It doesn't take much to wipe me out at this point.

Some people might think that now that I'm home, everything is all right again—that I'm well—but there's still a lot of work to do. It takes a long time to rebuild your body. Can you imagine starting over from square one? I think a lot of people wouldn't even know where to begin. I just hope I'll be able to function normally by the summer; that's what I'm hoping for, anyway, because there's a bunch of stuff I can't wait to do.

Incidentally, I ordered my tickets for the Ulver concert in Lillehammer in May. I decided that I just couldn't stand saying, "No, I probably won't be well enough." Because how boring is that? I ordered the ticket, so we'll see. If I can't do it, I can't do it. (But that's not going to happen!)

There's about a month and a half left before I have the three-month checkup. I'm looking forward to it and dreading it at the same time. I'm looking forward to it because that's when all the medical restrictions on me will be lifted. I'll be "free" again. (I'll also get to remove the ugly tube that irritates me so much—the one used to take blood samples.) And I'm dreading it because it's always possible they'll find cancer cells in my new bone marrow.

For whatever reason, today I feel confident that I won't have a relapse; there's just no reason to think I would—and that's good. I love days when I'm positive. Some days my outlook is a lot bleaker. After all, a relapse is always at the back of my mind. Especially when you hear about other people having relapses. I feel so sorry for Bengt Eidem, who just had a relapse recently, four years after his bone marrow transplant. I've also heard about other people who are in the midst of a relapse, and I think about them a lot, and about the people who are still lying at the hospital and fighting their diseases.

I'm thinking in particular of Svein Kåre, who's in bed at the hospital now, fighting. Please post some kind comments on his blog at www.svekn.blogspot.com.[6]

---

6 Svein Kåre Handeland died on March 2, 2009. Anne Marie wrote the following on the blog they shared: "Svein Kåre—my beloved husband and Johanne's wonderful father—died today at 9:20 am." On the same day, Regine linked to their blog under the title "Life is so unfair."

Knock me down and I get up again
Thursday, March 5, 2009

I've been pretty miserable lately, and haven't been up to much. I couldn't do a lot for the physical therapist on either Tuesday or Wednesday. But even though I'm making slow progress, I'm incredibly happy just to be home without any infections or other complications. It's almost a month until the three-month checkup. Then I'll finally get to move around in public again! I'm looking forward to having that option again, even though it will also be pretty weird, I think. Everything's going to be strange when I start living normally again. After all, I've been "isolated" for more than six months now. I'm imagining it will be a bit difficult at first—because I'll be unfamiliar with so many people, etc., but it's probably doable. I hope people won't stare at me.

There isn't much for me to do right now. I hope I'll have enough energy to take a walk in the forest, or even just go down the street now that the weather is so nice.

My mom and my sister and I invested in a sewing machine. I'm a terrible seamstress, but I'm super excited about learning how to sew some outfits. We have some old clothes up in the attic that could easily be altered into something wearable. It'll be fun to try.

Otherwise I'm taking photos around the house (now that I can't go very far) and at some other nearby places.

I have to admit that I'm feeling pretty lonely these days. Some friends are really good about visiting, but others aren't so good. And there's also always a couple of other friends who just can't visit because they're sick. I guess I could go visit them, but I don't usually have much energy.

A new perspective

Thursday, March 12, 2009

Today I went to the movies with my mom and grandma. We had the whole theater to ourselves, and didn't have to pay at all either! (Thank you so much, nice theater man!) We saw *The Orange Girl*. It was really good, and I definitely recommend it if you haven't seen it yet. Going in, I didn't know exactly what it was about; I just knew it had gotten good reviews. So it was a bit surprising that part of the movie was about a man who died of cancer. It made everything so much more real, and it was really moving.

The blood test I took today was just good enough; my blood count is sinking, but that's pretty normal. If it drops much further I'll have to get a blood transfusion, so I hope it doesn't come to that.

A few days ago I got a letter from the county. I opened it and started reading. I've been invited to the "award day" at the Festiviteten[7] in Kristiansund. I wondered why I'd been invited, but when I read further, I saw that I'd actually been nominated for the "youth prize"! I wasn't expecting that! I was obviously pretty excited, and I wondered who had nominated me. There's just one small problem though: The prize ceremony is on Saturday, and for the time being I'm not really supposed to be around crowds or people. But I really want to be there! So I decided to go. We discussed it with the event organizers, and they'll put a table way in the back, apart from everyone else, for us to sit at. We'll also go in after everyone else, so that I won't have to stand in line or mingle with a lot of people. I don't know how much it will help, but . . . you only live once after all, and who knows, the doctors could have bad news for me tomorrow.

I went for a walk in the woods the other day. I took a bunch of pictures while I was there, but only a few of them turned out. It's always like that. You have to take a lot of pictures to get a few good ones. During my

---

7 Kristiansund's cultural venue.

walk I also got a chance to see what's happened to our forest. The place where my friends and I used to throw a tent together and camp, the place where we had so much fun, has been completely destroyed. Now it's just dirt and rocks. Luckily some of the best parts have been saved, like the meadow with the creek. I hope it stays that way. The forest gives people who live in the city a chance to really experience nature; it gives them a chance to get away from city life—to feel something real, something that hasn't been made by human hands. And if we continue like this, later on there will be nothing but streets and houses. That's crazy! Why can't they just leave it all alone? Don't blame me when, ten years from now, you find out that the forest has completely disappeared.

In the course of my walk, I came across some people in the middle of a conversation. They were saying how great the lots would be. I was furious, and of course I had to spy. Do they have any idea what they're doing, what they're giving up? I don't get it.

The awards ceremony
Sunday, March 15, 2009

A bunch of you are probably wondering if I won the youth prize or not. Unfortunately, no, I didn't. I was disappointed, as you'd probably expect—after all, the award was worth 15,000 crowns, and that's a lot of money, at least for me. There were a bunch of strong candidates, but the ones who ended up winning were the ones who win every year (and so I wasn't very happy about that). It was a group of dorky gamers that has a LAN party[8] every year. I thought the gymnasts should have won instead. After all, they've gotten a lot of attention lately. They performed at the Norwegian Youth Festivals of Art and Norwegian Talents.[9] Really talented girls! Even if I didn't win, it felt really good to be nominated, which is an honor in itself.

This wasn't just a big deal because of the prize money; it was also my first trip out into the real world in over half a year. It was strange at first, but felt natural after a while (incredibly enough). I saw a lot of familiar faces, but many people didn't recognize me. Some did though. It was also fun to get dressed up for something again. Even if I don't have any hair to fix, I still felt good. The hat isn't that bad after all. And I think my hair is getting ready to grow again. I'm not the only one who thinks so either. Dark dots and an itchy scalp are good signs. It will definitely come in at some point, but it's hard to wait. I'm very impatient when it comes to things like this. Hope to have a few sprouts by summer, so I won't have to cover my head when it's hot out.

I tried taking a self-portrait earlier today, and I felt pretty good about it, considering I had to do it with a camera phone. You don't necessarily need a good camera to take good pictures, and you don't

---

8   Gathering of people who set up a LAN (Local Area Network) in order to play computer video games.

9   Talent show similar to *America's Got Talent.*

Self-portrait taken with a camera phone on March 15, 2009

really need an expensive editing program either. Creativity is the most important thing.

The walking wounded

Monday, March 23, 2009

I found out that I might still be able to finish my junior year of high school, and stay on track for graduation. I really hope I'll be able to! I know that I can finish two courses over three months if I really put my mind to it. I'm going to register as a candidate in international English, history, and philosophy. It's going to work. I'll do everything

I possibly can to avoid having to stay on for an extra year. I'm not into the idea of starting my senior year of high school when I'm nineteen, and going to classes with a group of sixteen- and seventeen-year-olds. There has to be another solution. Besides, it feels completely wrong to do an extra year just for two classes. That would just be silly.

Time really seems to drag on, but all of a sudden I realized it's less than a month until my three-month checkup. I'm not really dreading it that much; in fact, I think I might even be excited for it. It's definitely going to go well. I know it will. And after the check up I'll be free. That's going to be so disorienting. I have a feeling that I'll feel like a criminal for even going outside, and I'll definitely still be afraid of coming down with something. I don't think that's so strange though, considering how hysterical everyone around me has been about this kind of stuff since this all began.

Speaking of catching something, my sister has a cold. It's not her fault, though, poor thing. It just happens, but even though I try not to dwell on it, I really am scared about getting sick. I get a fever from everything, even just from a cold. And if I get a fever that goes above 100.5 degrees, it's back to the hospital with me. I really hope that doesn't happen. I guess I have to try to just stay away from her for a while. It's important to just get through this period without any fuss. My body *should* be able to deal with a cold, but it would be better to avoid it.

I'm really looking forward to the summer. I've got tons of stuff planned, and it's all pretty big for me. Stuff like

- The Ulver concert,
- The Quart festival,
- A Stockholm trip, and
- RaumaRock[10]

---

10   Annual outdoor rock festival in central Norway.

I think this is realistic—if not, I wouldn't have even bothered to day-dream about it. I'm pretty self-aware, for those of you wondering. And I'm tired of people telling me what I can and can't do, because I'm the only one who actually knows. Instead, people should look toward the future and tell me instead about what they think I'll be able to do then. I've decided just to walk out of the room if the nurses and doc-tors start talking again about how I could hit a wall, etc. They always say that, but I have no intention of hitting a wall anytime soon.

It's kind of fun to look at what people search for before they find my blog. Even if it's nothing special, it's still interesting.

1. reginestokke
2. regine stoke blog
3. allogeneic stem cell transplant
4. ulver concert
5. blog regine
6. epilepsy
7. face your fear
8. heart palpitations, stomachache

The epilepsy thing seems a little weird though. When did I ever men-tion that in my blog?

I'm considering starting a new blog after my three-month checkup. After all, this blog is supposed to be about the disease, the treatment, etc. So I think maybe it should end when the disease ends, and then I could start writing about my "new" life on a new blog. What do you think?

No hair? No problem!

Tuesday, March 24, 2009

As everyone knows, friendship is incredibly important—*especially* if you develop a serious disease. Then, you need all the support you can get!

Some people are just naturally supportive and easygoing. Anyway, I'm pleased to report that in my case, at least, I had a lot of friends who didn't make me feel forgotten when I got sick. Some of them visited me at the hospital, and others kept in touch via text messages, etc. As long as you care, it doesn't really matter what you actually say.

People who get sick—people like me—are still totally normal (except for being sick). We have the same personality that we did before, and we like to do the same things that we did before we got sick. The only difference is that, often, your appearance can change. That's especially true for cancer patients. Some people who get chemo gain a lot of weight, while others can't manage to eat at all during their chemo cycles, and they get super thin. And as everyone knows by now, you lose your hair. That's what everyone associates with cancer: hair loss. I mean, what's the first thing *you* think of when you hear the word *cancer*?

Nevertheless, it seems like the hair loss thing scares a lot of people. I mean that people get scared of the ones who lose their hair. That's my theory anyway. Because what other reason could there be for people not coming to visit? Right now, I'm cancer free, so it can't be the cancer they're scared of. So what are they actually worried about? A lot of men lose their hair at some point, and lots of men shave their heads for fashion or other reasons. But what if a woman loses her hair? Are people more scared of a woman without hair?

In addition to the hair on our heads, we also lose our eyelashes and eyebrows. We also tend to get thinner, and some women lose their shape entirely. In other words, we lose a lot of our sex appeal. And for a lot of women, this winds up being a profoundly traumatic experience. (It was for me.) And it's not very surprising when you consider how obsessed our culture is with appearances. When we become less attractive, some people wind up looking down on us. People talk about me and say: "Poor thing, she lost all her beautiful hair." But what about everything else? Losing your hair is a pretty small loss, in the grand scheme of things. (And just to clarify, I'm not necessarily saying it's any easier for men to lose their hair.)

A lot of people I know get their hair done two or three times a month, and of course they care a lot about how they look. When people say they look like they don't have eyebrows, or that they're having a "bad hair day," I start to wonder what they think about me. I also wonder how these people would handle losing their hair.

I manage to get through it because I know it will grow back. Sooner or later.

But I wonder:

Would you date a person who had no hair?

Would you have enough courage to support your friend if she or he got sick?

What's more important: how you look or who you are?

A lot of these questions have simple answers, but for some people it's actually not that obvious, and that's why I ask.

Regine's post and her questions generated 96 comments. Included here is a selection of those comments, including some of Regine's replies:

Completing two subjects in three months sounds insanely tough, but you're tough, too—so it wouldn't surprise me if you were able to manage it. Otherwise, this thing about hair . . . My roommate had beautiful black hair with awesome curls when we met. But after a few years he got alopecia areata, that is, he lost his hair in large clumps, and eventually also lost his eyebrows and some of his eyelashes.

He was obviously crushed when he found out that his hair wouldn't ever grow back. It's also kind of weird when he meets old acquaintances who don't recognize him anymore, because he looks so different. But for me at least, it doesn't matter. He's the same, so what difference does his hair make?

—*Else*

One of my girlfriends got leukemia, and she had a really tough time with it, with lots of hospital stays, etc. It was right in the middle of the second semester of our senior year, when everyone was super preoccupied with school stress and graduation. I visited her at the hospital a few times, but it was a long trip and I didn't have enough money to travel to Oslo very often, so we mostly just texted. But now that she's basically recovered and is trying to readjust to normal life, it feels more difficult to connect with her. It's as if the whole period of her illness is lying between us like a chasm, and I don't really know what to do. I don't know if I'm allowed to ask about her disease, or if it's something she'd rather put behind her.

I understand that it's frustrating when people seem "scared," but I'm not so sure it's just the hair. I think the lost hair is a symbol for the fact that you've been through hell, and people are reminded of that when they see you. For some people it's probably a kind of elephant in the room—something that no one talks about because they don't exactly know what to say or do. We Norwegians are just so afraid of conflict. I think it would help if you took some initiative. Maybe talk a bit about your experiences throughout the illness, and try to make it less threatening. Say what you said in the previous post—that you're optimistic, that you've got a positive outlook, that there's so much you want to do, and ask if they want to come with. Then you'll probably see them visit more. ☺

—*Heidi*

Yes, but now I'm back home and the worst of it is behind me. I'm not going through a difficult period, so I don't understand why it's so difficult to know what to say. It's still not an excuse.

—*Regine*

I stood by my best friend during her whole illness. There were times when she looked like hell (for lack of a better word). It was difficult to see her like that, obviously—so helpless against the almost constant pain. But what did that matter? She was someone I really, really cared about. At the same time, there was nothing I could do to help. Sometimes she couldn't do anything except just lie there. I tend to scrutinize people pretty carefully when I first meet them, but I try not to let those superficial judgments—whatever they might be—stop me from getting to know that person better.

For a lot of people the changes to your appearance won't be the most difficult thing to handle. The challenge for a lot of them will be finding the right words to use with someone who is going/has gone through something so serious.

—*Anonymous*

Good entry! In my family there's a condition called alopecia areata. You lose some or all of your hair. If I got it I wouldn't care, though, even though my hair is my best feature. If someone teases me about cutting it or shaving it off, I take it really seriously and get really scared. But I know that if it really comes down to it and I do lose my hair, I'll just have to keep living my life, and try not to care too much about what other people say or what they think.

Because just like everyone always says, it's what's inside that counts!

I asked my boyfriend what he would do if I lost my hair. He said, "What would I do? It's not your hair that I love, it's you!"

And I would definitely have supported my friend if she'd gotten sick. If they're your friends, you should support them, no matter what!

You're an amazing girl, Regine! ☺

—*Stine Merete*

Stine Merete: You're so brave for not caring about it! It's important not to worry about it either; it may not even happen.

Your boyfriend sounds great, too—he accepts you as you are. ☺ You're lucky.

—*Regine*

Do you want to help?

Wednesday, March 25, 2009

There was an article in the local newspaper about how there's a real shortage of blood donors. I skimmed the article and didn't catch everything because I was pretty busy that morning. Later in the day, though, my grandma told me that I was mentioned in the article, so I had to check it out. This is what it said:

> Domino Effect
> When cancer patient Regine Stokke blogged about her illness and agreed to talk to the newspaper about her experiences, the hospital was rewarded with an immediate response: More people began to register [as blood donors].

It's crazy to think that people had registered as blood donors after I told my story! That's great. I couldn't help feeling proud when I read that. Registering as a blood donor is so important. A lot of people have accidents and lose large quantities of blood, and every day more and more people are diagnosed with cancer. Blood donors help make it possible for people to survive both traumatic accidents and cancer. Maybe some people don't realize this, but blood transfusions are an important aspect of cancer treatment, if I can put it that way. Chemo destroys not only the malignant cells but the healthy cells as well, which makes your blood count drop, along with your blood platelets. And blood platelets are important as a means of controlling bleeding.

You can register as a bone marrow donor when you sign up to donate blood; but when you register as a blood donor, you don't automatically become a bone marrow donor, too. You have to eventually check another box on the same form, and I encourage everyone to do it. Even though most people succeed in finding a donor, there are still a lot of people out there who have to wait anxiously to get the help they need, maybe because one of their parents is overseas, or for some other reason. People with rare tissue types (the determining factor in finding a bone marrow donor) sometimes have to wait a long time before they eventually find a donor, and in some cases, they don't ever find one. If you have a serious disease, this is a critical issue. These individuals need new bone marrow to survive, and in most cases they need it as soon as possible. The longer you wait, the more chemo cycles you have to go through to keep the disease under control.

Maybe you don't know what being a donor entails? Maybe it seems kind of scary to you? But the fact is, being a bone marrow donor is simple. Here's some more information.

Do you want to donate bone marrow?
Only blood donors can sign up, so contact your blood bank. As a volunteer donor, your tissue type must first be determined. This procedure is similar to a normal blood test. After your tissue type is determined, you will be registered in the bone marrow registry database. When a person needs a bone marrow transplant, they will identify a person with as similar a tissue type as possible. Blood type is not relevant. Stem cells are first harvested from the donor in connection with the transplant, not before. The number of people that are chosen to give stem cells is about one to two per thousand a year.

You can withdraw as a donor at any time before the patient's treatment begins. A reason for withdrawing is not required.

Stem cells can be harvested from your bone marrow and from your blood.

How do I give stem cells from my bone marrow?
How is bone marrow harvested?

The harvesting of bone marrow is carried out at a hospital experienced in harvesting bone marrow. The bone marrow donor is under complete anesthesia. After that a needle is inserted in the back of the pelvic bone on both sides. The bone marrow, which looks like blood, is removed with the needle and collected in a blood bag. Only a small amount of the donor's bone marrow is removed, and it is used within a few weeks. The harvesting takes about an hour. The donor may return home the next day.

Does the donor need pretreatment?

No, there is no special pretreatment. However, the donor must start fasting at midnight the evening before the harvest.

Is it painful to donate bone marrow?

All donors feel some pain and tenderness around the hip bones for some days after the harvesting. One should be a bit careful with heavy lifting and strenuous physical activity for a week. There will be only very small scars, if any scarring occurs at all.

Is it dangerous to donate blood marrow?

If you are healthy, there is very little risk associated with bone marrow harvesting, and complications are rare. The donor will always undergo a thorough physical exam before the harvesting and will be given a detailed explanation of all aspects of donating bone marrow.

How do I donate stem cells from blood?

How can stem cells be found in blood?

Normally, stem cells are found in the bone marrow, but in some situations stem cells can also be found in blood after special treatment. In this case, the donor receives a shot with what is known as stem cell growth factor each morning for four to five days, which stimulates stem cells to flow into the blood stream. A stem cell growth factor called G-CSF is currently being used. G-CSF is a substance normally found in the body that stimulates stem cells. When enough stem cells have flowed into the blood stream after the G-CSF treatment, the stem cell harvesting is started. The stem cells return to the bone marrow shortly after treatment with G-CSF ends.

How are stem cells harvested from blood?

Stem cells from blood are harvested with the help of a apheresis machine. The procedure is carried out at a hospital with significant expertise in the use of such machines. The blood is withdrawn in a manner similar to blood donation. It is then centrifuged in the apheresis machine in such a way that the stem cells can be removed. The blood is then returned to the donor's body. The procedure takes a few hours, and may be repeated the next day to yield enough stem cells. Just a small portion of the stem cells are removed, and these are used within a short time.

Is it painful or dangerous to donate stem cells from blood?

It is not much more uncomfortable than giving blood and the risks are very small. As the procedure takes some hours, you may become a bit tired. The blood circulation and blood values are monitored carefully, and the apheresis is stopped if the donor feels unwell.

Is there any discomfort or danger linked with G-CSF injections?
Little risk is associated with daily shots of G-CSF. Almost everyone gets side effects in the form of bone or muscle pains. Many become fatigued, and some also get a bit of fever and/or headache. The discomfort can be alleviated with Paracet or stronger medications. Most people can continue to work during the G-CSF treatment, while others take a few days off from work. Everyone is given a thorough physical examination and informational session before the treatment.

Spring, 2009

Another unpleasant surprise
Thursday, April 2, 2009

My blood count has been dropping lately, and today it fell even further. My immune system also seems like it's getting weaker, so we decided to call the doctors at Riksen. They told us that I should get a bone marrow test so I won't have to just sit and wonder if something is really wrong. So that's what we did, and it went really well. The doctor at the hospital in Kristiansund is great. It was painful (of course), but it went really well compared to the other bone marrow tests I've had. Was given a lot of anesthesia, so I felt pretty woozy afterward. The test will be sent to Riksen so they can look at the results and see if there's a reason the blood count keeps dropping.

This doesn't necessarily mean anything's wrong. It could mean that a virus is developing, or maybe that I just need to stop taking some of my medications. So yeah, it's not necessarily a sign of a relapse. My blood has been tested for cancer cells, and they didn't find any (which is a really good sign), and I don't feel very sick right now either. Hope for the best!

All that being said, I was definitely scared when they told me I needed another bone marrow test—and it doesn't help when your family gets so anxious, too. We're going to try not to make anything more dramatic than it needs to be. The doctor at Riksen said a lot of patients come in with decreasing blood counts and have to take bone marrow tests. So it's not exactly unusual. Anyway, I'm optimistic.

I wish someone were here tonight
Friday, April 3, 2009

I wish someone were here when I feel afraid.

I wish someone were here while I wait for answers.

I wish someone were here when I fear the worst.

I wish someone were here when I feel lonely.

I wish someone were here tonight.

Terrible news

Saturday, April 4, 2009

Today I woke up to terrible news: I've had a relapse. The bone marrow test didn't look very good, and showed some immature cells. It hasn't gone very far, so the doctors suggested I stop taking one of the drugs that weakens my immune system. The general objective right now is to create some GVHD antibodies. That way, my immune system might be able to expel the sick cells on its own. Unfortunately, as it stands, I don't have a very good chance—even if steps like this do give us some small hope.

So now we just have to wait two weeks to see if anything happens. It's risky to stop taking this medication, and it could have deadly results. If this doesn't work, there's also been some talk of injecting cells from donors to stimulate GVHD production. I could get really sick from that kind of a procedure, but right now we can only wait and see.

If nothing works, I don't have much longer to live. Another transplant is out of the question because it wouldn't do very much and my body probably couldn't handle it anyway. Who would have thought this would happen?

I'm devastated, and so is my whole family. Life is so incredibly unfair—and now I just have to sit at home and wait to die? I don't have words to express how cruel this seems . . . How are we supposed to get through this?

I'm also crushed by the thought that, after I'm gone, my family will be left to deal with the fallout on their own. It's heartbreaking to think that they have to stay behind without me, with just their sorrow. Because really, how is anyone supposed to handle losing a family member?

The plan

Monday, April 6, 2009

No one in the family is taking this very well. Friends and even acquaintances—people I've just met once or twice—are sending me consoling messages. And I'm so thankful for everyone's consideration, whether I know them well or not. As far as I'm concerned, if you take the time to show that you care, that's enough. I'm overwhelmed when I think about how many people out there are thinking about me and wishing me well. It means so much.

I can't stop thinking about my family—especially my sister. I'm so worried about them. I don't want to be the cause of their unhappiness. Maybe it would have been better if I hadn't been born in the first place, so that they wouldn't have to suffer through this crippling sadness now. It's unbearable. I'm probably the one who's handling it best. I just try to make myself as indifferent as I can possibly be; I think that's the only realistic way of dealing with this.

You probably think I'm being really negative today, and you're probably right. We talked to the doctors at Riksen earlier, and they haven't given up on me yet. The relapse is still at an early stage, so I've stopped taking the immunosuppressing medication, and in about two weeks we'll find out if that's having any effect. The doctors will do everything they can for me. They also took this news pretty hard. They have a tough job, but they're also obviously doing something that's hugely important. They're going to have a meeting about me next Tuesday, I think, to talk about what they can try next, and what they need to be prepared for.

The reason for cutting the immunosuppressing drugs is so I can get a rejection reaction (GVHD). That's my only hope now. GVHD will allow my immune system to attack not just my body, but also the sick cells. I'll probably get some reactions within two weeks, but nothing's for sure. There's no guarantee it will work. No one knows.

My other option, if this doesn't work, is to inject/infuse lymphocytes from donors. For people not familiar with this practice, lymphocytes are donors' cells that can help me to create GVHD on my own. I've heard of people with similar diagnoses to mine who've had relapses after three months and who have survived through this method. The doctors won't say whether or not they think it will work. They just don't know. They only know that there's a chance. No one can predict the future, so there's no use just speculating. The doctor we spoke with also mentioned a third possibility, but she didn't say what it involves. So I guess we'll hear more about it later, if it becomes necessary.

You're probably still wondering why they don't just give me another transplant. The doctors talk a lot about how risky it would be, and I know that it's a complicated process, and that a new transplant might just not work. But personally, I feel like I've got nothing left to lose. I've heard of people overseas who've had two transplants and still survived. They're still alive today. It sounds like a transplant might still be the fallback if nothing else works. They've never done two transplants on one patient here in this country, even though it sounds like it was considered in a few cases. Anyway, as long as they try everything they can, I'll be satisfied. Whatever the result, that's what really matters.

It's risky to cut out the immunosuppressive drugs. I could suffer from a serious immunologic attack that could kill me. But at the same time, these attacks are still important for me to get. The doctors would prefer not to treat me for them, too.

I honestly thought that my case was hopeless. The other people that I've talked to in my situation have been sent home to die. And thankfully I haven't gotten that advice yet!

Keep wishing me good luck!

And many did just that. In total, 353 readers commented on Regine's last two entries, among them conservative party politician Bengt Eidem, who is afflicted with leukemia and who wrote the book Deadly Serious:

Hi, Regine!

I just discovered your blog today. I was on Svein Kåre and Anne Marie's website and read about a girl named Regine who'd recently had a relapse. I went right to your site and for the past hour I've been getting caught up on your story. I'm so impressed by your courage. And I love the way you write. Your posts are sad, wise, funny, and always tremendously engaging. I think that despite your struggles, you manage to put smiles to a lot of people's faces. It's a true pleasure to read your blog.

At the same time, it certainly wasn't a pleasure to read about the latest developments. But, for now at least, it's encouraging to know that the substances the doctors are using and developing will enable people to survive these really dangerous situations. (I just wish they'd start using these substances sooner—like right now, with you!) Regine, I don't often write about my gut feelings, but I think you're going to survive. I refuse to believe that your time has come.

In many ways, you and I are kind of in the same boat right now. It looks bad, but there's still hope for us. When you write about your indifference, I recognize myself, but when you optimistically describe your treatment options, I recognize myself there as well. So you and I have a lot in common, and for now at least, we also have LIFE in common.

Let's hold on tightly to that. And let's beat back the immature cells that are trying to overtake our bodies!

—*Big hug from Bengt Eidem, Trondheim*
P.S.! Go moose! :)

Oh, Regine, sweetie, I felt twisted into knots after reading this! Your birth was one of the best things that ever happened to your parents, so don't ever think that they'd be better off without you. Think of all the happiness you have given those around you! Don't lose hope! ☺

—*Jenny Cecilie*

Dear Regine!

Ever since you were born, you've made every second of every day wonderful for your parents and your family. Regardless of what you may think right now, the memories that you share with everybody around you are worth their weight in GOLD, and those memories are something that they will never want to be without.

Much luck in the days ahead—it's so great to see all of the support you have; in the meantime, I'll be thinking about you and yours. Kisses to you!

Keep plugging on like you've done all along! YOU are a wonderful person and your blog provides a huge service to tons of other people. You're a true role model. ☺

—*A big hug from Johanne*

Dear, dear Regine!

I frankly don't know what I should write to you now. I felt faint when I read your entry, and am getting unbelievably frustrated. Jesus, this is so damn unfair!!

We're thinking of you, Regine!

The doctors at Riksen will have to put their heads together and come up with something very clever. They've managed to work miracles for others before, and they can do it again! If you aren't ready to believe in miracles yet, I'll believe for you. I can't wait to hear about your improvement.

—*Many hugs from Maren-Sofie*

I had a brother who got cancer when he was ten or eleven years old. He died when he was sixteen. We couldn't do anything about it because when he had his third relapse, the cancer had spread through his whole body. Everyone knew he was going to die—he had anywhere from two weeks to a month left. But we made his last days his best. I miss him terribly, because he was the only one I felt I could trust. But I still carry many great memories with me, and they comfort me when I'm sad, since I know he'll always be with me in one way or another. I just want you to know that I know what it's like to lose a beloved family member. And you must not blame yourself in any way. But with all this support and compassion, you're definitely going to make it anyway! There's so much love and support out here for you, and trust me: That means something. That means a lot.

—*Anonymous*

Thanks for all the great comments everyone; it means so much to me! For people wondering if you can write about me, go ahead—that would be just fine. ☺

Bengt Eidem: I also heard about your relapse via Svein Kåre and Anne Marie's blog. I was really upset when I read about it, because you're one of my heroes, and I was really hoping it wouldn't happen to you—or to anyone else, for that matter. I read your book when I was waiting for the transplant at Riksen, and it was really, really inspiring. I understood that it was possible I wouldn't survive, but after reading your book, I felt like I was much better prepared for everything I had coming. Your book gave me courage.

I think you're right when you say that we have a lot in common. I hope that we both get better. We have to believe it's going to happen, even if it's difficult at times. (Especially with the mood swings: One day we want to give up and don't care anymore, and the next day we want to fight on forever, and have complete faith that the next procedure will be the one that works.) If you're reading this now, it would be so great to know how you're doing, because I'm very concerned. I've been wondering ever since I heard the terrible news.

—*Regine*

Hi again, Regine!

I'm doing well. I'm at home and I'm almost pain-free—so two of the most basic criteria for happiness have already been met. ☺ Got a high dose of chemo as a start to my treatment in February. In March and April I went for two and a half weeks of daily radiation treatments. Last radiation is tomorrow and then I'm on Easter break. Gonna be celebrating a city Easter in Trondheim, so I'm hoping for good weather.

Then it'll be exciting after Easter, there'll be a lot of tests and consultations between St. Olav's and Riksen, and after that we'll have a better sense of what lies ahead, and what we still have to do.

I will definitely keep up with your life and health via your blog, and I'll keep my fingers crossed (and my toes) for us both. In the meantime, happy Easter!

—*Hugs, Bengt*

An entry dedicated to my blog readers

Tuesday, April 7, 2009

I just wanted to take a minute to say how truly grateful I am for all of the support that you, my readers, give to me each and every day. Every word means so much to me, and helps to keep my spirits up. I was in a pretty dark place over the holidays, and maybe I still am, but your kind words help me to keep hoping. I love you all so much—even those of you that I don't even know.

I've also gotten some beautiful gifts from some of you. Ida and Maiken sent Easter eggs and a nice card. The card was unbelievably well done. Everything inside the egg was delicious, and the drawings of me at Quart[1] put a big smile on my face. Martin's mother knit socks for me and wrote me a really nice card. It made me so happy, and (incredibly) the socks fit perfectly. She even knit my name on them, which made them extra special. Thank you so much!

Truth be told, though, the cards and gifts are nothing new. Throughout this whole process, people have been incredibly sympathetic, and I've received a ton of presents from family, friends, and even my mom's colleagues. I've gotten so many bouquets, cards, money, and wine—and again, I'm so thankful for everything. Martin has also given me lots of gifts: roses, CDs, movies, and really nice cards. Every time he gives me something, I can't help but cry; it makes me so unbelievably happy. But of course you don't have to give me a gift to show that you care. Kind and supportive words are more than enough.

Without you I could never have gotten this far!

If you have a second, you should definitely take a quick look at the film Martin made (and which he dedicated to me). Martin is unbelievably talented, and this film is totally special. I would love for you to see it, and I guarantee that you'll get something out of it. Please leave a comment for him, too—it would make him so happy!

You can see the video (which is a little over three minutes long) here: www.youtube.com/watch?v=hu133xtiQyM.

---

1 Quart is short for the Quart Festival—an annual music festival in Kristiansand.

Regine's entry generated 95 comments, including many compliments for the film. Martin also wrote an entry:

Your blog's become an ad for my movie. ☺

I don't understand why this had to happen . . . After everything that you've been through, I finally thought it was over. That you were free. I thought that now, when we got together, we wouldn't have to worry about cancer, or chemo, or the latest test results. That the next time I'd need to comfort you, it would be because you missed the bus, or because you didn't win a contest (although that's not very likely, since you come in first place no matter what☺.) But apparently lightning *can* strike twice . . . .

Last Friday, when we stayed up late chatting online and talked all about our plans for the future, everything seemed perfect. Even as late as Saturday, five minutes before you called, I was stopping at the wine store to pick up a bottle of wine for you—and then the asteroid hit, and time stopped, yet again.

But . . . but no matter what happens now, and how difficult things get, we have to do what we can to enjoy ourselves. There is clearly hope, and we'll get though this together! You're everything to me.

Love you, Regine.

Yours,

—*Martin*

Under the title "Fear of Death," Regine wrote the following on her PC on April 10 (not previously published):

Fear of death

Friday, April 10, 2009

What are you supposed to do after you hear that you're going to die? It feels wrong to go home and just wait. You don't want to lie in bed and just watch yourself falling slowly apart. When the doctors give up, is it worth it to try other methods? Lots of people would probably try to contact hospitals in other countries, or try alternative treatments. But if nothing can be done, what do you do?

I got some very bad news last week: I've had a relapse. They discovered that 10 percent of the cells in my blood marrow are immature. That's the news that I had to wake up to on Saturday morning. The Easter holiday had finally arrived, and I'd already made so many plans. Not just for Easter, but for the whole year. I was going to go to concerts, and festivals, and I was going to start working as a journalist at the local paper. I was going to start school again in the fall. Then, suddenly, all my plans went down the drain. There are so many things I want to do, but I feel like my time is running out.

Although I've had a relapse, it doesn't mean that there's no hope. The doctors still have some options for me. But I don't feel like I have much hope left in me. My reserves are small, but they're still there. And it's important to keep believing that things can turn around, because otherwise I'll just go crazy. I just don't want any more bad news. My body might be able to keep on fighting, but psychologically I've got nothing left to give.

In the meantime I try to do things that I love. I have to use the time that I do have as best I can. First and foremost, I try to spend as much time as possible with my family and friends. They mean everything to me, and without them I would never have gotten this far. And I'm so thankful that I have them, and that they're there for me. After all, I'm still the same person. I'm not just a cancer patient. A lot of people probably see me as "the girl with cancer," but I don't want to be that person. I want to be normal again, even if only for a minute. Completely, totally normal. It's funny, but it's almost like I forget about everything else I have going on when people talk to me like a normal person, and when they behave completely naturally. Most people don't know what to say or do when they meet someone who has cancer. And although I can understand that, it still isn't very pleasant, and I don't think other cancer patients like it very much either.

When I'm not spending time with my family and friends (or even when I am), I also love to paint, take photos, take walks, and listen to music. I also love to write. It's amazing how much you can express through words and images. I've become a much better painter since I started working at it. The different brushes and color options can actually be really hard to manage over the course of a painting, but it's still super fun to try and learn on your own. I usually don't have anything specific I want to paint; I just start something and see where it goes. You definitely don't need good technical skills. I'm terrible at drawing. I think it just depends on creativity. If you're creative, there are no bad ideas. And I love it when I finally feel satisfied with something I've done. It's hard to think of anything else that feels so gratifying.

But more than anything else, I love photography. I love to be outside in nature and take pictures of whatever catches my eye. For me, when you're out in nature, there's hardly anything that isn't beautiful. Unfortunately, I haven't been in very good shape recently, so there haven't been many trips outside. I hope things improve. I feel energized when I take walks in the forest—when I'm able to just listen to the sounds, smell the smells, and see the incredible beauty all around me.

It's impossible to describe what nature is: It's so many different things—but for me, there's nothing better in the world. That's why I can't understand why we're ruining it. The forest next to my house is my favorite place in the world. I've always loved it. When I was little, my parents had to take walks with me in the forest in the middle of the night to get me to stop crying. Now someone is trying to tear it down to make a profit. I don't like that at all. In fact, I hate it, because in some ways I think the forest and I share a kind of identity.

As I die, the forest dies too. At the same time that the cancer is spreading, so are the houses. It's Easter break now. Construction is on hold. Maybe the cancer will take a break, too? That's what I'm hoping for, and it's the only thing that can save me, too. Plan A has to work now. Cutting out the immune suppressing drugs has to stop the cancer. The new immune system has to work; they have to get rid of the cancer cells that are in the marrow. If not, I'll die.

I don't want to die, but at the same time I have the feeling that pretty soon I won't be able to take it anymore. I'm tired of fighting. I've tried just about everything there is to try. When the chemotherapy didn't work, I had to have a bone marrow transplant. Everything looked like it was going well, all the way up to the follow-up three months later. Then, our greatest fear became our new reality. And now all anyone can do is cry. That goes for me, too, even though it's the people around me who are taking it the hardest. In the end, they're the ones who will have to live with the grief if I die. I'm scared for them. Because how well can anyone handle losing a family member, or a best friend?

What is death, when it really comes down to it? Most people can't even begin to say what they think it is. And of course no one can really know. I'm not religious, but one day at the hospital I talked to

the hospital pastor there. He didn't care if I was religious or not. We just had a conversation about life and death and other difficult topics. I was surprised both by him and by myself. We managed to put words to some profoundly mysterious things. We talked about the incomprehensible. Since I'm not religious, I don't believe in life after death. I think it's like an endless sleep. That it all goes black. That one doesn't feel anymore, that one doesn't see anymore, that one doesn't get to experience anything anymore. Life goes on, but we don't. My mom thinks that the reason why all the good people on earth are taken from us is because they're being gathered to create a better place. That's a really beautiful idea, and I hope she's right, and that's the way it is. Because the world isn't a good place. People starve to death, people fight wars, people kill, people get sick, people die.

Most people don't realize how good their lives really are. When we're healthy, when we're doing well, we waste our energy on feelings of dissatisfaction. I wonder why. Because when our lives are turned upside down, it doesn't matter how dissatisfied we felt before: The only thing we care about is surviving. There's no meaning to life. There's no reason for anything that happens.

How can there be a reason for a good person's death, for diseases, etc. It's fanatical to believe there's a meaning. You just have to accept that things are the way they are. There doesn't need to be a reason. At the same time, that doesn't mean you can't create your own meaning. The key word is *love*. If you don't have love in your life, you don't have anything to live for. We live because of our love for our family, for our friends, for nature, for music, for a certain hobby, for animals, and for boyfriends and girlfriends. That's when there's meaning in your life. That's my opinion anyway.

Waiting for death is dehumanizing. To feel your body just getting worse and worse. To have to wait for answers. For the only answer that matters: Will you live or will you die? Most teenagers spend their time worrying about how they've done on a test, but others—like me—wait to find out if they'll survive long enough to have another birthday. The world is unfair. For those of you who go on to live a long and happy life, I want you to try and give something back to the world. Think of all those other people whose lives are spent in suffering. Give. It's unbelievably important.

Out on a walk

Tuesday, April 14, 2009

Things are going okay, even though we're all still struggling with the tragic news. I try not to think about it. I do things that I enjoy, and behave just like before. I spend time with friends, paint, photograph, etc. Painting is really therapeutic for me. It's especially fun when you notice your technique improving after doing the same thing several times over. A canvas can express so much.

Around the time of her relapse, Regine wrote this poem:

The sun begins to fade.

Darkness is coming,

Good souls waste away,

Dark souls triumph,

Moonlight

Takes the fog in and

Trusts

In a better time.

Hope, stagnated

Retreats shyly.

Windblown sins push

Against the rain, against the tears,

Covering every hearse.

Light is failing

Nature's pull

Toward salvation

Saves the world.

The journey is long.

This tree holds new life. This tree holds

Hope. In the tree lies the source of life.

I hardly notice the disease. That's probably the reason why I've managed not to think about it as much recently. I still haven't had any reactions to the changes in my medication, but then again, it's only been a week. I have to wait another seven days or so. I'm anxious to hear what the doctors will say after their Tuesday meeting. I'm not really expecting that there will be much to report, but I'm scared to death of getting more bad news. I'm also dreading the next bone marrow test. Am not sure when it will happen, but definitely within a week. What if the disease has progressed?

In other news, Martin and I went for a nice walk today. We took photos and had some fun. Martin's also a really good photographer. You'll get to see some of his pictures, and you can see my paintings later, if you're interested. Go to www.smirr.deviantart.com/gallery to see more of my photos. I also uploaded some of Martin's photos there.

I'm dying

Tuesday, April 14, 2009

The doctors don't think they can do anything more for me except give me chemo to prolong my life. That means I don't have much longer to live. Without the chemo, I wouldn't even make it to eighteen. I don't know why they don't want to try the other alternatives they mentioned. I also don't know why they won't try out a lot of the things that have cured other patients. Right now I'm just feeling desperate and sad, and I have no idea what I should do. I'm going to die. What am I supposed to do in the meantime? I absolutely refuse this slow torture. I feel in my body that I'm getting worse and worse. I refuse to rot away like a vegetable. I refuse to just lie there until I can't talk anymore.

I feel like I'm in great shape physically, and I just don't understand why they're giving up on me like this. It's so damn unfair.

I'm healthier now than I was before the transplant, so I could definitely tolerate another round. I know I could. But they refuse to try. Receiving chemo just to lengthen my life is the dumbest thing I've ever heard of. What kind of a life would that be? A life in quarantine and sadness, just waiting for death? No way. Hell no.

Regine's entry and subsequent front-page features in Dagbladet *and the* Kristiansund Daily *generated 1,125 comments on her blog. Here's a small selection.*

Is there anything we can do to change their minds? And weren't you given a reason? It's just terrible. They can't do that!! Not to you. You're too young, too healthy. ☺ Ok, now I'm just crying.
  —*Kamilla*

This is totally wrong . . . I'm sure your parents will try to get you the help you need. Don't give up. Things will work out! We've started collecting money so you can travel overseas if you need to—so don't forget that we're all behind you. Everyone in Kristiansund thinks about you daily and loves you, you know. Keep your head up, Regine . . . Fight back with everything you have.
  —*Hug from Marianne*

Ask people you know (and even people you don't know) for help in finding out what alternative treatments are available and what you need to do to get them. We're also thinking about you in Averoya, and in the blogosphere. Marianne—if you start a collection, there are a lot of us who will contribute, both with money and with getting the word out!
  And Regine, one can't help being moved by you and touched by your words. In the midst of all this, you have to try to live a bit, too;

you have to try not to put all of your energy toward fighting the disease. Do things that you enjoy, and be with people that you like. As much as I want to, I can't promise you that everything will go well, but I really hope so, with all my heart.

—*Warm hugs from Hestiaverden*

According to the patient rights laws, since you are not in agreement with the current treatment plan, you are entitled to a new evaluation. The doctors can't possibly have the right to just give up, especially without even giving you an explanation as to why. It's totally unbelievable. If you call the cancer line they might be able to answer some of your questions; at the very least, they'll definitely know a bit about options for treatment overseas. I'm supporting the people who proposed starting a fund for you, and I'm sure there are many others who would love to do the same! Everyone deserves a chance, and it's totally shocking that the doctors don't seem prepared to give you yours! Don't back down!

—*Anja*

I just don't know what to say. What an awful thing to hear! You're an incredibly strong girl and really deserve so much more. Continue to stand up for yourself and demand everything that can possibly be of help. They can't just give up on such a young life. I really hope there is a way out of this, and that you get to live the life you've fought so hard for.

—*Anne Marthe*

More info

Wednesday, April 15, 2009

I've had another talk with the doctors. They don't think they can do anything else for me, as they already said. They don't think that a new transplant would help. They don't think there is anything at all that can cure me. That's the reason they don't want to try anything else. Instead, they think it's better for me to receive chemo once the disease enters my blood, even though that's not much help. It won't lengthen my life very much either. It's unlikely that I'll make it to my eighteenth birthday.

I appreciate all the comments on this blog. And I'm grateful that people want to collect money—but I wonder if it will really help now. It's not as simple as just raising millions and traveling overseas for treatment. What we need help with is finding a hospital that will review the case, and figure out if they can actually help me. Do they think I have a chance? Is there something new they're willing to try? Do they think there's a treatment that makes sense?

I need specific hospitals. (Germany? The US?)

If there are any hospitals that might be able to help, I would love to hear about them.

A little message and a thank you

Thursday, April 16, 2009

I really appreciate all your comments and concern. It's completely overwhelming; I don't know what to say. But the doctors at Riksen have been totally incredible. Don't put the blame on them. They are just doing what they think is right. They have, after all, done a lot for me; they've done everything they could, according to them. They're basing their decisions on all of the available subject literature, research, experience, scholarship, other doctors overseas, etc.

The doctors at Riksen say I am close to 100 percent incurable. But I know that people in my situation have recovered and gotten well. I've received mail and read about them myself. Isn't it worthwhile to give it one more try?

We've decided to get my medical records, translate them, and ask one of the doctors here if he can help us make the transition to another treatment center. We want to have a new evaluation. Maybe there are some doctors out there who think there is hope? I just can't come to terms with giving up. There must be something . . . even if the doctors say there isn't.

This sounds incredibly strange and freaky, but I actually told my parents before the transplant that I would get through it, but that I would have a relapse after three months. That's pretty sick. I also had a sighting on the way up to Trondheim for chemo. I saw an American flag. I had a quick glimpse of it while I was looking out at the forest. (I probably sound creepy, but it's true.) Probably dumb of me to even mention it.

In any case, I really appreciate your comments and emails, etc. But there's something I need to say: I've received so many responses on email and text that it's a bit much. If you would like to leave a nice supportive message comment for me, you can do it here on the blog. It's hard for me to respond to email and text because there are so many. I've already had 68,000 page views just today. I don't want to offend anyone, but I hope you understand. I really appreciate it.

I think there was something else that I wanted to mention, but I can't remember it now. Anyway, I'll update you as soon as I know more. I'm also open to hearing about suggestions for hospitals abroad, etc. I'll check out the ones that are recommended.

By the way, was there someone who said my ears should be burning since everyone is thinking and talking about me? Well, my ears have literally been tingling since yesterday!

A visit from *Dagbladet*[2]

Thursday, April 16, 2009

Today I had a visit from *Dagbladet*. A journalist and a photographer were here. They were really friendly and spent a lot of time with me. The interview will probably be aired tomorrow. Watch it!

The doctor in Kristiansund agreed to contact some hospitals in New York for evaluations. Hoping for a positive answer!

Newspapers and such

Friday, April 17, 2009

Today there's already been a lot of action. A lot of people have called; a lot of people have sent messages and email. A pervert called me and said he was jerking off. Sick. And yesterday a girl called me the devil because I wasn't a Christian. (I thought that was really spiteful.)

Anyway, I was really pleased with the articles in *Dagbladet* and the *Kristiansund Daily*. There will also be an article in the online version of *Adresseavisa*. I think there will also be a video of me on the *Dagbladet* website.

Other journalists have contacted me, but I've had to decline those interviews because of other plans. It makes me feel bad, but sometimes that's just the way it is.

I got a call from a really nice man this morning who asked me if I wanted to do an exhibition in two months. That made me so happy. I hope I can make it until then.

---

2   *Dagbladet* is one of Norway's largest newspapers. It's done in a tabloid style, and on Fridays *Dagbladet* publishes a special issue devoted to pop culture and young adult issues.

Today I'm going to paint with Else.[3] I hope it will be fun. I'm also trying to decide if I should let NRK More and Romsdal[4] come and film us; I'm not quite sure yet. (Update: I just invited them.) There's a lot going on right now, and I know that I have to be selective; I hope I don't overdo it or make any big mistakes.

NRK and TVNorge—update

Friday, April 17, 2009

By the way, you can see me on TVNorge tonight at 6:00 pm, and on NRK1 at 6:40 pm. If you're interested. There is also a video available on *Dagbladet*'s website.

It's been a really busy day—so many emails and Facebook posts and texts and calls! Luckily, I was able to relax and paint a bit over at Else's house. She's an amazing woman. I'm still sitting here, and we've had lunch and really enjoyed ourselves. It's been a good break from all the stress. I had to turn off the telephone because it wouldn't stop ringing.

Update: TVNorge didn't show the feature about me. I don't know why. Maybe they'll show it later?

That aside, the Facebook group dedicated to my situation is called *Vi som skal kjempe for Regine Stokke.*[5] They're doing a collection auction. It's serious. If the money can't be used for me, it will either go to a nonprofit that does research on myelodysplatic syndrome, or it might also be used to better the conditions of children and adults with cancer.

---

3   Artist and art teacher who commented on Regine's blog in November.

4   Local TV news stations.

5   In support of Regine Stokke.

Update: Now you can read about me in Swedish newspapers. My story has apparently spread like wildfire: You can find it online in the April 17, 2009, edition of the paper.

On bringing out the best in people
Saturday, April 18, 2009

Maybe a lot of people are taken aback by the fact that I make so many media appearances. A lot of people probably think I'm starved for attention or something (and I'm sure that there are also a lot of other people who think it's great). I just think it's important to make people aware of the issues. Many young people feel alone in this type of situation. In a small city, you rarely find more than one young cancer patient. And it's so incredibly hard to have to live through this type of situation. You feel as if no one understands you, and you feel like it can't really be happening. And I totally understand that! You have to go through something like this before you can understand what it's really like, and understand what it's like to live with this crippling sense of uncertainty. "Will I survive this?" you ask. And it's a thought that affects all cancer patients (and others who are seriously ill).

This type of thing helps to bring out the best in people. People get involved; people contribute. You don't always have to contribute with money either. It's enough to just be a supportive human being. It's enough to show up, and simply show that you care. It's incredibly important for people to get involved with things that are outside the realm of their own experiences. There are plenty of healthy, smart, capable people out there who can really be of service. There are so many people who suffer every day, who need your help and support, both in terms of money and also just in terms of human fellowship.

And that's why I'm encouraging you to do something about this—those of you who can.

Something that didn't come across very well in my interviews is that I'm very concerned with getting people to register as blood and bone marrow donors.

It's hugely important, and I've written about this issue before. I hope people just go out and *do it* instead of dragging their heels and "thinking about it." That one simple act can help to save lives. And isn't it rewarding to do something for others?

There have been so many write-ups about me in the media recently! I saw some more today. You can read more about me in today's editions of the *Kristiansund Daily* and *Dagbladet:* www.dagbladet.no/2009/04/18/nyheter/innenriks/sykdom/kreft/kreftforskning/5794831/.

As I mentioned earlier, they're taking a collection for me. My hope is that they raise a ton of money for myelodysplastic syndrome research and for improving conditions for child and adult cancer patients. You can read more about this on the Facebook page "In support of Regine Stokke." A web page will be set up eventually, and I'll get back to you with more information about that later.

By the way, I'm on the top of the list at www.blogg.no.[6] Incredibly cool, even if it doesn't really matter much.

In my next entry I was thinking of posting some of my paintings—especially the ones from my session yesterday at Else's house—at the Undertow gallery.

---

6   Blog-publishing service that posts "top lists" of its most read and active blogs.

Video blog

Saturday, April 18, 2009

Oistein Monsen (*Dagbladet*) filmed me while I was taking a walk. So before the post about my paintings, here's a quick video blog:http://sinober.blogg.no/1240068800_videoblogg.html

Edit: By the way, I was on TV Norge news at 6:00 pm in case anyone saw it. I have no idea if they'll rerun it or not. Do they repeat the same news show all evening? Anyway, it focused on the same stuff as this video blog, but covered some other things as well.

Exhibit, book project, etc.

Monday, April 20, 2009

I'm so fortunate to have my own photo exhibit at *Nordic Light*[7] next week. The annual event is held here in Kristiansund, and my exhibit will be in the Old Expert Hall on Kongens Plass. I'm really looking forward to it.

My exhibit will be called "Face Your Fear." I hope it will add something really special to the exhibit. It's happening next Wednesday.

This is really a dream come true for me. Thank you so much, Ann Olaug![8]

Also, a man contacted me about doing a book project. It seems like it would be made up of mainly photos and poems. Incredibly exciting!

My other exhibit will be on June 27 in Sunndal. I hope I'll be able to participate in that one, too. If not, someone needs to organize and set up everything for me. Whatever happens, though, this is another dream come true.

---

7 Annual one-week international photography event.

8 Ann Olaug Slatlem is a volunteer with *Nordic Light*.

I'm so thankful for the people who helped to make this happen. It means so much, and feels really fulfilling.

Here are two pictures that will be the centerpiece of my exhibit at *Nordic Light*:

The blood test results were bad today. But we expected that. After all, I had a relapse. But I hope things will turn around soon. My body's under attack, and the disease won't just disappear. I'm waiting to be rescued.

Paintings

Tuesday, April 21, 2009

Clearly I'm not an artistic genius, but I still have a great time when I'm painting. And isn't that what matters? I'm glad you're interested in seeing them. Here they are[9]!

Clothing sale—update

Tuesday, April 21, 2009

Update: New product descriptions have come out, and now you can see the reverse side of the sweaters, which will have some writing on them. The writing on the sweatpants will appear on the back of the legs. See www.beltespenner.com for more information.

Line Victoria[10] had the idea that we could sell T-shirts to make some money for my support fund. Beltspenner wanted to participate as soon as they heard about it, and they've already started making some sales. The image is from a photo of my eyes that I edited and submitted. Anne Marthe wrote the slogan on the back (which is

---

9 See artwork on page 127.

10 Line Victoria Husby is the program director at TV2 television station who followed Regine's blog from the beginning.

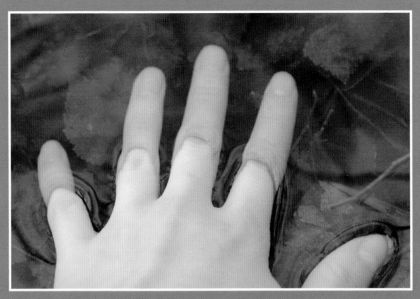

Two of Regine's photos, entitled "Drowning" and "Dead Girl Walking" respectively.

pulled directly from my blog): "Face your fear. Accept your war. It is what it is." I think the T-shirts are pretty awesome, and so are the other clothes, too. You can get the T-shirt in both men's and women's styles. They also offer pants, hoodies, and tank tops—and all the proceeds will go to my support fund. A BIG thank you to Beltespenner and special thanks as well to Thomas Adams, who's responsible for of all this! Totally incredible. You can read more about the campaign.

All the clothes are available in sizes small to extra-large, and are available in several colors.

Treasure every day
Wednesday, April 22, 2009

I have to admit that all the media attention surrounding me has been stressful, and it's been difficult to decide which offers I should say yes to. Some places have also written about me without my permission, which isn't very cool (even if they were good articles). Thankfully it's starting to quiet down now. I'm in no way starved for attention, but I *am* very involved in spreading my message. I'm hoping that after a good day today, I can spend a nice evening with my girlfriends and just relax. I never know when I'll have to go to the hospital again, so it's important to treasure every day.

It's a good thing I'm not sick, because my immune system is really bad right now. I'm getting pretty worried about that. Your white blood cell count shouldn't ever go into a free fall.

I think they need to do something. And I just hope there's something that *can* still be done.

A lot of you are probably wondering if I ever got an answer from the hospital overseas. I haven't. So I have no idea what they think about my situation—and whether or not they think there's any hope.

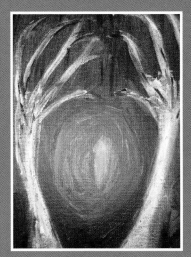

I was lucky enough to get in touch with a Swedish woman whose son had exactly the same diagnosis as me. The Swedish doctors gave up on him when he had a relapse after his bone marrow transplant. A few different measures were taken to cure him, including a new transplant, and he's still alive today. Stories like this are really important for me to hear, and I'm glad this woman reached out to me. I hope that I can imitate that boy's success.

On another note, there's something I need to correct. The photo exhibit I talked about that was supposed to be in Sunndal is actually in the Ora prayer house (it's not a religious organization). It's being organized by Jon Riiser, and it's on June 27 at noon. I also hope that some of you will come to *Nordic Light* next Wednesday.

By the way, the clothing sale is going really well. Remember that you're supporting a good cause! This is great.

I'm actually kind of worried that people will get sick of me after seeing so much of me in the media. But the thing is, it wasn't me who went to them; they were the ones who came to me, and I hope you understand why I agreed to talk with some of them. I'm really involved in the cancer cause, and I want to make sure I do what's best for myself and for others in the same situation. I hope you have a great day, and a big thank you to everyone who's getting involved! I really appreciate it, and you need to know that.

New treatment started today
Thursday, April 23, 2009

St. Olav's and Riksen have a collaborative treatment project that's starting up today. The treatment is relatively new, and no one knows how well it's going to work. It might be able to reverse the disease, but it's definitely not a miracle cure. The goal is to get to a place where I can get a new transplant, so this treatment is intended to just buy us some more time. It will take seven days, and it's happening here in Trondheim. I'm really eager to hear more about how it's supposed to work. No matter what, it will be of some benefit. If it doesn't turn back my disease, it will at least extend my life. Anyway, we're all really excited to see how it turns out. I guess you could say it's like an alternate version of chemo. Everyone's really pleased that the doctors have made it available, especially since I've got nothing to lose right now. The treatment can probably just be continued in Kristiansund on Monday. The best thing about all of this, by far, is being able to stay at home.

As I said, I'm now at St. Olav's for treatment. It's not very likely that I'll get sick, but I need to be here just in case something out of the ordinary happens. That's the risk with all treatments. You never know, and no one has any guarantees. Just after we got started with the treatment, Bengt Eidem came by to visit with his girlfriend, Kristin. It was so sweet. They're truly good people. We had a lot to talk about and we have a lot in common. He got some good results on his most recent set of tests today (hooray!), and he also brought a nice gift for me. A cute little teddy bear. I hope we can meet again. He said he hoped so, too.

One step at a time

Saturday, April 25, 2009

I think the treatment's going well—no complications yet. And that's great! The goal with the medicine is to help the bone marrow generate more healthy blood cells and at the same time kill the immature cells. It will be interesting to see how it goes. In any case, the medication tends to work for most people. I'm very curious. Those who are interested can go here to read more about the drug: www.vidaza.com.

I had another set of visits from Bengt and from *Dagbladet* today. The interview will most likely be printed tomorrow. It was a really pleasant conversation at least. It's an important issue, and I'm excited about seeing an article about Bengt and me. I received a gift from the journalist and photographer. They bought the TV series *Entourage* for me. I need a few things to watch now that I'm at the hospital. My father and I are going to see *Dead Snow*[11] on the big screen today. (A little black humor never hurt anyone.)

I want to take a quick second to thank the RaumaRock festival for their amazing gift. They sent me festival passes, T-shirts, photos, a letter, and a lot of other stuff, too. How sweet! I'm really looking forward to the festival. One way or another, I'll get there! That's my goal, and it's important to set goals for yourself. I get depressed if I just sit around and dwell on how sick I am and how hard things are for me. Plans are important, but they need to be realistic, too. I think that in general I manage to keep things pretty reasonable.

Quick update
Sunday, April 26, 2009

Update: Someone asked if I could do a question-and-answer post. Maybe that's not such a bad idea? As far as I'm concerned, you can just ask away, and I'll try to answer as best I can.

---

11   Movie about Nazi zombies in the snow.

Safe at home

Sunday, April 26, 2009

I finally made it home, and I feel great. It's just as easy to continue the treatment here as at the Kristiansund hospital. It only takes ten minutes a day. Still, it was amazing to meet with the St. Olav doctors and nurses again. They're incredible, and we had a lot to talk about. Not only are they nice, but they're also super-talented! Just wanted to say . . .

You can access today's interview in *Dagbladet.*

Continue sending in your questions. Ask all you want!

On the same day, Regine writes the following in her diary (not included on her blog):

I love love and affection. I live for affection and love. But right now, at this moment, I don't want any new people to start liking me. A lot of people like me when they get to know me. And now I have to pull back. I don't want to hurt anyone when I go away. And that's what's in danger of happening, I think.

Admitted

Friday, May 1, 2009

Unfortunately, I've been admitted back into the Kristiansund hospital. I've got a high fever and extreme muscle pains. No one knows what's going on yet, but they took a lot of tests. Have started taking antibiotics, which we hope will take care of the problem. (It's also possible that these are side effects of the medication.)

Started getting sick a few days ago. I had a visit from Sofsen[12], and it was super nice. She's an awesome girl. I wish I had been in better shape when she was here. Will have to try again later!

I also got to take part in the photo exhibit opening. (Luckily.) I wasn't in very good shape at the time, but in a way I really had to go. And I'm really glad I did.

So I was admitted on Wednesday, and so far things are not getting any better. I'm really worried. No one knows what it is yet. I just want to go home; it's better to be sick at home than to just lie here, sick and waiting. They can't do anything anyway. My sister's confirmation is this weekend, and I'd like to be at home for that at least. I'm so scared that this thing—whatever it is—won't go away, and that they won't find out what it is. I'm on antibiotics, but it doesn't seem to be doing much. Had a fever of more than 104 yesterday, and it looks like it's heading in the same direction again now.

I was totally dazed at the exhibit because I was starting to get sick. It's too bad it turned out that way.

I wasn't too impressed with the fact that *Dagbladet* said that I was "sentenced to death." I'm sick of people only talking about how I'm going to die. No one knows that yet, especially since I recently started a new treatment. Things look bad, I admit, but I get really upset when people write inappropriate comments on my blog. Someone actually sent me a message saying he wanted to come to my funeral. Don't people have hearts?

Regine's entry led to 414 comments, for the most part supportive. Many had also read Dagbladet's *headline "Cancer patient Regine is praised*

---

12   Blogger and Regine's friend.

by Morten Krogvold"[13] with the subtitle "Photo legend describes seven-teen-year-old's photographs as totally amazing." Here's a small selection, followed by a response from Regine:

Hi Regine,

It made me sad to read this post. Hope that things get better soon. Remember that people are people (for better and for worse), and everyone reacts and even thinks a little differently. Your openness has provoked thoughts and feelings in people that they may not have even known that they had. Some people are really impulsive and others are more thorough and some are maybe not quite "well." The comments will probably be like that, too. Rise above these comments and use your energy on something that matters (like taking care of yourself and your family). I wish you all the best.

—*With kind regards, Tore*

Get well, Regine! You'll clear this hurdle soon—I know it! In the meantime, there's a real downside to being the focus of so much attention: You'll get a lot of dumb comments from people who don't know any better or who have real psychological problems. So don't pay any attention to them. You've accomplished so much already, and dis-played real wisdom and an ability to think through some profound questions about human existence. I'm also undergoing cancer treat-ment and have learned so much from you already, even though I'm now an old woman of sixty-seven.

—*Warm thoughts from Unni*

I had a functionally impaired daughter who was also given a "death sentence" by her doctors; they felt she would live a year at most. So

---

13   Artistic director of *Nordic Light*.

every day while I was walking around, I was also consumed with the idea of her death! But we need to focus on life, not death. New drugs and treatments are being developed all the time, and you have to be open to the possibilities they may offer. I'm sending tons of positive thoughts your way, and I know that thousands of others are doing the same.

I hope the fever goes away and that you have a good day.

—*Grete*

What great feedback from Morten Krogvold! That must have been so wonderful to hear—and it's fully deserved as well. Have only seen your photos that are posted online, but they are truly powerful and very well done.

Some people don't think very carefully about what they say. Rise above these comments, and focus on the positive feedback instead! You'll get well, Regine! That's the way it is. ☺

—*Ingeborg*

A SMALL REQUEST TO EVERYONE HERE: Regine is not just "the girl with cancer." Regine is Regine, and she happens to also have cancer. There's a big difference. She's a totally cool and fun girl—with values and opinions that are distinctly her own. She has so much to offer! She's tough (with real backbone), and isn't a "poor, little, sweet" girl. Yes, we can PITY her situation. But she doesn't need to hear "POOR YOU" all day, every day, because she KNOWS that she pulled a short straw here. Rehashing it over and over again is just rubbing it in. And yes, she *is* sweet—but she's also tough. And to those who keep posting things like "Awww . . . dig your blog!" . . . What is there to dig!? The way she writes, I hope. Because she's talented. But Regine is blogging to share a message. She's not writing so that people will pat her on the head and say "Pooor little thing" and then go out and get drunk and complain the next day because they have hangovers.

And for those who focus on death the whole time. What a twisted fucking (excuse my French) focus!??? Christ, focus on some of the good things instead.

Thank you!!

—*Sofsen*

Just wanted to tell you that you're doing a world of good for others through your blog and your fight with cancer.

Last time I went to the blood bank, the nurse told me there had been a big surge of sixteen- to seventeen-year-olds who had read about you, and who wanted to give blood. They'll definitely return to give blood when they're eighteen. And then there are probably many, many of those old enough who have given blood because they heard about you from somewhere else.

You're making the world a better place, Regine! I think of you often and hope everything works out in the end! Enjoy the confirmation!

—*Stina*

When will you die?

—*J*

Thank you so much for all the nice comments!

J: Are you a total shithead, or what? "*When will you die?*" Maybe you'll die tomorrow in a car accident—you never really know. No one knows exactly when they'll die. Do you ask just so you can rub in how bad things look for me? I feel like the negative comments are getting more and more frequent, and I honestly can't understand why.

I really appreciate all the positive ones (and luckily they're the majority)—they mean a lot! But at the same time, I can't help getting upset by the negative ones, and maybe that's why people post them. Some people just don't respect others, and don't know what's important in life. If only they knew what it's like to live with this fear. They probably wouldn't be so high and mighty then. Unfortunately though, life is unfair and diseases affect the most innocent—and I'm not just thinking of myself. There are so many people here in Norway and around the world who have been struck down by things like this. All the other cancer patients I know truly deserve to live.

—*Regine*

Answer from the US

Tuesday, May 5, 2009

The doctor from Kristiansund called and said that she'd received an answer from the US. My mom, my dad, and I eventually went down to the hospital, filled with anticipation. We'd already been waiting about two weeks for an answer. The US doctor wrote that he agreed with many of the Riksen hospital's conclusions and felt that my prognosis was bad—that I didn't have a good chance—but that he was willing to treat me if I was in good condition and didn't show any specific signs of illness. The treatment would then involve some experimental chemotherapy, which could lead to remission (a state in which my bone marrow would consist of less than 5 percent cancer cells). And then after that, if the disease did go into remission, he would have to give me a new bone marrow transplant. If it was still an option for us, I could go see them so that they could assess my health and cells with their own eyes.

The answer was what we expected. It's clear at this point that I have a disease with a pretty bad prognosis—we definitely realize that.

But if the doctors are willing to try again, why shouldn't we take that chance? Because even though the chances are slim, it still might work.

Anyway, now we're struggling with our final decision. Should we continue the treatment here, or travel to the US?

We're going to Trondheim on Thursday to talk to the doctors, and thought we could discuss it then. It's important that all the experts give us their viewpoints. We'll go where the treatment is best. If we find out that it's better to continue the treatment here, we'll stay here. Everything is up in the air right now, but if the US becomes a possibility, we need to head over there pretty soon. This particular hospital is located in Texas, and it's one of the world's best for cancer treatment.

We're also waiting for an answer from a hospital in England and another one in Germany. It will be interesting to compare the responses.

Luckily I'm starting to feel better now. I haven't had a fever at all today, and that's great. I also got to participate in my sister's confirmation, which made me really happy. It was great. A very successful day. With a little help from the home nurse, I could be back home for most of the weekend.

Answers to questions—part one

Thursday, May 7, 2009

Early tomorrow I'm traveling to Trondheim, where we'll have a talk with the doctors. We'll be discussing the previously mentioned hospital in the US, along with some other things as well. The medicine I just received doesn't appear to be working, and I'm starting to get really stressed. If something is going to happen, it has to happen soon. When I get back, I'll update you on what's going on. Here are answers to some of your questions.

Ane asks:

Question: Have you considered writing a book (when you get well) about everything that's happening now?

Answer: Yes, I'd be very interested in (and excited about) a book project later on.

Etthjertetoindivider asks:

Question: Have you written a will?

Answer: No.

Question: Are you scared of dying?

Answer: Yes.

Question: If yes, why are you scared of dying?

Answer: Because I have so much more I want to accomplish here in life. I want to live more, see more, experience more. Isn't that natural?

Question: Do you think I'll get to meet you one day?

Answer: Never say never.

Question: If yes, would you give me a hug?

Answer: Since I'm totally paranoid about bacteria and stuff like that, most likely you would not get a hug. ☺

Question: What do you think about what NN[14] said about you several blog posts ago, when he tried to make himself look like a great guy?

Answer: I thought they were incredibly childish entries. There are more important things in my life right now than having the most read blog in Norway.

Question: What do you think about him?

---

14   On April 17 Regine's blog moved from the twentieth most visited blog on www.blogg.no to the second most visited blog, and on the same day, NN asked his blog readers if she deserved a top spot on the list. NN blogs about fashion, makeup, and his life.

Answer: I don't know him personally, so I probably shouldn't say too much about what I think, but he's not exactly my type, is one way to put it.

Question: Which blogs do you read daily?

Answer: Maren-Sofie's, Anne Marie's, and Sofie Frøysaa's.[15]

Question: Are you going back to school?

Answer: If I get well, I would probably go back to school.

Question: What kind of work do you want to do?

Answer: Psychology, photography, or journalism.

Martine asks:

Question: What do you think happens after death?

Answer: I think everything goes black, like in a kind of eternal sleep and then that's it—you just don't exist anymore.

Question: Are you close to your family?

Answer: Yes.

Question: What's your best memory from childhood?

Answer: I have so many good memories from childhood. If I had to choose one special memory it would have to be when Malin and I created an imaginary friend. He was a polar bear who needed food every day. We visited him every day to cook food for him.

Question: The worst!

Answer: When I was given a hard time because of how I looked.

Question: Who would you most like to be stranded with on a desert island?

Answer: All of my best friends.

Question: Which person/people mean the most for you?

Answer: My family, my friends, and my cat.

---

15 Maren-Sofie blogs about living with ALL (acute lymphoid leukemia); Anne Marie is the wife of cancer patient Svein Kåre Handeland, who passed away in March 2009; and Sofie Frøysaa is the blogger known here as Sofsen.

Oda asks this question about giving blood:

Question: Which precautions do you have to take with regards to alcohol consumption and smoking? (I don't smoke myself, but maybe others are wondering about this?) And what about kissing/sex, etc.? Are there other things you are not allowed to do? Could there be consequences if you break any of those rules?

Answer: I don't think there are any special precautions. The most important thing is to be healthy and not to have any contagious diseases. A physical exam will be done to see if the donor meets the requirements. It's very important not to break the rules; it can have consequences for the one who gets the blood.

Marisve asks:

Question: Which experience would you like to relive?

Answer: I wouldn't mind reliving all the concerts and festivals I've been to with my friends, and more generally I'd love to just go back and relive all of the great times me and my friends have had together. I wouldn't mind going on all of our family vacations again either.

Silje asks:

Question: Where do you find inspiration? Where do you get the courage for all this?

Answer: I get inspiration from music, from nature, and from myself—from my own thoughts and feelings.

Ms. North asks:

Question: Do you have a favorite photographer?

Answer: I really like Peter Beste's photographs. I also like Matt Mahurin.

Anonymous asks:

Question: I have a few different questions about your disease. When you got chemo, you lost your hair. Did it fall out gradually? Do you lose absolutely all the hair on your body? Like your eyebrows and eyelashes, and under your arms and legs?

Answer: It took a little while before everything fell off. Yes, it fell out gradually. At first I only lost the hair on my head, but after a while I also lost my eyebrows and eyelashes. It took about four months before absolutely all of it fell out.

Question: How are you affected by your disease on a day-to-day basis? Do you really notice it? Are you in pain or are you sick a lot? Or do you just have a kind of general sense of the disease? A general anxiety?

Answer: Of course I notice it! Every day. I can't go to school. I can't do things that other people take for granted. I have a weak immune system, which means I have to watch out for infection, which means I can't be in places with a lot of people. I'm not in a lot of pain, but I'm really weak, and things that wouldn't even make a normal person tired make me exhausted.

Question: Do you think it's okay for a seventeen-year-old to get a "death sentence" from her doctors?

Answer: Of course it's not okay, but if there's nothing they can do, then there's nothing they can do. I feel like the doctors should do everything they can, and after that it should be up to the patient if he or she wants to try alternative treatments.

Elizabeth asks:

Question: What has been the best thing, if anything, about having this disease?

Answer: I would say that the best thing is that it makes you put a greater value on life; it makes you enjoy every day more than you did before.

Question: What are you most scared of?

Answer: I'm most scared of having to go through a hellish decline, with lots of pain and suffering. And I'm also scared of death, of course.

Question: What was the first thing that occurred to you when you found out that the doctors had given up on you?

Answer: Isn't that obvious? Of course I thought that I would die and that there wasn't any hope, and that it was really over.

Question: What do you think of all the attention you're getting (both positive and negative)?

Answer: For the most part the attention has been positive. It's helped me persevere and keep a positive outlook. The support I've gotten has been incredibly important. Some people give me negative comments, but there are people who are simply dumb and ignorant and who maybe just lack the capacity to be compassionate (or care for anyone at all).

Question: Are you really as strong as you seem to be? Where do you get courage?

Answer: I have highs and lows, and sometimes I'm weaker than at other times. You learn to be strong in this type of situation. You don't have a choice.

Beate asks:

Question: Have you played any sports? If so, which ones?

Answer: I've danced, boxed, and played soccer.

Question: Favorite band/artist?

Answer: Ulver, Enslaved, and Wardruna.

Caroline asks:

Question: What do you usually do at the hospital when you aren't getting treatment? Do you read a lot and stuff like that?

Answer: When you aren't getting treatment, you're usually not at the hospital. ☺ But maybe you're thinking about when I *am* getting treatment? Then I usually just watch TV to make the time pass. Other than that, there's not very much to do.

Ine Amalie asks:

Question: What was your first reaction when they told you about your diagnosis?

Spring, 2009

Answer: I got totally scared, and was sure that it was the end. My head was spinning with thoughts about treatment, the prognosis, etc.

Question: What's it like to have no hair (I think it suits you not to have it, but I'm wondering what you think/feel about it)?

Answer: It's incredibly unpleasant. I feel naked. I liked having my hair so that I could hide behind it sometimes. I truly miss arranging my hair, brushing it, washing it . . .

Question: When you get well, do you have any plans about what you'll do?

Answer: I'm very careful about having plans and dreaming, even if I do let my mind wander sometimes. Right now I just want to live, do the things I want to, and spend quality time with the people I like. I also want to contribute something to the world. I want to work toward improving the lives of hospital patients, and I also want to help cancer patients who are struggling. And of course I want to travel around the world and take photos.

The rest will come later!

Get rich or die trying
Thursday, May 7, 2009

The medicine I've been on hasn't been very effective. It can take a long time for it to work, and under normal circumstances I'd need to have several cycles, but things are at the point where we just don't have time for that. The disease keeps advancing, and now it's totally out of control. The blood sample the doctor looked at was full of cancer cells.

We found out that the best thing to do is to go ahead with a high-dose cycle. We have no idea if it will work, or if I can tolerate the treatment, but we think it's best to try. It's just not an option for me to go home to die. We're trying anything that might work. The new plan is for me to have two chemo cycles to get me into remission. After that they'll give me a new transplant—*if* everything goes well. I really hope the chemo gets rid of these cancer cells so that I can have the new transplant. We're starting on Monday, and things are getting urgent. The doctors in Trondheim didn't think there was an advantage to going all the way to the US, since they're able to offer the same treatment here.

It's not going to be easy to start on such a tough treatment again, but I know it needs to happen.

I wish there was a miracle cure, but unfortunately there isn't.

I hope that at some point I'll be in as good a mood as I was in the picture below. But that seems unlikely right now . . .

Guest post
Friday, May 8, 2009

One of my readers really wanted me to open the blog up to a guest blogger. And who better than Sofie Frøysaa? She wanted to write a post for the people who've left me negative comments. Personally, I really like what she's written, and I'm thrilled that she supports me as much as she does. Luckily most of my readers are positive, intelligent, and kind people, but when you have a blog that's become this popular, more and more negative comments come in.

Sofie Frøysaa—you mean so much to me. You're the best!

WAKE UP!

D ear readers:

My name is Sofie Frøysaa, and I, like many of you, have followed this blog since Regine started it last November (n.b.: I take full responsibility for this entry).

Most of you contribute with motivational, supportive comments. Most of you show compassion and wish Regine well—as you would expect, right? However, there are some idiots out there who take out their own anger and frustration on Regine. This entry is for them . . .

Not only am I a regular reader and admirer of Regine, but I'm also her friend. That's why I get fed up and angry (not to mention sad) when people unnecessarily drain her energy by tossing crap in her comment box.

It's no secret that NN produced the most pathetic blog post ever, entitled "Drama in Paradise." This post of his focused on the famous top ten list at www.blogg.no. In it, he asked his readers if they thought Regine deserves to be on this charming list of top bloggers. (It should also be mentioned that he lets very few of the comments sent to him appear on his blog. That's why it's just the icing on the cake that he now dishes out such nasty comments.)

Clearly, what's most important to Regine right now is her popularity and having as many blog readers as possible. This is obviously the whole reason for her blog. All PR is good PR or something like that. (Oy, I forgot for a second that this entry is addressed to people who probably don't understand irony. Sorry.) Another asshole made an idiot out of himself in the comment box just yesterday. Whenever that guy opens his mouth, or turns on his computer, he's actively reducing the average social intelligence among Norway's population. He did say sorry though. (So in other words: There is hope! Otherwise, I never would have written this entry.)

Today I came across yet another impressive comment. A girl writes, "I feel like you seem so sour and fed up when you answer the questions." So that's strange, is it? My dear: How would *you* have reacted if you'd gotten the same news as Regine? Would you have shrugged your shoulders and smiled? I'm pretty sure you don't understand the seriousness of all this. In a completely brutal and unfair way, this is a matter of life and death. I lost my mobile phone last week (flying home from seeing Regine, in fact). I got bitter and fed up just about that. It's in those types of meaningless disappointments that people get "sour and fed up." That you even chose those words is completely amazing. Do you think people get SOUR when they live with cancer? Have you heard of perspective before? No? That's what I thought.

And when it comes to the questions that Regine gets, they're not all written by Shakespeare, if you know what I mean. To pull out just a few recent examples: "Are you scared of dying?" "Do you think it's okay for someone who's seventeen years old to get a death sentence from her doctors?" "What will you do if you hear that there's no hope for you, and that you'll die in a month?" Do you just want to rub it in? Why is it that so many people focus on death? The best one was probably: "Rest in peace." Don't you think that Regine is totally aware that the worst could actually happen here? Why not encourage her to think positively? Why not just take a second to point out that as long as there's life, there's hope. She'll get through this!

If there's one person who deserves a place here on earth, then it's Regine. If there's one person we can learn from, it's Regine. If there's one person we need to cheer on—yup, it's Regine. She's "only" seventeen years old, but she's dived deeper into life than most people. She's seen life at its worst, but she still holds onto her courage. She teaches us to value life. She teaches us to see life from another perspective. She shows us that life is a valuable gift. That we only get one life on this earth, and therefore we need to be the best people we can possibly be.

Regine is an exemplary human being. It is unacceptable—in fact it's downright shameful—for people to take their own frustrations out on her. Some people are probably, in an absurd and pathetic way, just jealous that they'll never accomplish what Regine has already accomplished at the age of seventeen.

When I was four years old, my mother taught me that if you don't have anything nice to say, then you shouldn't say anything at all. What I'd like to propose is that going forward we all live according to the Cardemom Town law,[16] and focus on what really matters here in life.

If anyone has questions or angry comments in response to this post, then respond on *my* blog—not Regine's.

Risking it all

Saturday, May 9, 2009

The weekend was good, in spite of everything else that's going on. Before I start the treatment on Monday, I'm trying to enjoy myself as much as possible. Tonight I'm going to have a nice dinner with my family and enjoy my time with them. I spent a lot of time with Martin over the past few days, and that was—as always—amazing. I try to do things that help me to forget my illness, if only for a little while. The best thing that my friends can do for me is make me

---

16   From the children's book *When the Robbers Came to Cardemom Town* (Thorbjorn Egner, 1952). Residents of Cardemom Town live by the law "You shouldn't bother others/You should be nice and kind/And otherwise you can do as you please."

forget. But still, I'm dreading Monday more and more. It won't be easy to start that awful cycle, but it has to be done. I have nothing to lose, so I may as well give it all I've got. The doctors at Trondheim agreed that I should start a high-dose cycle. They're going to do everything they can to get me through it, but it will be tough. We all know it.

Arrived safely

Sunday, May 10, 2009

After three and a half hours in the car, I'm finally in Trondheim, at St. Olav's hospital (yet again). Thankfully, nothing will happen until early tomorrow morning. But then it will be full-speed ahead. First a bone marrow test, and then after that the chemo cycle starts. It will be interesting to see how many cancer cells have taken up residence in my bone marrow now, but the chemo cycle will start no matter what the results are. The cycle will last five days. During those five days, I'm counting on being totally knocked out by the chemo, as usual. The days afterward will be worse. Then there will probably be another bout of blood poisoning in store for me, which is a truly awful thought. It's a good thing that we now know a little more about how my body reacts, so the right antibiotics are probably already on hand. The color of the chemo drugs I'll get are white and blue. I've had the same combination before, and it worked. I hope it does now, too. Why shouldn't it? We just have to wait and see. After having had the blue chemo, I've developed a total distaste for all kinds of things that are blue. Even blue slushies make me want to vomit now.

Something is seriously wrong with Norwegian health care

Monday, May 11, 2009

Some of you have probably heard about Espen Steen. In January 2007 he found out that he had intestinal cancer. He started chemo and radiation therapy and went through several operations. Later he learned that the cancer had spread to his liver. He continued with the chemotherapy treatments, but the results were bad. Several operations later, he was told that the cancer had also spread to his lungs. At that point there was nothing more that the doctors could do for Espen Steen. He was advised that his cancer was incurable.

Espen did not want to give up so easily. After researching several alternative clinics, he found Dr. Burzynski, based in Houston, Texas. That clinic had had good results treating the kind of cancer Espen has. But the treatment costs money, and Espen needed financial assistance. The treatment is available here in Norway, too, but it's not used to treat Espen's specific type of cancer. Therefore, the treatment isn't being offered to him here. Instead, he needs to travel all the way to the US and then pay huge medical bills.

Espen is apparently getting good results from the treatment. Go to www.espensteen.com to read his whole story. He would probably appreciate if you could contribute with anything at all, especially since he and his family can't afford to pay for the treatment.

So far so good

Wednesday, May 13, 2009

The chemo cycle is underway and so far it's actually worked better than we expected. Originally, the plan was to do a five-day cycle from Monday to Friday, but now it's not certain that I'll need the Friday session. We'll look at the blood test results tomorrow. You never know what's happening in the bone marrow before taking a test, but according to the blood tests the cycle has had a really good effect, and the doctors seem to be really surprised (in a good way).

When I started the cycle, my white blood (leukocyte) cell count was 26. A healthy person would have a count of three to ten. These numbers indicate if there are a lot of cancer cells in the blood, but if the number is high, it can also indicate an infection. For a person with cancer, these numbers will just rise and rise if they're not treated. In one day, they fell from 26 to 5—a really incredible drop which indicates that the cycle is working well.

In about two weeks they'll give me a new bone marrow test to see how many cancer cells are left. That will be a long day.

So far I haven't had significant reactions to the chemo. My appetite isn't the best, but I manage to get some food down. And luckily I don't feel nauseous at all! Otherwise I'm just a little tired. The doctors say I'll have some aches next week, and that's also when I'll probably get blood poisoning. But it's possible that I'll be able to take a trip home right after the chemo is finished. Maybe for the weekend. I hope so. If not, it won't be for a while.

Martin is visiting. He spent the night here at the hospital. It's nice to have a visit from someone besides my parents (but of course it's nice to have them, too).

Yesterday I went into town right after I had the chemo. I went to the movie theater, where they also have an eclectic group of films available as DVDs. I bought David Lynch's *Blue Velvet*. I really liked it. Thumbs up!

I also found out from Ann Olaug Slatlem (who's been so kind and who organized just about everything for my exhibits) that Morten Krogvold showed some of my photos to his photographer friends— and that they really liked the photos! That's super exciting—it makes me so happy to hear stuff like that. I also sold some photos, but I'm not exactly sure how many yet. I think they'll also become available for sale online eventually. That would be great.

Don't forget about the benefit concert at 6:00 pm!

Thursday, May 14, 2009

I just wanted to remind you all about the benefit concert tonight at Tahiti at 6:00 pm. It's going to be amazing, with music and dancing and more. Unfortunately I can't be there, even though I'd love to go. I'll probably get to go home tomorrow, and I'll have my last dose of chemo in the morning. I hope that those of you nearby will make it to the concert. Just to clarify: All the money that's raised will go toward MDS research and to improving hospital conditions for young and adult cancer patients. Many people think that the US has a miracle cure (which they don't), and always tell me that I need to get treatment overseas. In Norway my treatment is totally free, and I hope that will continue. If there are changes, I'll let you know.

Something that's pretty sick is that I had 90 percent cancer cells in my blood before I started the chemo cycle here. I've never had so many in my blood before. My bone marrow was 26 percent. It probably wouldn't have been long before I died if they hadn't started the treatment on Monday. So now, after the treatment, there aren't many left in my blood, and hopefully the same is true for my bone marrow, but you never know for sure until you get tested. I'm hoping for good results; I'm feeling optimistic myself, but of course I don't want to count my chickens before they hatch.

I went to a café today with Martin and my dad. It was nice. We ate nachos and had some cookies for dessert. It's nice to have a change from the hospital while I can. Tonight we'll probably watch another David Lynch movie. They have a big flatscreen TV at the hospital that they can wheel into my room, so in a way, it's kind of like going to the movies. Very cool stuff!

She stands in the corner

Sunday, May 17, 2009

So, I made it through the weekend; that's not bad. It was so great to get to be at home. I haven't had any side effects yet, and I'm trying to enjoy myself as much as I can. My immune system has hit rock bottom—so there's no good news there. So now I'm just waiting for the fever to start. It could happen any time, but luckily I'll be at home and won't go to the hospital unless I get ill. It's not guaranteed that I'll come down with something, but it's very likely, and then I need to deal with it right away.

May 16 was a good day. I was outside and barbecued with my friends, and kicked back. The weather was good and we sat outside for hours.

As usual, I went to the hospital first thing today. I have to get blood platelets[17] every day, since I run out of them so fast, but the process doesn't take long, so I'm not complaining. The rest of the day looked promising. I even put on my folk dress[18] and went to Grandma's house to say hi and have food and cookies. And after that I met some friends at the park.

Things didn't go so well there (for reasons I won't go into) so I decided to go home. Martin ended up coming over, and after that the day quickly improved. I thought I'd be in a bad mood for the rest of the day, but Martin always makes me happy. We drove around a bit, and I bought some junk food. We parked somewhere, found a bench, and just enjoyed the nice weather. It was lovely.

I'm glad I didn't dwell on the fact that, based on my prognosis, this will probably by my last May 17.[19] I don't want anything to do with those kinds of thoughts.

I also want to give a big thank you to the band and to everyone who showed up at the benefit concert. So far I've only seen clips from the concerts, but what I did see looked amazing. It's inspiring when so many people get involved, and show support. Totally incredible. They raised about 11,000 crowns!

---

17   Platelets help stop bleeding by forming blood clots. With leukemia, the abnormal white cells crowd out healthy blood cells, including the platelets.

18   Traditional folk costumes that vary from region to region.

19   Norway's national holiday.

A long day at the hospital

Tuesday, May 19, 2009

So, my fever started yesterday, as we had expected. But luckily I got to enjoy the weekend. My good friend Silje was visiting me when the fever kicked in. Luckily it wasn't overwhelming. We drove to the hospital in Kristiansund to get the antibiotics, and my fever went down pretty quickly. Am glad I avoided the chills; they're brutal. Things seem to be going well now, but you never know.

I don't know when I'll get to go home yet. If my condition stabilizes, I definitely can. But no matter what happens, I need antibiotics three times a day, and I need blood transfusions almost every day. It's been a long day. It took three whole hours for me to get the blood even though it was already ready in the blood bank. It almost seemed like they'd forgotten about it. I also had to laugh when the nurse asked me how the thermometer worked. I assume most people have seen a thermometer before.

Martin is visiting and keeping me company. It would have been really boring to sit here alone and stare at the ceiling.

I'm hoping to go home for a while tonight; that would be ideal, anyway. And in general I'm counting on this going well. Anyway, nothing serious yet! I feel pretty good.

Oh, I also wanted to let you all know that my photos are for sale on Facebook. All proceeds will go directly to my support fund. With regards to the support fund, I really think a lot about how to use the money. I think it's important for cancer patients to be comfortable and happy while they're at the hospital. I've learned from people that hospital conditions for adults are quite bad. There are few (if any) activities or facilities. It would be great if you could suggest things we can do! It's all about being creative.

So go online and check out our Facebook group page. And people who don't have a Facebook account can see the photos here: www. smirr.deviantart.com/gallery/

Keep in mind that not all the photos here are for sale, and sometimes they have different titles.

Orders can be sent to annolaug@online.no.

From Ann Olaug:

Welcome to Regine's fantastic and powerful photo exhibit on Facebook. Some of the world's best photographers visited the *Nordic Light* photo festival in Kristiansund and were in awe of Regine's work. Congratulations, Regine! You should be SO PROUD!

The photos will be for sale on Facebook for as long as Regine wants. If you have any questions regarding the exhibit, or about purchasing photos, just contact me at annolaug@online.no.

—*Ann Olaug* ☺

Answers to questions—part two
Thursday, May 21, 2009

Better late than never. Finally, here are the answers to the second round of questions . . . . ☺

Tonje asks:

Question: I have a question about your disease, and I totally understand if you don't want to answer. I was wondering what your symptoms were at the very beginning? What made you decide to go to the doctor? I wish you all the best; you're going to manage this.

Answer: First, I was incredibly dizzy, my ears were ringing, and I just felt weird. Later, I had a serious flu right in the middle of summer. And after that a sinus infection. I had severe headaches for many weeks, a lot of UTIs, and a sore throat. I was so weak that a lot of times I came close to fainting. I couldn't hold myself up. When I was making breakfast, I needed to sit on a chair because I couldn't stand. Right before I was diagnosed, I also had some bruises on my feet, and bleeding in my gums. I don't know how many times I went to the doctor, but they never found anything.

Eirin asks:

Question: What's a transplant? What does it do and what do the doctors do? How does it work? How did you react when you found out that you had cancer? Could you show us a picture of yourself when you had hair?

Answer: I'll try to explain it simply, so that you/everyone don't need to read a whole page of medical jargon. Stem cells from a donor are injected into the patient's blood. After two to three weeks, the stem cells find their way into the bone marrow and start producing healthy blood cells. The stem cells can be harvested from either donated blood or bone marrow.

My first reaction was to burst into tears.

Ane asks:

Question: Do you have/have you had any pets, and if so, what kind? And what are their names?

Answer: I have a cat named Josefine. We also have a rabbit named Sniff, but he's my sister's responsibility, even though (for the most part) my parents take care of him. Right, Elise? ☺

Question: If you had the choice of traveling to the Mediterranean for a week or $1 million, what would you pick?

Answer: I would choose the million, obviously. ☺

Question: What kind of music do you like?

Answer: I mostly listen to rock and metal, but I also listen to a bunch of other stuff.

Problematic asks:

Question: Did you have a blog before you got sick?

Answer: I had a blog before, but it didn't last long.

Question: What's your favorite period of Ulver's long musical history?

Answer: I actually like almost all of Ulver's music, but of course there is some that I'm more into than others. I especially like *Bergtatt, Kveldssanger,* and *Teachings In Silence.*

Violaine asks:

Question: Do you sometimes have trouble sleeping if you get bad news?

Answer: Yes.

Question: Do you have a favorite book?

Answer: I really like *Angels and Demons* by Dan Brown.

Lisa asks:

Question: How did you react when you found out you had cancer?

Answer: Badly.

Question: When did you find out?

Answer: I think it was August 23, 2008.

Marianne asks:

Question: When you get totally well again, what's the first thing you'll do?

Answer: I just want to enjoy life, and do what I want to do. Enjoy freedom.

Question: Have you always been this compassionate?

Answer: That's a hard question. I do know that I've changed a lot since I got sick.

Anonymous asks:

Question: What will you do if they tell you there are no more options and that you'll die in about a month?

Answer: There wouldn't be much that I could do.

Mali asks:

Question: Is there/has there been a thought that is/has been difficult to tackle? How has this thought (if it exists) changed since you became sick?

Answer: Death is hard to relate to. My thoughts about death haven't actually changed. I've always been scared of dying.

Johanna asks:

Question: Where do you get your strength?

Answer: That's hard to say. I've wondered about that myself. It probably has something to do with having a good support system.

Question: Do you feel that you've benefited in any way from being sick?

Answer: I've had a lot of new life experiences. Good ones and bad ones. So I would have to say that I've gotten something out of this. I think I've become a better person.

Question: What are you passionate about besides donating blood and bone marrow?

Answer: I'm very passionate about saving natural spaces. It's so sad that they're cutting down the forest behind my house. I'm also passionate about stiffer penalties for people who torture animals.

Kristina asks:

Question: Did you have symptoms long before you went to the doctor?

Answer: Yes, for about three months.

Question: How do you manage to be so positive and happy?

Answer: I found out a long time ago that I don't get anything out of being negative. It just makes everything worse. So I mostly try to be positive and happy. ☺

Question: Are you scared of sleeping?

Answer: No. Why should I be?

Moox asks:

Question: A fairly interesting question: A few months ago, the doctors told you that your cancer was terminal (and if I remember correctly, the conservative politician was told the same thing). You now have a very popular blog and it now seems like they've changed their mind. They're going to try treating you. This makes me wonder if their original decision was made due to economic/administrative considerations, instead of medical ones?

Answer: I'm not receiving treatment now because of my popular blog. It doesn't work that way. It was the Riksen hospital that decided to give up on me. Now I'm at St. Olav's for treatment; I'm their responsibility now.

Signe asks:

Question: How long does the treatment last?

Answer: It's hard to say. It depends on how well the treatment works and what it's supposed to accomplish.

Maja asks:

Question: When people get into a situation like yours, and have their lives threatened by a disease, can you give us some tips? How do you think it's best for people to act toward you? What's good to hear, and what should people NOT say?

Answer: These are really good questions. It's most important to show support and to show up—and almost all of my friends have done that. It's also nice to just be treated like a regular person. I like it when friends make me forget that I'm sick. Definitely avoid dumb questions about death. It would also be good to try and put yourself in the sick person's situation (even if you can't ever completely understand it); that might keep you from asking obvious questions. The worst thing is when people complain to me about trivial things. Like a bad hair day, for example. You should definitely avoid doing that.

Kristin asks:

Question: How do you want to celebrate your eighteenth birthday?

Answer: If I wasn't sick, I probably would have gone drinking with friends and enjoyed myself. That would have been great.

Marte asks:

Question: Are you a Christian?

Answer: No.

Question: How did you experience the transition to "hospital life"? Were you scared of shots and other stuff like that, or have you gotten used to it now?

Answer: I've never really been afraid of shots, even though I know how unpleasant they can be. I don't need that many shots because I have a Hickman catheter. It's located above my breastbone and can be used to take blood tests and deliver medications. The transition was tough. It was a pain to have so many people around me all the time. I had no privacy—something I really need. I wasn't alone for ten weeks. It was a pain to be woken in the middle of the night by nurses who came into my room, and it was a pain to be woken up at the crack of dawn to take blood tests. It was also exhausting to have to drag around the stand that I was attached to, where they hung the chemo and the fluid.

Question: Do you watch a lot of TV? What are your favorite shows?

Answer: You're condemned to life as a TV slave when you get sick. I love *Twin Peaks*. It's not on TV anymore, but you can buy it on DVD. It's brilliant.

Question: What's the high point of your day?

Answer: It varies from day to day, but it's always nice when friends come to visit! ☺

Ingvild asks:

Question: I'm not sure if you mentioned this already, and that I just didn't catch it, but do you know how you got this disease?

Answer: It was totally random. It could have happened to anyone.

Isabell asks:

Question: If you recover completely, and all your dreams come true, is this an experience you would have rather not had, or do you look at it as a kind of character-building life experience? How has it changed you as a person?

Answer: That's a difficult question. I've changed a lot as a person, and a lot of my views have changed. But I would rather not have had this experience.

Photo documentary

Friday, May 22, 2009

Today I was out with Per Erik and took photos. It was so nice! It feels like I haven't taken photos in ages. The weather was fantastic, and we had a beer together outside.

("I took a photo of frozen ice," I said at one point. I actually said, "frozen ice.")

Being outside today shows that we've gotten the infection quickly under control, and I haven't had a fever for several days now. (Luckily.) But my immune system hasn't gotten any better yet, so things could still change. On the other hand, my blood percentage went up today all by itself, and that's a sign that my bone marrow is starting to work again. So maybe my immune system will go up soon, too. I hope so.

I'm on my way
Tuesday, May 26, 2009

So I drove up to Trondheim on Sunday. I had an appointment for a bone marrow test. Actually, I wasn't that nervous this time. The doctors warned us in advance not to expect too much. My cells haven't "woken up," so I don't have that many cells yet. I think they said they only saw fifteen, which isn't much! But on a positive note, the fifteen cells that they did find were all healthy! They didn't see any cancer cells! That's about as good as things can be for now. So we drove home again on Monday afternoon. I had a headache and felt a bit giddy. I always get headaches after anesthesia.

So what's next? The tentative plan is for me to stay at home for two weeks and get a bit better before my second bone marrow test. It's too early to know if I'm already in remission, but we'll know more in two weeks. Ahh, I'm *really* looking forward to being at home. They told me I had to come in quickly if my white blood cell count goes up suddenly, but we have to be positive and count on that not happening. Being home for two weeks means that I can

1. go to the Ulver concert this Saturday; and
2. celebrate my birthday at home next Saturday.

I'm so happy! I really hope I manage to stay healthy enough for both of those. You're probably thinking that this was excellent timing, but as usual I'm worried about getting too optimistic.

After the bone marrow test next week, we'll hear more about next steps. I'm pretty stressed right now, since everything is still up in the air. I want them to plan the next transplant. They obviously need to do it differently this time, since it didn't work last time. But I'm worried that nothing's going to change.

The doctors also talked about wanting to put me on Vidaza again. I'm skeptical, since it didn't work the last time. After I started taking it, the disease really took off. I don't want that to happen again. But I also understand why they can't plan another transplant until they know whether or not I'm in remission.

I hope I'll have a better sense of what's next after the next bone marrow test, and I hope I agree with the plan! But whatever happens, for now I'm just focusing on enjoying my time at home.

I love looking through old photos right now. It brings back good memories, but at the same time it makes me sad because it feels like that part of my life is over. See how good I look in sunglasses (not)!

The wanderer
Thursday, May 28, 2009

E arlier today I went to the movies with my parents. We saw *Angels and Demons* (a fantastic movie!—but of course the book was much better). Have you read the book/seen the movie? I love Dan Brown's conspiracy theories, and hope his next book comes out soon. We had the movie theater to ourselves, and got to see the film for free. Thanks so much to all the theater employees! It blows my mind that so many people care enough to organize something like that for me. And it's not very often that I can go to the movies these days.

Dress up

Regine age three with newborn sister Elise

Later, I met Anne Marthe and Eli Ann. We watched three episodes of *Twin Peaks*. I think I've gotten them hooked on the series. It's just brilliant.

I also just want to give a quick thank you to the fans of the Kristiansund BK soccer team. They raised more than 9,000 crowns during today's game against Alesund. Great initiative!

The only thing I'm not happy about in that article is that they wrote that the Norwegian doctors have given up. That's not really true, even though they're not sure where the transplant will happen (if I get that far).

I've worked on some new photos. Here are a few of them.

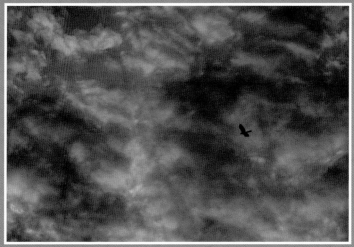

Summer, 2009

Summer, 2009

Ulver—the concert

Monday, June 1, 2009

After a lot of planning, everything was all set for the Ulver show on Saturday. They were going to be performing at the Literature Festival in Lillehammer, and this was the first time in fifteen years that Ulver was playing live, so people from all over the world came to see them. (Some even came from as far away as Alaska and Brazil.) It was definitely an historic evening for Ulver fans.

And I was lucky enough to get to go backstage before and after the show!

It was so cool. I got to meet all the band members, and they were all really nice. I was a little nervous and didn't know exactly what to say, but it wasn't really a problem. They were down to earth and didn't take themselves too seriously—which I liked. It was very special to meet them!

I'm so glad that I could even make it to the show. I never thought it would happen, but it was great to just get away for a while.

I bought myself a *Shadows of the Sun* LP. It came in a wooden box, and I think only a thousand copies were printed, so that's pretty cool (not to mention expensive).

I thought the show was good, and the sound was incredible. They should have played longer! They also had some really affecting videos that worked as a kind of background to the show. The first one was a rebuke to author David Irving,[1] and showed how awful things were for Jews during the war.

---

1   Writer, historian, and holocaust denier.

Regine and Ulver band members Kristoffer "Garm" Rygg and Tore Ylwizaker at the Lillehammer Literature Festival, June 2009

P.S. It looks like my bone marrow has started working again. My immune system has also gotten a lot better, so that's good news. I hope I can stay healthy enough so I can stay home all next week, too. I've already made plans for my birthday—so there!

A thank you to some great people

Thursday, June 4, 2009

In this entry I just want to take a second to say thank you to Beltespenner.com) for all the work that they've done. Thomas Adams (the man behind the company) has given me so much support. He and his employees have worked hard to create clothes to benefit my support fund, and the amazing thing is that they're not taking any money for it. The profits go directly to the support fund. Isn't that amazing? It makes me think that the world isn't such a bad place after all (and it's not—thanks to people like Thomas Adams!).

As of now, they've sold about 1,500 pieces of clothing. That means we've made over 100,000 crowns. It's so exciting to see that people are buying the clothes. I never thought so many pieces would sell. Thank you so much to everyone who has supported the project!

Just think how much money there will be in the support fund. It means so much to me, and I'm sure it means a lot to other cancer patients and their families as well.

I really want to give some money to Thomas Adams and his team, but right now all I can do is thank them. I hope they know how much it means to me.

One other thing: Don't get upset if it takes a while for the clothes to arrive. You'll get them sooner or later. It's a lot of work to print all of these clothes!

Today is my birthday!
Saturday, June 6, 2009

Yes! Today's the day—I'm finally eighteen. Who would have thought I'd make it! I'm so glad I started treatment; it means there's a real chance that I'll live longer. If I hadn't started, I probably wouldn't be sitting here today. It's a thought I can hardly get my mind around. I've waited so long for my eighteenth birthday and now it's finally here (even though it's not quite like I thought it would be). Before, I used to look forward to turning eighteen so that I could buy alcohol, drive a car, vote in elections, and basically be a normal and independent adult. And I can pretty much do that now, but I can't really enjoy the benefits like a normal person can. But on the other hand, my eighteenth birthday is a symbol that I'm still alive, and that I'm going to continue fighting against this horrible disease.

Earlier (on Friday), I went out to dinner with Martin just like we'd always planned. It was really nice—and the restaurant was almost empty, which worked out well.

Later today I'm going to celebrate with my best friends. We're eating at Peppe's, going bowling, and later we're going to my house for some drinks. I'm really looking forward to it!

Oh, I almost forgot to mention that, thanks to Ann Olaug, I met Morten Krogvold yesterday. Ann's been amazing and has come through for me in so many ways. (Thank you so much, Ann!) It was great to get to meet Morten. He's a really knowledgeable and interesting man. He was also very engaged and sincere with me. I really appreciated that.

© Silje Sund

Photo of Regine taken by her friend Silje Sund for a school project on donating blood

Am posting a photo of me that Silje Sund took for her final exam project. She decided to do a project on donating blood. You're very talented, Silje! I'm sure you'll get an A!

By the way, I'm not going up to Trondheim on Sunday after all. Things look good right now, so the trip can wait a few days. I don't know exactly how long, but I'll probably go some time next week.

During the following days, 1,300 blog readers congratulated Regine. Here's a small selection:

Dear Regine: Happy birthday and congratulations with your battle. I'm following your blog and I'm really impressed. I think you'll win this fight (as a 58-year-old grandmother, I have to believe it)! Your biggest strength is the positive attitude you and your family all share. St. Olav's Hospital in Trondheim is very professional, and you're in excellent hands there (I know this firsthand, from when my daughter was sick). Keep it up, Regine, and things will work out in the end!!
   —*Hug from a grandmother in Hitra*

My dear young lady,
   Turning eighteen is a milestone for most people. It means that you can drive, buy alcohol, and vote in elections. But for you it's even more important. A lot of people were afraid that this day would never come for you. Your family, your friends, and after a while, all of Norway, shared your fear and horror—although of course they weren't able to fully put themselves in your situation. In your blog you've given us insights we would otherwise never have had, and given us a glimpse of your painful reality.
   Now the day is here. You've won for now, and there are thousands of people hoping that you have many more birthdays ahead of you.

Being as strong and courageous as you are, you'll continue fighting, and we'll keep on admiring you.

It might sound crazy, but my hope is that today, on your birthday, you have the chance to let yourself go and stop fighting; let other people care for you for a while. Then you can go back to your struggle tomorrow. On your birthday I want you to eat birthday cake and open presents and just enjoy yourself and your loved ones. I want you to let your cares go, and just be happy and "normal" for a while. There will obviously be many normal days still to come. And many difficult days, too, when you'll need to be strong and clever and tough. There are a lot of us who follow your story, who think of you, and hope and believe that you'll get better. But today is YOUR day. Enjoy every second of it.

As you know, I think a lot about you, and my whole family is following your progress.

And although I've said it before: A big happy birthday, especially to you, but also to your mom, dad, and little sister—and the other people closest to you.

I'm so incredibly happy for you.

—*Hugs from Hestiaverden*

You're the most beautiful, the prettiest, the loveliest, the strongest person I know! Again, happy birthday, my dear Regine! You make the world a better place!

—*Sofsen*

Regine, I smile a little every time I visit your blog, and I also get sad and upset that cancer is allowed to exist. But Regine, because of you, and your courage, I don't despair for long. Because I know you'll win this fight, Regine! No one can measure up to the strength you've shown so far. I wish you an incredibly happy birthday today, and hope you have a truly fabulous day!

You deserve it. And much continued happiness, darling girl.

You're wonderful!

—*Hug from Johanne, fifteen years old*

A big happy birthday! ☺

You've inspired me! I've registered as a bone marrow donor, since I was a blood donor before.

I went to St. Olav's on Thursday to give blood, and while I was there I gave bone marrow samples, too—they'll be tested to determine my tissue type.

I hope I can help someone like you!

—*Olav*

Hi there!!!

A big belated happy birthday!!!! Wish you all the best!!!! I often think about you and peek at your blog . . . You're incredibly strong (and I think of your loved ones too). You're all so impressive . . . Say hello to your parents for me . . . Even if we didn't get to spend a lot of time together, I really valued the contact we had in Oslo . . . I miss SK . . . and I'm happy that YOU are hanging in there and getting a chance to experience more of what you want!!

—*Warm hug from AM*

The best birthday party ever
Monday, June 8, 2009

Thank you so much for all the birthday wishes! They made me so happy. I've never had so many congratulations before! I'm sorry if I missed any questions in the entries below, but there are so many comments! So if you didn't get an answer, just go ahead and ask again.

So, about my birthday, first of all, I celebrated with my closest family. We ate food, had some cake, and really enjoyed ourselves. I got a ton of great presents (and money, too)!

Later on, I celebrated with my best friends—and that was just totally unbelievable. It's the best birthday I've ever had. Just one thing was missing: my health. It was an unforgettable evening. First we went out to Peppe's for pizza and got a private room so that I didn't have to be surrounded by too many people. And after that we went to the bowling alley—it was so much fun, even though I came in fourth place (out of six). After the game we went to my place, and that's when the party really got going. Good drinks, good company, a camera, and sentimental '90s music turned out to be a perfect combination. We played all kinds of CDs and ended up dancing and singing all night long. I don't think the night could have been any better.

Thank you so much, everyone, for all the gifts and birthday wishes.

The key to the gate

Tuesday, June 9, 2009

I'm traveling to Trondheim again tonight, and on Wednesday morning I'll have another bone marrow biopsy. The fun is over for now, and it's time to get back to reality. We'll get a lot of questions answered, but we'll also have to make a lot of new decisions about how to proceed. It makes me really uneasy when the doctors don't even know what they'll try next. Maybe another cycle is in the cards to get me in complete remission, but we won't know anything about anything until we get the test results back.

And what happens after that? Will I get donated lymphocytes?[2] Will they try giving me Vidaza[3] again? Will I get a new transplant, and if so, when, and how? How many of the decisions will be up to me, and how tough will the choices be?

The fact that the future is so uncertain wears me out emotionally even if I hardly ever show it. Yesterday it occurred to me that no one has asked me how I'm actually doing. Maybe they think I don't want to be asked. Maybe it's also because I seem so happy and satisfied now. And who knows: Maybe I would just have told them that I was doing fine.

Don't misunderstand me. I'm happy and I *am* fine, but I'm also struggling psychologically. I'm always trying to get rid of dark thoughts, and pushing them away. I'm pretty good at it sometimes, but they're always there; even if no one else can see them, they're still there. When I ignore them, they just accrue into a huge ball of frustration and terror. And eventually that ball will just explode, and everything will come out.

Yesterday I went to a café with Anne Marthe, and afterward we went for a walk around the city. It was really nice, but I still couldn't keep my mind from reeling. I was thinking that I should do things like this more often. I should be as free as everyone else, and I should be able to do what I want all the time. But I can't. If my transplant had been successful, I would have been cured by now. I would have been able to start my new life now. But instead I have to live with this uncertainty again, and start a risky treatment. It also doesn't help that a certain doctor at Riksen told me my cancer is incurable. I think about that every day. Is there anyone out there who actually thinks I'll get well again?

---

2   A type of white blood cell that makes up approximately 25 to 35 percent of circulating white blood cells in human body.

3   Drug used to treat certain types of MDS.

Some bad news

Thursday, June 11, 2009

I wish all news was good news, but that's not the way it is. On Wednesday I had a bone marrow biopsy. The results showed that there are still way too many cancer cells left in my bone marrow. The chemo hasn't had the effect that everyone was hoping for. There's about 10 to 15 percent left, so now things look really bad. It became a day full of drama for my family and me. (It didn't help that the doctor cried, either.) It seems like there's no hope. My bone marrow doesn't produce enough for me to start a new high-dose cycle. The doctors say it would kill me. So I'm going to start a low-dose of chemo pills on Monday. The doctors have gotten rid of the cancer cells this way twice before. That's saying something, but now the chances are really small. Still, it could keep things under control so the bone marrow might be able to get a bit stronger and enable me to start a high-dose cycle again.

They said that we shouldn't give up hope, but I'm not sure that I have much hope left. I've hoped and hoped, believed and believed. I've tried to be so positive the whole time, but now I don't know if I can do it anymore. Nothing seems to be working, and I'm getting desperate. I'm so scared. There's nothing I can do. It's so awful for me to see that I'm getting worse and worse without anything working. I don't want to die yet, but right now things look really bad.

Many readers were powerfully affected by Regine's post, and 637 people wrote comments. Here's a small selection followed by Regine's response:

You're allowed to give up hope once in a while; there's nothing wrong with that. Sometimes things get to be too much. Don't feel guilty. It's totally normal! Everyone needs a break sometimes. Maybe it's hard to take a break from your thoughts, but sometimes I get the impression that you feel you're responsible for keeping yourself up, which you are in a way, but you're also allowed to wallow for a bit and take a break from being so strong. It's important to be positive, but sometimes it gets to be too much—and that's when you're allowed to sit down and cry and rest. At times like that, you don't have to get up again until you're ready. Hope will wait until you're ready for it again.

—*Anonymous*

That's sad news, Regine. And I understand why you're down in the dumps; everything looks bleak right now. But you have to try to find your strength again. The strength that we all admire so much. Find it and FIGHT! You won't die yet, darn it! You have many years left to live. I visit your blog several times a day, and I'm rooting for you with all my heart.

I'm looking forward to the entry about you being totally cured. Because that entry WILL come. Anything else would be totally impossible. ☺

—*A neighbor who's rooting for you*

Dear Regine,

I can't claim to know how you're feeling, because nobody looking in from the outside could ever know that. But it's heartbreaking and totally awful—and I think it's that a lot of people who comment here on your blog forget that you're actually only eighteen years old! Of course you're scared and sad! Who wouldn't be?

I walked by St. Olav yesterday and wanted to go in, sit by your side, give you a big hug, and just be there for you and show my support.

I also must say that I often think of your parents and the desperate situation they're in. To see your children sick and scared is a horrible feeling, and you want with all your heart to trade places with them. I'm a mother and I know that a parent would happily do anything for her child. So, my dear Regine, is there anything we can do for you? Anything at all? There are a lot of us who think about you and your family and pray that you'll get well. Find the strength to keep fighting. We're hoping that faith really can move mountains.

—*Biiiiiggggg hug from Sarah*

Scream, be angry, be fed up, cry—get it out and don't bottle it up. It's brutal to always have to fight against fear and despair. It's not always about being strong. So keep taking baby steps and one day, maybe way down the road, you'll be well again. Things can still get better, Regine. They have to.

—*LH*

Dear Regine,

No, no, and NO! ☹

This isn't what I wanted to hear.

I feel SO sorry for what you're going through, and would gladly switch places with you, because I've already been alive for 30 years more than you, BUT this HAS TO go well in the end.

HANG IN THERE as much as possible, and we'll do what we can. You're in my thoughts every day (even if I don't post comments that often).

I hope you have good friends you can talk to; in my own experience, things are better when you have someone who can listen to you and just be there for YOU.

—*BIIIGGGG warm, encouraging get-well hug from Olaf* ☺

185

No. NO. This is very hard to hear. I feel tears welling up in my eyes, because I can hear how scared you are in what you write. It's heartbreaking.

But there's still hope—keep that in mind.

I really want to wrap my arms around you, but I know you're lucky and already have your loved ones with you. Say hello to your mom, dad, and sister.

—*Warm hug from Else*

Thank you so much for all the comments! I read them, but unfortunately I can't reply to all of them. I hope you understand that. But I appreciate them all so much.

A lot of people ask me if I have someone to talk to. I don't get anything out of talking to psychologists. I talked to the hospital pastor twice and that was really helpful. But I'm totally fine with sorting things out on my own.

I'm happy just to be out with friends and to do other things like that. Simple things. That's enough for me.

A lot of people asked me if there's anything they can do for me. I appreciate that, but it's more than enough that you're writing supportive messages on this blog. ☺

—*Regine*

The voice from the tower

Saturday, June 13, 2009

The days after the bad news have gone well, in spite of everything. The period right after you get painful news is the worst I think. But after a while, you have to just shove it all aside—all the pain and sorrow. There's no other choice. If you went around constantly thinking about the pain, you'd go crazy. It works best for me to suppress those painful thoughts for as long as I can. Then, later on, if you just break down and can't stop the negative thoughts from swirling around, so be it. That's what works for me, anyway.

Since I'm in such good shape, there's nothing stopping me from doing the things I enjoy—at least for now. I went shopping the other day and bought myself a lot of clothes (and a short-lived feeling of happiness). Actually, I wonder why I still buy clothes, because a lot of times I feel like I don't use them anyway!! I've also spent my evenings with the people who care about me. Watched movies. Yesterday I painted, and today I took some photos. I was happy with the results, but my painting isn't done yet. When it comes to painting, I'm no artistic genius.

Made of glass

Monday, June 15, 2009

Today my blood values were about the same as they were on Wednesday. So they're stable. My immune system has gotten better, and luckily my blood condition hasn't gotten much worse. It's hard to know where to go from here. The doctors are really wracking their brains, and they have endless discussions about next steps. What can I tolerate? What will work best? They're working on a compromise, but that isn't always easy. I need something that will be effective, but it also needs to be something that my body can tolerate in its current condition.

They changed the plan a bit after my immune system improved. There was no pill cycle today, but tomorrow I'm going to start taking a chemo drug called Cytosar instead. I'll get it intravenously for four days. After meeting with the doctor today, I started to feel a little more upbeat. It sounds like this has a better chance of working. We know the Cytosar will kill the cancer cells, but we don't know how

many; no matter what, though, it'll have some kind of effect (I think). It sounds like it's much more effective than the pill cycle, but it's hard to know for sure.

In any case, the Cytosar worked well for me in the fall, but I received it in large doses. Hopefully it'll work well now, too.

Life is so fragile. You go around thinking you'll live forever. Unfortunately, it's not really like that. Everyone has a hard time coming to terms with death. I can't think of anyone who is comfortable with dying. But what would be best: to live forever, or to die just once? I don't think it would be so great to live forever. Obviously it's not a practical question—just a little thought experiment. Death is something we all have to face one time or another, young or old. We all have to go through the same process. I wonder if people are just as scared of death when they're old? Or do people eventually just realize they've lived their lives and that's it? No matter what, I think it's more frightening to face death when you're young. But whatever the case,

I feel like I've experienced a lot so far, and that's better than being old and not having gotten anything out of your existence. Imagine looking back on your life and thinking, What have I actually accomplished? That must be an awful feeling. I really would have liked to accomplish more, and I know I would have if I'd gotten well. I would have had a ton of new experiences, and made a real difference in the world. Well, we just have to keep our fingers crossed—even if a complete recovery seems so out of reach.

Quick status update
Friday, June 19, 2009

Hey there! Many of you get a little worried when I don't post anything for a while—so just wanted to let you all know that I'm safe and sound. The chemo cycle started on Monday and ended today. I've been pretty exhausted these past few days. I've also developed a mild fever. My body aches and my stomach hurts, too. I'm pretty sure the chemo is the reason why. My blood values aren't too bad—or I should say that they're good for me, but for others they would be catastrophic. My immune system has improved, so that was a pleasant surprise at least. I'm assuming the values will start dropping again soon because of the chemo. I had to be at the hospital for five hours today. First blood tests, then medication for the nausea, and then chemo. After that I had to have two bags of blood. At the end they did an ultrasound of my heart to make sure everything was okay. I was totally worn out after all that, and had to take it easy for the rest of the day.

On Thursday, two cool girls from the paper came over. They're doing a profile of me for the weekend edition of *Dagbladet,* which comes out next Friday, June 26. The reason I agreed to do it was that it sounded like it was actually going to be a good interview. The questions were really personal, and I felt like I was able to actually communicate a bit more than I normally can about who I am and how I think. That was the objective anyway. I'm looking forward to seeing the result. It was pretty different from the other interviews, which just focused on my blog and my disease. I think it'll turn out really well.

I've started making plans for the Quart festival. I really hope I can go! I can't say for sure if I'll be able to or not; it depends on how the treatment goes and how I'm feeling. But I hope that we can come up with a solution so that I can go. The festival manager promised me two tickets and a hotel room. How great is that!? If I can go, my best friend, Eli Ann, will come with me. I'm worried it won't work out, but I'm still looking forward to it, in spite of my doubts. Imagine seeing Slash live! Not to mention Marilyn Manson.

I'm struggling to answer all the mail that I've gotten, but rest assured that I'm doing all I can!

A toast to Quart (and the wig)
Wednesday, June 24, 2009

I hope everyone had a lovely St. Hans celebration![4] I know I did!

A few days ago I came down with a bad case of the stomach flu. Why can't people just wash their hands after they use the bathroom? How gross! It resulted in another trip to the hospital, but now I'm well again.

Today has been great. I had the house to myself and had a visit from the world's loveliest person, Eli Ann. We barbecued and had an amazing time together. Sausages are so underrated. We popped open some champagne (trust me—it was called for), and we toasted to the Quart festival next week, and to me wearing a wig. Yes, you

---

4   Midsummer celebration.

read that correctly. Actually, I hate wigs, but today I missed having hair so badly that I decided to put on one of my two wigs. I think it worked well!

The tickets and the hotel for Quart are pretty much in order and they're both being paid for by *Dagbladet*. (Thank you so much!) I hope I manage to stay healthy, and that my treatment doesn't get in the way. I'm counting on everything working out!

What do you think of the wig? Does it look real? It's made of real hair. I wonder whose hair it used to be. Have you had a good day?

Glorious summer

Friday, June 26, 2009

I barbecued again today—this time with Karina and Silje. We made the world's best meal, complete with marinated chicken filets, chips, béarnaise sauce, and salad. It was *so* good. We tried champagne this time, too but it didn't work out as well, so we had some sodas instead. After eating we went inside to watch *Hostage*. (Ack! It's super intense!) Then we had strawberries and ice cream for dessert. A wonderful day!

Do you think wearing a wig violates a kind of taboo? I somehow feel like it does, but I'm not sure why. I wore a wig to the hospital today and finally avoided all the stares. That felt good, so I've decided to give the wig a second chance. It actually looks pretty good. And I feel much better when I have it on.

I've been thinking a lot about people who permanently lose their hair. It's probably awful not to have hair. Can people actually get used to it? I haven't. Society today is obsessed with looks. It's really hard to find a good wig. I probably tried on twenty of them when I was looking. None of them were like my real hair, and most of the styles were ugly. Totally old lady. They should have a better selection. The word *wig* leaves a bad taste in my mouth. Why can't they just call it . . . I don't know . . . but something else.

Would you wear a wig if you lost your hair?

Which wig do you like better?

Regine's story continued to move more and more people. The members of the art rock band Ulver—who had recently conquered their collective stage fright and played live for the first time in sixteen years—were among them. On their home page, under the title "We did it. Faced the music. And you," they wrote:

Regine Stokke, a brave girl sentenced with MDS/AML. Our burdens are nil compared to yours. We are glad you did make it to the concert and that we got to say hello to you. It is truly astounding how you manage to smile in the face of such adversity. Forgive us our pathetic coquetry with death. We don't know what else to say.[5]

---

5   This was posted in English on their website.

Some people who followed Regine's blog saw Ulver's comment, and others read Regine's interview in Dagbladet, *but most of the 466 comments posted in response to Regine's June 26 entry answered the question of which wig she should wear to the Quart Festival. Here's a small selection:*

Hi there, Regine. You know what? You're just as lovely with hair as without hair, and I think you should wear whatever feels right. If you feel best with hair, then wear a wig!

Wearing a wig is something that has to feel right for the person wearing it. Whether or not you can get used to it . . . I don't know: Some people probably can, and for some people it's probably a relief to wear one, while for others it's totally wrong. We're all different in that way, too. ☺

I lost my hair after chemo, too, and I got two wigs that were totally fine, but I never managed to feel completely comfortable in them. One of them was pretty similar to my original hairstyle, but I felt like something wasn't quite right about it. I used it once in a while, but only when I was out in public. Then one day I realized that I wore it to spare people from having to see me without hair—and that's when I stopped using it.

Both of the wigs you have on here look great on you, and it's good to be able to vary the style.

Do what feels best to you, Regine! Hope things are okay with you these days!

—*Hug from Lise*

I just read your interview in the Friday edition of *Dagbladet*, and I have to say, Regine, you're totally smart (wise, even!) and have a beautiful, beautiful soul.

After getting to know you and your story here on your blog, and hearing more about you through the papers, I've learned a lot. You've given me so much! You've actually made me want to be a nicer, more satisfied person—and to be kind to those around me.

I don't believe in God, but once in a while I pray anyway, because it's a way to express sorrow and longing. And I've prayed for you, you beautiful girl! I'm cheering for you! Don't stop believin'!

(I like the wig with curls the best. ☺)

—*Anne*

No, not at all! Wigs can make a big difference for people struggling with hair loss, regardless of their gender.

The one on the left is best, even though you look beautiful in both photos. ☺

—*Thomas*

I like the one on the right best. And you shouldn't be scared to wear a wig. Just think about Tina Turner—she's worn wigs for as long as I can remember. ☺ And that lady rocks. You do, too!

—*Kjersti*

Quart is just around the corner!

Sunday, June 28, 2009

Tomorrow we're traveling down to the Quart Festival. The plane leaves around 2:30 pm and I'm packing up my stuff as we speak. The festival starts on Tuesday and it's got an incredible lineup.

The bands I'm going to see are:

-Slash & Friends,

-Marilyn Manson,

-Volbeat,

-Placebo,

-Skambankt,

-Familjen,

and a few "small" bands.

It's going to be so great! I'm looking forward to this just like a little kid.

It's going to be totally wild. A huge thank you to *Dagbladet* and to the festival manager for covering both the hotel and ticket costs.

I also want to thank my parents (of course), and the doctor in Trondheim who helped make this possible for me. I have to go to the hospital in Kristiansund on Wednesday to take a blood test, but it will probably go well.

Our hotel is ideally located, right in the middle of town, so in addition to the musical acts at the festival, we'll be able to enjoy some summertime in the city. I'm looking forward to sitting on the grass, listening to good music, and having a beer.

Any of you going to Quart?

Slash & Friends

Wednesday, July 1, 2009

Yesterday I saw Slash & Friends, and they put on one of the best shows I've ever seen. For those of you who don't know, Slash used to be the guitarist in Guns N' Roses. He's one of the best guitarists ever.

I can start by telling you that we actually had the chance to meet Slash at the airport on the way to Kristiansand. He was standing right there in front of us. We couldn't believe it! Then, when we got on the plane, he was sitting in the row right behind us. We mustered up the courage to ask him for an autograph, and Slash said yes, albeit a little hesitantly. We also asked him to take a picture with us when we landed, but he was too busy. At that point, though, we'd also seen Perla Hudson—Slash's wife—and Ronnie Wood,[6] who were also on the plane.

We arrived at the hotel, and unbelievably enough Slash & Friends were staying there, too. So awesome! We got to take a photo with Zig Zag, another guy who used to be with Guns N' Roses. We'd already done so much in one day, and it was still early! We were in heaven.

Before the concerts we went shopping and bought a bunch of cool stuff. The weather was good. We had a pre-party at the hotel and were feeling pretty good by the time the concert started. We were so lucky to have gotten photo accreditation. That meant that we could stand in front of the fence and take photos of the band. Of course we were focusing on Slash. It was an incredible show.

There were about 20,000 people there, and in no time the whole place was going crazy. The show got really strong reviews later on, and I think they were totally justified. The band played hits like "Paradise City," "Sweet Child o' Mine," "Paranoid," "War Pigs," "Honky Tonk Woman," "Knockin' On Heaven's Door," and "Whole Lotta Love." Some of the best songs in the history of rock! Fergie really surprised me; she was really talented!

We took photos during the first three songs, but then we had to move further back.

Otherwise we are *thoroughly* enjoying our time at the Quart Festival with VIP passes.

Tonight there will be even more to look forward to.

---

6   A member of the Rolling Stones.

Slash performing at the 2009 Quart Festival

I filmed a video while they played "Sweet Child o' Mine." If you decide to check it out, don't look at the video—just listen to the music.

Volbeat, Placebo, and Marilyn Manson
Thursday, July 2, 2009

Another incredible night. We saw so much cool stuff today. The best part was getting to see Marilyn Manson. What a show! That guy is totally amazing.

Here's a few pictures from the concerts.

For Eli Ann, Regine's best friend, the Quart concert festival was also a precious memory. Included below is her description of the time they spent together at the festival:

Every summer for the few last years, we've gone to the Quart Festival. Not much can measure up to sitting around an evening campfire after having spent a warm day going to concerts and eating ice cream on the grass. It's become a tradition we really look forward to, and one that we carefully plan for—usually way in advance. This summer though, everything was different.

On a beautiful midsummer's evening not too long ago, Regine and I sat on the veranda at home. We had sausages on the grill and had popped some champagne. The Quart Festival was just a few days away, but up to that point we'd barely made any plans at all. It was like we were afraid to look forward to it, because we were so scared that the trip wouldn't happen. Maybe Regine would get too sick to go, and maybe the treatment would get in the way. There was a lot that could have broken up our plans—however much we looked forward to them.

Marilyn Manson performing at the 2009 Quart Festival

Regine's photos from the Quart Festival

But a few days later, dressed for summer and bubbling over with excitement, we arrived at Gardermoen airport to catch the plane to Kristiansand. And then, to our great amazement, we saw Slash heading toward *our* plane. We looked back and forth from him to one other and back again. Was this really happening!? When we finally got on the plane, we were like two fourteen year olds: We were giggling (nervously) and we couldn't stop. We could hardly believe it. So even before getting to Kristiansand, the trip was already a success. For an hour we were sitting within an arm's length of one of our favorite artists. From time to time, we looked eagerly between the seat backs, just to make sure he was still there. We talked about all the stuff we were going to do over the next few days. We had no idea how fantastic it would turn out to be.

Later on, we took a seat on the bridge in the middle of town and had an ice cream. The sky was clear, the sun was shining, and we were just people watching. A boy holding an ice cream cone was balancing on the edge of the bridge—a tiny bit of wind would have sent him right into the water (and we wondered just how much wind it would take). There was also a middle-aged man who took off his shirt before lying down on the bridge to work on his tan—silver grey chest hairs and all. We just smiled. There are crazy people everywhere, doing crazy things, and there are a lot of milder eccentric types, too. Regine snapped a photo of a swan bobbing on the water near the docked boats. Swans actually mate for life, and when one of them dies (so they say) the other one dies of sorrow. The swan was resting so peacefully and gracefully in the choppy waters. We were fascinated, and talked about how animals are more intelligent than people in some ways, with their well-developed instincts and senses. There's a lot we can learn from animals.

Because Regine only has a small supply of strength right now, we took a lot of small breaks between shopping, concert-going, and restaurants, just so that she doesn't get too tired. We also visited the hospital a few times to take blood tests. Regine decided that she doesn't want to know too much about the results. If there's bad news, we don't want it to ruin this well-deserved vacation.

A lot of people have recognized Regine, and she appreciates it when people come up to wish her well and tell her how much they like her blog. But she also just wants to blend in with everyone, and she wears the wig to help her gain a little anonymity for a while. At the hotel, Regine cuts and arranges the wig like she wants it, and with newly styled hair, she goes out into the world without getting stopped by the press or stared at. The press has been following her since we arrived, and we can't help but laugh at their quizzical faces whenever they think they might have recognized her, but aren't sure.

Regine got a VIP-pass, and I'm lucky enough to get to share it with her! So now we get to take photos of some of our favorite bands right from the edge of the stage without being crowded out by tons of people. For the Slash & Friends show, we were able to find a good position up in front, but then we just had to wait (anxiously) for them to take the stage.

We were standing with journalists and other press people, and it was pretty easy to pick out the real fans among them. The cameras were poised, and we knew that eventually we'd get to see one of our favorite acts up close. It was just hard to wait. Finally, though, Slash & Friends got on stage. The festival exploded in light, and cheers from the audience behind us blended in with the music and covered us like a blanket of sound. We took photos like we were pros. Between photographing, we looked over at each other and shared wide-eyed, ecstatic smiles. We shouted to each other, but our words kept getting drowned out by the guitar distortions and the bass vibrations. Words can't capture what it was like, but Regine's expression said it all. Her eyes were beaming with happiness, and at one point she just mouthed the words

Regine and Eli Ann sitting on hotel steps in between concerts

"This is crazy!" And that's exactly what it was. Slash moved to the edge of the stage and put one of his feet on the monitor and, in authentic hard rocker style, went off on an insane solo. We could just barely see his eyes behind his dark sunglasses. Regine pulled my head toward her and yelled, "He probably recognizes us!" We burst out laughing and decided that he really was looking at us (regardless of whether or not that was actually true). After listening to a few more songs, we decided to sit on the grass, have a beer, and just enjoy the music in the summer evening. One hit after another filled the Bendikbukta stadium. There were two guys right next to us who'd had way too much to drink and were rolling around half naked on the grass. We just laughed and shook our heads. They probably weren't even able to remember the next day which bands they saw. Oh well—too bad for them!

The festival could not have gone any better so far. Being able to just enjoy the music feels so incredibly liberating after everything that we've gone through.

For the first time in forever, Regine's felt like a normal teenager. We had lunch under a parasol earlier, and we both agreed that summer in Southern Norway really is idyllic. (Whenever we order food here, we always end up getting club sandwiches.) In the afternoon, we went for a walk around the shopping area and wound up loaded down with shopping bags. Our legs got achy after wearing sandals for so long. We're tired and happy—which means laughing cramps are never far away. And before the concerts, we've been getting wine and cocktails at the hotel. The music is always on full blast, but we do our best to drown it out with singing.

We've spent a lot of time at our window, where we have a full view of the hotel bar and outdoor restaurant. Most of the groups playing at Quart are staying at our hotel, and our cameras and room keys are ready to go in case we see someone we know. When we do spot someone, we run right over to the elevator (which always seems to take its sweet time—we end up standing there and hopping around impatiently until it comes, and when the doors open again to let us out, we waste no time in racing out to the terrace). When we first checked in at the hotel, Ron Wood was already sitting at the bar. (We weren't exactly surprised.) Then, at the end of every day, we lie in bed talking about everything we've seen and done. We share thoughts and theories about all kinds of things, and the atmosphere is unforgettable, even if thoughts about the disease are never far away.

We're both surprised—and very happy—that Regine's been able to take this trip, as per our tradition. This time though, we've got a hotel instead of a tent, and room service instead of a barbecue, and we agree that this really is "an event of a lifetime" kind of thing. These are precious memories that will always be part of us.

Vidaza today

Monday, July 6, 2009

Arrived home from Quart on Friday. As I said, it was totally incredible! So great that I got to go! I was in pretty good shape too. I managed to do most of the things I wanted. Went to concerts, went shopping, ate outdoors, etc. I don't think I've been this active since last summer. It's incredible to think about. Quart definitely turned out to be the event of the year, or maybe even the event of a lifetime if you ask Eli and me.

Meanwhile, the recent blood tests are showing signs of a turn for the worse. My immune system is getting worse and my white blood cell count is rising. Not good, but that's how the disease is. And we know from before that my bone marrow is full of cancer cells, too. The doctors in Trondheim thought it would make the most sense to start me on Vidaza today. It could work, and if it does, it would be the simplest solution. If it doesn't work, they have to start trying some other methods. Very risky methods. But for now we just have to wait and see. Experts from other countries also think this is the right course. One thing that's good is that the blood platelets have gotten started. You have to consider everything that's positive. But of course when something goes well, something else inevitably goes wrong. I guess you can't ever get everything you want. In general, I'm not doing anywhere near as well as I was at Quart. I bet it's because I was so active there. I think it really had an effect. My blood percent is low, too. At this very moment I'm at the hospital getting blood.

That aside, I think it was very cool of Norway, Inc., to give me tickets for the upcoming Metallica concert in Oslo. They wanted to pay for my tickets, travel, hotel, and meals. Isn't that incredible? Eli and I are planning to go. It's always possible that the treatment will get in the way, or that my condition will worsen, but I'm hoping that it will all work out.

I was pretty surprised that people recognized me at Quart—even when I was wearing a wig! It was actually kind of nice to hide behind a wig. No one stared or anything. I felt like a normal teenager again, and I got to escape from reality a bit. It was so amazing to get to take photos of the stars, too. Not many people get that opportunity. I'm so glad you liked the photos I took. I only put up a few of them; there's a limit to how many concert photos I can post, before I start hitting the B-roll. A lot of people asked what kind of camera I use. It's a Nikon D70. I didn't do much editing on the photos from Quart, but the editing program I use is Adobe Photoshop.

By the way, I forgot to mention that there are two auctions going on right now at the online auction site QXL. The Kristiansund camera club is sponsoring them. The proceeds will go to my support fund. Thank you so much!

On July 9, 2009, Regine posted her diary entry from April 27 on her blog:

Diary: Monday, April 27, 2009

I hate it when people tell me they're dissatisfied. Dissatisfied with what, I wonder. You shouldn't complain about your life to someone who's hanging on by a thread. I don't appreciate others taking life for granted when I would love to have even a small portion of what they have ahead of them. I don't want to talk to those people; I block them out because they sap all my energy.

Why don't they say something nice instead, and tell me that I'll get well. I like to hear that, even though sometimes I react negatively to those kinds of comments, too. ("How do *you* know?" I think.)

I'm struggling with how I should feel and what I should believe. I'm kind of ambivalent. Will I live or die? Am I on a voyage toward the darkness of death? Or am I heading toward light and life? Nothing is determined yet.

I'm indifferent. I don't want to live or die. I think it's better this way. I shut out feelings of despair, sorrow, and terror. I don't get anything out of them. I hold things at a distance. But deep inside I know they're there.

I keep myself busy because I'm stressed. I have to do something all the time just to avoid those impossibly intense emotional reactions. I'm not detached; I'm just tired of all of this. Tired of fighting for something that should be a given: life.

I'm so sick of *trying*. I question deep down if this will ever work out, and while I still hold on to hope, I've lost my confidence. Hope has faded so many times. Do I dare hope again?

I'm struggling to feel anything at all. Even when I sometimes start to feel happy, I know that I'm really not. It's a superficial happiness, a strange, hollow feeling that's hard to describe.

People say that I have to believe things will get better—as if that will make me get well. If only it were that simple. I've experienced the world's dark side. I've seen so many people suffer—including myself—that I've had to stop believing in this being a "good" world. There can't be meaning or a reason for all the bad stuff that happens. I get angry at people who try to convince me otherwise. No, life has no meaning. That's what I say to people, and it's definitely true. The fear of no longer existing never goes away. I'm afraid to leave the world and I don't want to do it. I think about my family, and about my friends. I have to fight for them. I can't leave them behind with that sorrow. I have to try everything I can, despite how bleak everything looks. I'll try to convince myself that the treatment will work, but for now I just have to wait.

But waiting is a horrible experience with something like this: It's a time filled with uncertainty and terror. No one knows what will happen. I have one foot in the grave, and while I'm hoping to get out, doubt holds me back.

Regine's entry resulted in 237 comments. Here's a small selection, including Regine's responses:

There are definitely more people than just me who are rooting for you. You're not alone in this. I really feel for you. If there were anything I could do, I would do it. But I feel like all I can do is hold out hope for you, and believe in your cause. With respect to you, I *do* believe in goodness, so I hope with all my heart that everything will work out. But, Regine, even if you're scared, anxious, etc.: You must not stop living. Think about all the fun things you could do during that time when you're sitting around feeling scared. I'm not saying you should listen to me. You probably think this is a dumb comment; I'm only fourteen, and I probably shouldn't be writing since I don't know anything about this, but I just don't want you to stop living. Don't stop enjoying yourself, and doing what you want to do. You never know where the path will lead, and I hope with all my heart that everything works out! You're an inspiration to us all! Don't forget that.
—*Silje*

Little Silje: Thank you so much! Even though you're "only" fourteen, as you say, you show incredible insight into other people's situations.
—*Regine*

The meaning of life is contained in people just like you, Regine. What you give to so many people is what makes you immortal. You're making an impact. That's why it isn't a question of time. Of course you want to do everything there is to do. Of course you want to live. But even if your life isn't as long as an old woman's, it's still a whole life. With your fantastic blog, with your wisdom, openness, and the strength that you share with us all, you have accomplished more than many people can dream of. I hope and believe you will make it, and get well.
—*Helle*

I sort of understand how you feel, since I have a terminal form of cancer myself, and I can only be treated for a limited amount of time. Luckily I'm forty-nine, so I've gotten to live for a while, but I'm absolutely not ready for the end. I think it's like that for everyone, regardless of age. When things get tough, I think about everything I'll get to avoid when I'm gone—all the bad and unpleasant things in life. I guess that's kind of gallows humor, but it helps a bit. At the same time, I try as hard as I can to steer my thoughts away from what's painful, and it works really well. I read this quote once: "The deeper the sorrow, the deeper the silence"—and that's how it is. You write so beautifully, so movingly, and so directly about some of the most difficult things there are: disease and death. It helps me because then I understand I'm not alone. Hold tight to life for as long as you have strength and as long as you can. I feel you have it in you! Hugs and kisses from someone unknown to you!

—*Ann-Kristin*

"The fear of not existing never goes away."

That sentence almost knocked me out of my chair. I don't know, it was just so . . . powerful. God, I'm getting totally emotional. ☹ I'm sitting here sobbing . . . Typical me! But this time there's a good reason for it!

—*Vilde*

Thank you so much for all the nice comments. I'm speechless. I'd like to answer each and every one of you—many of you write so fully and deeply. I hope you know I really appreciate it, and that it means so much to me.

—*Regine*

A little update

Tuesday, July 14, 2009

So I'm done with the Vidaza cycle now. It went smoothly this time! The only side effects so far have been some pretty mild stomachaches. But that's all part of the deal right? Thank you so much for all the kind comments to my last post—it means so much to me! Some of you almost wrote complete letters, and I really appreciate your taking the time, because a lot of you are really profound and insightful writers. I'd like to answer each and every comment, but that's just not possible. I'll respond to your emails soon. I just haven't been up to it these last few days.

I haven't done anything really interesting recently. Eli and I have just been watching a ton of movies, though, and we also went out to eat one day (which was so nice!). From what I can tell, the blood test results aren't that bad right now. My blood percentage and blood platelets are stable, and my immune system has improved slightly. On the other hand, the white blood cell count is also rising, and that's not good. They're going up evenly and steadily and I'm scared they'll "take off" like last time. That would be catastrophic. It's spooky and ominous to see them just going up and up. The plan is to repeat the cycle in two weeks. Hopefully we can stick to it but it's hard to know for sure.

I received a guest post today by email. I think it'd be nice to repeat because the writing was really good, and the woman who wrote it has a gripping story to tell. Maybe that will be my next entry.

Guest post

Wednesday, July 15, 2009

I received an email from a woman named Ashild. She really wanted to do a guest post here on my blog. Ashild is forty-six and has a lung disease. She's been waiting eight months for a lung transplant.

Thoughts on extreme sports, the sports award ceremony, and show biz

Extreme sports

Have you ever considered that the idea of "extreme sports" can be applied to a lot of activities that you won't necessarily see at the X Games?

The impulse that encourages us to take risks and "let the chips fall where they may" informs a lot of our decisions. Doing what you want, or even what you set out to do, can cost you your life and your health. You don't even have to climb a mountain, cross a roaring river, or navigate a treacherous forest for disaster to strike.

And I'm not talking about broken hearts and pain and love and that kind of thing.

I'm saying that for some people, just leaving the house takes incredible mental strength: It exhausts them more than a long walk in the mountains would exhaust a healthy person. And for some people, it's a greater act of courage to just express an opinion to a new acquaintance than it is for someone else to deliver a lecture to a packed auditorium. For some people it can be so physically demanding to go to the theater that they have to prepare themselves for longer than a pro football player would take to prepare for a championship game. Some people have to rest for days after a trip to the mall, whereas some runners just need a few hours to rest after the New York

Marathon. The goals that we set when our health is bad are as unstable and ephemeral as the weather on Kilimanjaro.

So the basic idea I'm trying to express is that everything is a matter of courage; life is about taking chances, about embracing risk, about daring, about going beyond your limits, about tolerating uncertainty, about staying focused, and about knowing that, despite everything (or perhaps because of it) your efforts can have catastrophic results. On the other hand, it's just as likely that you'll wind up with a genuine feeling of victory. It all depends on your own starting point, your own assumptions, your own goals.

I know a few people involved in extreme sports these days. I cheer for them and raise the flag as high as possible—whether they finish first or last or not at all. Good luck to all who try!

The sports awards ceremony

Once a year, TV2 broadcasts its annual sports awards ceremony. Prizes are awarded to the most fearless of the fearless, the best of the best. Fame, honor, and glory are heaped upon athletes in a range of sports. These athletes are impressive; they have iron wills and amazing staying power; they're stars, and when they get a little luck, they win.

One after another they say thank you after receiving their awards. Thanks to family, coaches, and support systems—to everyone who backed them up and helped them achieve victory. "I could not have done this without you," they say. "Without you, I would not be where I am today."

They all share an uncommon willpower, lofty goals, incredible focus, stamina, and muscular bodies. They also share a large support system that cheers them on, and people in that support system put their own interests aside so that the athlete will have the optimal conditions to focus, train, test, sleep, and eat. And if the athlete struggles mentally, he or she has supporters and psychologists to help him or her get over the hump and find the strength and courage to press on.

Because in the sports world, it's completely acceptable for athletes to put themselves, their own needs, and their own goals, ahead of everything else. To expect that people around them will support, drive, cook, be kind, show interest, babysit, etc., so that they can focus all of their energies on their own career and accomplishments is a kind of culturally accepted egotism. These athletes have a self-centered focus that is noble, in its way, and no one thinks of their "assistants" as tireless or kind or self-sacrificing. If they're lucky, they'll get a special mention on an awards show at some point. At least, that's what they hope for . . .

Maybe you understand where I'm going with this . . .

Imagine if all of us who are sick or struggling with one thing or another received the same support!

Imagine if we had the same professional support network around to back us up when *we* got exhausted!

Imagine if we were able to accept help and support from family and our networks without anxiety or fear that we were being a bother, and imposing on their lives!

Imagine if we could be seen and recognized for the daily effort we make for our health!

Imagine if someone could see us as heroes, everyday heroes!

Imagine if TV2 had created an award ceremony for us! The survival athletes!

"The show must go on"

It's an age-old saying for artists and actors, and one of the oldest mottos for people in the circus. But it can also be a metaphor for life itself.

That's how I think of my health situation. It's a show that has to be carried on, day after day, no matter what shape or mood I'm in.

I drag myself to health consultation after health consultation. I have to answer tons of calls and emails to arrange consultations with doctors at one hospital or another, pick up medications at the pharmacy, straighten out issues with the Norwegian Labor and Welfare Service. Last week I was at the hospital for several days. Then there are the treatments, inhalers, and medications that must be taken every single day, and at the moment, I'm taking intravenous medication as well. Nothing happens by itself; nothing is arranged by itself. I always have to hang in there, drive myself everywhere, arrange everything so that things don't grind to a halt.

I wish the stage curtain could go down once in between, that I could pause the show, that a champagne bottle could be popped, and that backbreaking work could be rewarded with honor and applause. I want to experience the thrill that an actor feels, when the curtain goes down and the applause rises in the darkness.

But the analogy has to end somewhere, and fame in this case would preferably be substituted with health and happy days instead (which would continue for as long as the show needs to go on).

People in the industry say, "There's no business like show business." I'm happy that I didn't choose that path in life. It's enough for me to perform well in the show that is this life—even without the applause.

I'm an actor in the show of life, and the show must go on; I dislike sports awards ceremonies, but I feel like a top tier extreme athlete. What about you?

Sixty-eight readers commented on Ashild's guest post, among them Regine and Ashild herself, who wanted to provide some background to what she has written:

Thank you, Regine, for accepting my guest post.

I want to explain a bit more about what I wrote: I've been sick for a long time, and have lived through a merry-go-round of infections and downturns for several years. For a while now, I've noticed how people in the media (and elsewhere) always focus on healthy, athletic people who participate in spectacular events and competitions. This observation has made me want to celebrate the everyday heroes I know who have a courage and toughness that surpasses even that of the star athletes.

I was also inspired by some of the comments in response to your post about "everyday complaints." It made me reflect on how little others know about what it's like to live with a serious illness. That's why I pulled these entries from my blog. So that maybe other people can understand what we go through, and congratulate us.

Most of all, this is a tribute to you, Regine. You are a cool, tough, strong, brave, open, thoughtful, and incredibly mature girl!!!

And I'm cheering for you!

—*Ashild*

Ashild, I'm so happy that you're sharing this with us! You're a great writer, and you make a ton of really important points. I'm honored to share this entry on my blog. ☺ I wish you luck, and hope that things work out for you, too.

—*Regine*

The picnic
Friday, July 17, 2009

As you probably know, my blood tests are only heading in one direction these days. My bone marrow is saturated with cancer cells, and it has been for a long time. My white blood cell count is getting to the point where I'll probably need to have some chemo next week to just slow things down. After that I'll start Vidaza again. At least we have some sort of plan though; that's better than not knowing anything.

The weather was beautiful today, and Eli and I decided to go for a picnic. We went shopping, and then we made lunch and went out to the forest. It was so nice. It's always nice to just sit and relax with good food and nice weather. And after we came back later in the day, we started watching a series that Karina recommended. It's called *True Blood*, and it's about vampires. The first episode was cool and it seems really promising! It's always nice to have something new to watch, being the TV slave that I am.

Abandoned
Wednesday, July 22, 2009

I've been in okay shape lately. I thought the blood tests were going to be awful, but luckily they weren't! They're not great results by any means, but at this point they're better than average. The white cells haven't gone up much since Thursday, and that's good! As a result, the doctor thought I wouldn't have to undergo more chemo before they give me Vidaza again, and that's very good news. I'm going to start Vidaza again on Saturday—in a double dose, since I tolerated it well.

My blood status is as follows:

Hemoglobin: 10.7

Thrombocytes: 38

Neutrophils: 1.47

Leukocytes: 8.7

(No, I'm not expecting everyone to understand this.)

The Metallica concert is in a little more than a week. I'm actually allowing myself to look forward to it at this point. Plane tickets and hotel rooms have all been ordered. Will it actually work out? It will be a little scary to travel alone, even if Eli comes with me. After all, Mom and Dad have been everywhere with me since I got sick!

But it will be good to do something on my own for a change. I'm eighteen years old, and I've always liked being independent. (The disease kind of put a damper on my independence though.) If the concert works out and goes well, I'll be ecstatic; the only thing I'm scared of is getting swine flu. Wouldn't that be so typical?

Today Eli and I went out to eat. It seemed appropriate. My blood tests hadn't gotten much worse, and it looks like I'll be able to avoid the chemo we were planning for. I have to treat myself to things when I can. The food was so good.

Dead to the world
Monday, July 27, 2009

I don't have very much to say. I've been in miserable shape these last few days. Could hardly bear to see any visitors. The drugs are destroying me. My blood tests are going to hell, too. My immune system is okay, but what good is that if everything else is in full shutdown mode?

I wonder what will happen next. I'm absolutely sick of taking blood tests and then waiting for answers. Always bad news. I hate the waiting and the disappointment when I get the results. I lose a whole day, and then after I finally manage to pull myself together again, I just have to wait for the next disappointment. I've been feeling lonely lately. I'm scared that I'm going to die soon. I can't stand the thought.

I've been brought back to reality again. Dark thoughts are overwhelming me. I feel the tears coming. I want to live normally, to be healthy. The fact that it will never be my turn to get well is something I can't manage to accept.

Beauty

Sunday, July 19, 2009

Beauty is the warm summer air.

Beauty is water, running down the river.

Beauty is the scent of blossoming flowers in spring.

Beauty is the flavor of blueberries.

Beauty is friendship that lasts through thick and thin.

Beauty is sincere smiles from happy people.

Beauty is a blue sky.

Beauty is a starry night.

Beauty is cats rolling in the grass.

Beauty is the sound of rain hitting the ground.

Beauty is deep, dark eyes.

Beauty is innocence.

Beauty is love.

Beauty is insight, strength, and courage.

Beauty isn't always what people see on the outside.

Beauty is so many things.

What is beauty to you?

The voices
Saturday, August 1, 2009

There was no Metallica concert for me. I had a tiny bit of fever, my body ached, and I was in bad shape. That's just the way it's been lately. Luckily I'm starting to feel better. No matter what, I really appreciate what Norway, Inc., did for me. I even won a contest and was going to get to meet Metallica. How awesome would that have been? But they said they were sorry I couldn't make it and even dedicated "Nothing Else Matters" to me! I was speechless when I heard that. To me, that's a pretty big deal. Jan Erik from Norway, Inc., is going to send me a DVD of the concert, along with a guitar pick. (Amazing!) I'm disappointed that I couldn't be there. Jan Erik made so many arrangements for me, so I hope that he and the others had a fantastic time anyway. I'm just so sad I couldn't go. Metallica has been a big part of my life.

I went in for more blood tests today. The white cells have dropped to 6.2! That's good. I hope it stays that way. If nothing else goes wrong, I won't need to take any medicine next week, and then I can go to RaumaRock! Right after my relapse, I got a festival pass, etc., from the organizers, and earlier today we made arrangements to stay overnight. I have to believe it's going to happen. The festival manager is even going to arrange for a photo pass! Enslaved, among others, will be at RaumaRock, and they're one of my favorite bands. I wholeheartedly recommend their *Monumension* album.

Small rewards
Monday, August 3, 2009

There haven't been any changes really. The white cell count has gone down a little more. The Vidaza has really worked this time, which obviously makes me really happy. I have to struggle so much during the day, so it's good that something comes out of it. I've been really sick. People say, "Be positive, and do what you want." It's not easy to be in a good mood when almost all I can do these days is lie in my bed. I'm exhausted most of the time. I rest and rest but never feel fully rested. Every single day is a burden. My body can barely manage to support itself. The only time things are good is when I sleep, because then I don't have to feel anything. Feeling so weak does something to your psyche. I'm depressed every single day. I really hope I get better soon, because I don't think I can stand feeling like this much longer.

Taking a look in the mirror

Wednesday, August 5, 2009

Thank you so much for all your comments! I really appreciate it. I'm sorry if I sound a little rough every once in a while; it's hard to be polished when you're in a bad mood. My mood's a little better today, and my condition, too, maybe? I'm not quite sure. I hope things are headed in the right direction now. The festival manager asked if I wanted to be picked up by helicopter. Haha, how decadent! It makes me so happy when people do nice things for me. I said yes even though I'm afraid of flying. It will probably be amazing, despite my fears. I've decided that I *will* go to RaumaRock. I will. I will.

Will have blood tests again tomorrow. Traveling, even for a weekend, takes a bit of planning, but that's just the way it is. As long as the disease is in my body, I'll never be free. As a rule I only get a maximum of two to three days at a time that are hospital-free. BUT—it's better than being hospitalized on a full-time basis. I need to get blood before I leave, so that I can build up my strength. And maybe I need to get blood platelets too—I don't know. I hope the white ones haven't gone up. The fear of that happening never goes away. I hope the tests

Enslaved in concert (above) and Regine and Eli Ann with Enslaved band members at Rauma Rock in Åndalsnes on August 7 or 8, 2009

Photo from Regine's helicopter flight over Trollstigen (the Troll Path) on her way to RaumaRock, August 2009

are both good so I can leave and not worry about it; that would put me in a very good mood. If the test results are bad, I wouldn't be able to relax, even if I felt okay. I need some good news now.

Ready to go
Friday, August 7, 2009

Here I am, ready for RaumaRock! I'm sitting here *dreading* (and also looking forward to) the helicopter ride. It'll be exciting at least! This is going to be a crazy good day—and an amazing weekend. Enslaved is playing today, and I'm going to get to meet them! How cool is that? But even aside from that, there are a ton of other great acts playing tonight, and I can't wait to see who will be this year's surprise performers.

We'll talk! I hope you have a good weekend.

RaumaRock
Sunday, August 9, 2009

RaumaRock was such a fantastic experience! I'm so thankful. Markus (who was working there) took such good care of me, and did everything he could to help me have a good time. Everyone was so nice and they even gave us access to the backstage area! It was incredibly generous, and I'd never been backstage anywhere before that. Words can't describe how grateful I am for everything the people at the festival did for me.

We stayed at a hostel, and they were also super friendly and welcoming. There was an incredibly nice lady who organized everything so that it would be as comfortable as possible for me.

Otherwise, I just have to laugh at the fact that the Andalsnes newspaper snuck a photo of me when our helicopter landed. They put the photo on the front page, but I haven't seen anything quite so blatant in a long time. Oh well.

The helicopter ride was unbelievable. It was much better than I had thought it would be—just amazing. Much better than going by plane. It didn't even give me butterflies. We flew over Trollstigen, where we saw some amazing natural sights. What could be more beautiful than Norway's vast mountains? It left me speechless.

Of course I managed to get a urinary tract infection on Friday. We had to wait so long for a taxi, and it was cold outside. Then I had to take a trip to the emergency doctor at Rauma on Saturday to get some pills. But I was well cared for, and luckily things turned out okay. On Saturday I didn't have much energy, so I didn't do too much at the festival that day. The high point was definitely Friday evening! We were backstage for a while, and got to meet Enslaved. They were super friendly people and it was interesting to see the artists offstage. The concert was truly first-rate. They even dedicated a song to me, and I also got a signed CD and a sweater.

There were some blog readers who came over to me at the festival. I was so embarrassed that I didn't know what to say, but they were really polite and lovely. I was a bit uncomfortable when someone wanted to hug me though, because I shouldn't really have such close contact with people.

The future

Thursday, August 13, 2009

It's difficult for me to see a future for myself after all the bad news I've had. It's really difficult to sit and listen to friends talk about their future, what they want to do, etc. I never get included in those discussions. I don't enjoy talking about it either. It's a sensitive subject.

I know there's a possibility of getting well, but it's just so difficult to believe that. A relapse after a bone marrow transplant is usually the end for most people, but then you have some who survive. It depends on whether you have good luck or bad luck, and I've always had bad luck. First I learned I had blood cancer, but that wasn't all—it had to be a totally unusual and rare type that is difficult to cure. They say one misfortune rarely comes alone. I've been through tough cycles of chemo that have almost killed me. Three times I've suffered near fatal blood poisoning. And once I had such a serious lung infection that I ended up on a respirator, and my parents were told to take one hour at a time. But I got through all of it. Having to "learn" to walk again was no easy task, and I underwent a bone marrow transplant, too.

I'd hoped that I was done with all my bad luck. The transplant procedure went smoothly (relatively speaking), but then I had a relapse after just three months. When I spoke with the doctors at Riksen hospital I was told I was going to die. I still don't understand how I got through those days. I almost think my brain must have an off- and on-switch. Then there was a new hope on the horizon: Vidaza is the medicine that we have to put our faith in. It's the one that will move me toward a new transplant. Can't I have some good luck soon?

In all, 207 readers responded to Regine's entry. Many, like Bengt Eidem, wanted to encourage Regine as much as possible. Others wanted to give her advice about alternative treatments, something that GSC, who followed Regine's blog closely, reacted strongly to:

Okay, now I'm angry! Here come all the stories about successful treatments overseas. No two people in the world are identical. Nor are two patients identical. What works for one person could be completely wrong for someone else. Norwegian healthcare is respectable. Is there really anyone who doesn't believe that Regine's doctors are doing everything they can to get her well? I know a little about what Regine is struggling with and she doesn't need admonitions to persevere. Because she's hanging in there like crazy! If there's anyone who knows something about this, then it's Regine herself. I can't believe someone actually had the nerve to say that she has to persevere for those who read her blog! Shame on you! She has more than enough on her hands just fighting for herself, without pushing herself for us, too.

Continued good luck, Regine. You are phenomenal.

—GSC

Yes, Regine—you and your family DESERVE a bit more good luck soon!!! I think there are lots of people who have their fingers crossed for you. I'm so glad to see that you are "living life while you can" to the fullest. Festivals, concerts, helicopters, and much more. I'm positive that so far in your eighteen-year life, you have accrued more wisdom, more memorable experiences, and that you've been through more ups and downs than what most people can manage in 50, 60, 70 years. Continue living life while you can, Regine. None of us can predict when death will arrive, but we can do something about how we use the days we have. Persevere! I cross my fingers for you (and the Vidaza)!

P.S. Oivind Andre, in his last words to the outside world, encouraged us to "live life while you can." The blog contains a lot of life wisdom that all of us, healthy and ill, can benefit from reading.

—*Bengt*

A complete lack of energy
Sunday, August 16, 2009

Tomorrow it's time to start taking Vidaza again. I hate the thought of it. I'm so worn out and now I'll get even sicker. But it has to happen. Today I couldn't do much more than just lie in bed. It's so incredibly frustrating, when this is the only thing I can do. I so badly want to do things that give me some positive energy. I want to go outside and take photos, and I want to go on walks, but I just can't manage it. It's too hard. I hate not being able to take advantage of my creative side. This might be the reason why I'm so depressed right now, because I'm unable to do what I like. It's difficult to understand why I can't manage anything at all, but there's probably no other reason than the powerful dose of medicine I've been given. You're supposed to get used to Vidaza after a while, but it doesn't seem like it's getting any easier. And I get it so frequently. If I had been in good shape, it would have been so much easier to go through this.

Back to school—but not for me
Wednesday, August 19, 2009

Today's drive to the hospital was really hard for me, because we had to drive past my old school to get there, and today was the first day of school. I saw young students everywhere. I was also supposed to start school today. That was the plan anyway—before the relapse. Damn it, it's so unfair. Many people with cancer say they eventually stop thinking about how unjust it is that cancer struck them specifically, but I never stop thinking that. I wish it was someone other than me who was struck instead. An egotistical, but also very human thought. Who can really blame me for that?

The last few days have gone well. I received some blood on Monday, and my condition improved a bit after that. The cycle has just gotten underway and I haven't noticed many effects from it yet. Eli has visited me several days in a row, and I'm glad I have her around. She's the only one who's been showing up for me now that I need it the most. I wish I had more people to support me, but unfortunately some have left, and that's awful.

Eli and I have been baking and watching *True Blood* these past few days. We're hooked on baking and the series. By the way, we made the world's best smoothie yesterday, which really helped my mood.

Today I actually voted early. It's important to vote.

Regine's entry drew comments from 279 readers—most of them to express support and understanding, fewer of them to criticize her "wish" that someone else had gotten this cancer instead. Here's a selection from both sides, along with Regine's answers:

Hi Regine. I'm a married mother of four and I've followed your blog since I read about you in the paper. I'm a nurse, and I've also studied palliative care. Through your blog I've learned a lot about how a serious illness affects a young person. I've grown to like you from a distance. You have so much life inside you, so much to contribute, so much to teach us. I hope this cycle will help, and that you can avoid the side effects. I know these are just words, but I want you to know that I am someone who thinks of YOU often. Hug.

—*Laila*

My dear. I just have to write to you before I go to bed. You are often in my thoughts when I go to sleep. I'm so glad you have Eli, Regine. Unfortunately, it's true that a lot of friendships dissolve after a while, when the "newness" wears off. It's now that you need them, and I hope the ones who aren't there for you read your blog and realize how hurt, lonely, and bitter one can feel. You must know how much we in your family love and miss you right now. I hope you sleep well tonight. Thank you for managing to write some words to everyone who's following you. Good night, beautiful girl.

—*Hug from a mother/grandmother*

I think most people understand that your thoughts are human. There are many of us who appreciate how honest you are about what you feel and think. You show many different parts of the disease and give us outsiders a privileged glimpse at the insanity you have to endure. It's too bad that you have to receive dumb comments from people who preach about things they know nothing about, when you're being so honest and brave and mature, and daring to show the meaninglessness of this awful disease. Have been thinking of you in connection with the start of school around the country. It IS unfair. I'm glad you have Eli. And I'm glad to hear the last few days have gone well. I hope the treatment starts working now!

—*Respect and admiration from a stranger (26)*

Would it have been better if it had happened to someone else?? So, you are the world's best person, then? Everything is about you now, right?? No one gets to go to school and enjoy themselves if you can't?

—*E*

To the person who asked: "REGINE, how can you say something like that!!??" Um, maybe because Regine is in a true life crisis right now, maybe because she has CANCER, maybe because the doctors have given up on her, maybe because she's young and doesn't want to die, MAYBE . . . it's because she's a human being that she says things like this!!?

And of course it's unfair that you, Regine, should get this awful disease! It's completely unfair for you, your family, and your friends.

Give this horror to a mass murderer, a child killer, a pedophile, a mad-man instead! That would be more fair. Unfortunately though, the world doesn't work that way . . . I lost my dad to cancer when I was fourteen years old, and I understand what you're feeling! I wished it had happened to my best friends' fathers, my uncles, anyone—just not MY dad! These feelings didn't belong to an evil psychopath without compassion, but a normal, thoughtful fourteen-year-old girl. And today I've stopped walking around wishing that these people were dead . . . Regine, you are just human and you're allowed to have these thoughts! It's normal . . . I visit your blog every day and CHEER you on! And wish with all my heart that you get well and win this unfair fight! Regine, I love your honesty! It makes you so REAL. ☺
—*JEA*

Thank you so much for all the nice comments. ☺ It means a lot. I don't really think the ones who've left me are afraid of being infected by me; it's probably deeper than that. People were good at showing up in the beginning, but when things go on for a long time, it seems as if some of them don't feel like bothering anymore. Rebella: Thanks for your comment; good that you understand. ☺ E: That comment was just totally uncalled for. I suggest that you leave this blog and never come back. I'm being honest in here, and you have to be able to take it. I'm not saying that no one is allowed to enjoy themselves when I can't. That's the dumbest thing I've ever heard. I'm pretty sure if you had to choose whether you or I should have cancer, you would choose me. Tonje: Alternative treatments are not something I have thought of trying. I am already receiving treatment that I think is fine, but thanks for the tip.
—*Regine*

Dear Regine: Of course your thoughts are natural. We're all egotists, and if I had life-threatening cancer, I would also have preferred someone else had it. I'm sure of that. But that doesn't necessarily mean that you should wish cancer on other people. Some people are stupid, Regine, so let's just ignore them. When other people come and tell you what you should think or feel, you can tell them to go to hell. It's YOUR blog and you're not writing any ugly things about other people. My God, people have no idea what things are like for you. The closest I'll ever get to knowing how you feel is when I think about how my father, when he was sick with cancer, was up four days and nights in a row without saying a word. He was probably so sick with thoughts of dying. It was awful! He survived, and is now 100 percent healthy. I really, *really* hope that a miracle will happen for you, Regine. You're a person the world can't be without. So creative, so competent, so wise. When I compare you with other eighteen-year-olds, I know they seem materialistic and shallow by comparison. And I was like that, too. ☺ You have a lot to teach people. I've learned a lot from your blog myself. I'm healthy and I have my freedom. What in the world am I complaining about?? Small things . . . And I think more about that now. I'm thankful. Cancer could happen to anyone at all. My goodness, dear Regine, the darkness you are going through is unthinkable for me. There are a lot of idiots who leave harsh comments here, but believe me, Regine, 95 percent are people who care about you. It's sad that some of your friends have disappeared, but be thankful for Eli. ☺ More than anything else, I just want things to turn around for you, Regine. A long, BIG hug from me. ☺

—*Lise*

Dear Regine! You're worn out from the medication, and the reality of your illness is much more apparent now that the school year has started without you. So it's totally natural for you to feel depressed, broken down, sad, and angry that this has happened to you! And the sense that friends have distanced themselves as the disease has dragged on is seriously painful. It's completely understandable that you have no optimism or initiative left. Unfortunately, I don't think you can count on your readers necessarily understanding what your situation entails. You write fragments of your daily life, sometimes positive and other times sad and full of despair, and we readers have to try to read between the lines, and see past the words on the page. Some readers have the ability to sympathize; others don't (something that's painfully obvious in a lot of the comments). But I sincerely believe that most people want to offer you their support. If there are people who don't understand the burden you have to carry, then they should avoid saying anything—and I totally understand why you want those people to stay away from your blog. It's difficult to say something meaningful for the situation you're in. But I want you to realize that people who have experience with serious diseases can empathize with some of what you're going through. And there are still many of us here who feel for you and think of you and wish you nothing but the best. We're praying for a miracle.

    —*Greetings from Ashild*

"I wish someone other than me had gotten this cancer instead." I think that's an awful thing to say actually . . . Weren't you the one who said you have to "accept your war"?

    —*K*

Yuck, I get totally pissed off by some of the comments you get. Of course you don't want other people to get cancer; every functional human being understands that you wrote that in a state of deep despair. I have no doubt that EVERYONE in your situation has the exact same thought at one point or another. To write as openly and honestly as you do about your psychological and physical struggles shows how tough and bold you really are. It's so sad to read about your friends disappearing. Thank goodness for Eli! She really sounds like the world's best friend! Worth her weight in gold. It's when times are tough that you see who your true friends are. I hope that everyone who thinks they hate school reads this entry, and understands how lucky they really are. I'll cross every body part that's crossable for you, and I hope you soon get to hear some good news and have some good days.

—*Big hug from a neighbor who's cheering for you*

Wishing that someone besides you had cancer is the same as a healthy person meeting a seriously ill cancer patient and thinking: I'm glad it's not me. They're two sides of the same coin. It's totally natural—and not brutal or grotesque at all. It's a thought that demonstrates the basic human instinct for survival. The fact that some people can't tolerate your honesty is something I hope you can dismiss and rise above. They would think the same thing if they were in your position, but they probably wouldn't be brave enough to tell others about it. I hope your condition is still okay and that the cycle is doing what it's supposed to do. In the meantime, I have some smoothies to recommend: Try one with bananas, a lot of frozen blueberries, and a lot of vanilla yogurt. Blueberries and vanilla is an unbeatable combination; it tastes incredible. ☺

—*Jorn*

Thank you so much to all of you who made an effort to understand what I was saying! There are a lot of good and wise comments in here. I don't understand why people feel they absolutely have to provoke a debate with me. These are my thoughts and no one else's, and there's no need to sabotage them—especially if you have no idea what

I'm going through. These are thoughts that everyone has, but which hardly anyone says out loud. At least I'm honest. I'm tired of people expecting you to say, "Ahh, I'm so happy that this happened to me." I just don't believe in the sunshine stories of people who say things like that. If you don't have anything better to do than bring me down even further, then you must not have anything worthwhile in your life. That's tragic. I also don't understand how this K can claim that I write a lot of controversial things. She's the one being controversial here, not me.

Lillebeth: I completed the Vidaza cycle today. ☺

—*Regine*

I think very few people here understand what Regine has actually been through. Long-lasting cancer with relapses is a different animal entirely from your basic cancer case. First, cancer is not a single disease; there are at least 180 distinct types of cancers, most of which have subtypes and stages all their own. As such, cancer and cancer treatments range over a broad spectrum, which at the low end can involve only a small surgical incision (which may not even leave a scar) and minimal radiation treatment; those two simple, minor measures often allow for the patient to be healthy for the rest of his life. At the other end of the spectrum, however, patients are forced to actively fight against the cancer despite chronic ill health; they can feel their bodies being destroyed by the disease and worn down by the drugs and medicine, and they live in constant fear that the next doctor visit will be a death sentence.

Both descriptions are of "cancer," but they aren't even close to being the same thing. How anyone can justify a cruel retort when Regine shares her thoughts, her pain, and her experiences, I just don't understand. The people criticizing Regine for her comment that "I wish it was someone other than me who was struck instead" should just be happy that they aren't in a position to understand the long-term pain that serious cancer can involve. I've stood on the sidelines and seen what patients go through, but I can still honestly say "anyone but me!" Regine, you're an incredibly tough girl. I've read your blog for a while now, and I really hope you experience a change for the better soon! And more generally I just want to thank you for being so brave, and sharing your thoughts and experiences with us. Even if it's painful, even though it hurts, I'm really thankful for your giving so much of yourself to us. You've become the personification of what I'm fighting for, and your words inspire me whenever I grow tired or frustrated with my work.

—*The Researcher*

Hi Regine! ☺ I've been following your blog for a long time, mostly because my sister (Sofsen) asked me to take a look a while back, and since then I've read it as much as I possibly can. I often think about you and what you have to go through, and I still can't manage to mentally put myself in most of the situations you wind up in. I think Beate put it best when he said, "People are crazy." I think that hits the nail on the head. You really just have to keep writing. I don't see you as an "egotistical" person or as a strange person. I see you as a light in the dark. You bring hope to so many people. Christian suggested in the above that you should "think about all the people who have the same diagnosis that you do." Yes, you should remember them.

Think of the hope you bring them, and think of all the strength that you give to them. They see how bravely you're tackling a situation that most people would see as hopeless. You're fighting; you're standing up to the disease. And damn it, you'll succeed in knocking the shit out of it, too. And when that day comes, think about all the people who currently have the same diagnosis as you. Think about how many people will get a new spark of inspiration, and a new shield.

You'll show them that, yes, recovery is actually possible. So Christian: I agree with you. Regine really should think about all the people with the same diagnosis as her. The courage you show, Regine, almost brings tears to my eyes. Keep fighting.

—*Matias, a big admirer*

Hi Regine! I've been visiting your blog for a long time now but this is my first time commenting. I recently looked through a lot of the comments you've gotten, and it left a really bad taste in my mouth! Who are you to decide that what Regine feels and what she wants to discuss in her situation is wrong!? Who are you to define Regine as confrontational!?? Who are you to come in here and actually THINK that Regine is after fame and PR in the papers!!?? What the HELL(!!!!) is wrong with you?? What gives you the right to blog negatively about a person who is actually looking death in the eyes at such a young age?? Unfortunately, that's the way it is now: fame and glory and the number one spot on Blogg.no is what counts. What the HELL!!!?? Take a look in the mirror!!!! Get a clue! I won't even TRY to imagine myself in your position, Regine. I won't even try! I'm 31 and I have a beautiful five-year-old daughter. I'm so profoundly thankful for having gotten as far as I have today! And I appreciate every single day of my life! My mother died of cancer when I was fifteen, after sixteen(!!!) years of being afflicted. The doctors were beside themselves with amazement that she made it so long. I have a picture of her here as we speak, with a needle in her arm, smiling to the nurse who took the test. That's my mom. I was delivered by caesarian because of her health at the time. She promised herself she would see my sister and me get confirmed. Sixteen years! She made it. After my confirmation, she had achieved her goals and she died in the fall of the same year.

Sixteen years!! I still remember vividly how she lay under a comforter in the living room, sick, and with a high fever. I called a taxi to

Riksen myself (I was used to doing it after so many years of chemo). This time she knew she wouldn't be coming home again; she knew that it was the last time she'd see the place that she loved more than any place else on earth. She just knew it! Dad also probably knew it, although he didn't say anything to my sister or me. We thought it was just another trip to the hospital.

We're talking about willpower—the willpower that gave her sixteen extra years of life, and gave her some of her happiest moments on this earth. We're talking about going through chemo with a smile because she didn't want the people around her (who she loved more than anything) to get depressed! At the funeral, a good friend of hers said it best: Every year my mom went by this friend's house with an almond ring cake for Christmas. She even came by during her last year, with as big a smile as ever. "I managed it this year too . . . " she said.

The church was packed for her funeral. The taxi driver who used to take her to Riksen for every new cycle of chemo cried at the funeral, and his wife did too. I guess what I'm actually trying to say is . . . you're like her. You're a fighter. You see the silver lining in things that are too dark for most people to even think about! You have what it takes to survive, Regine. Mom had it, but unfortunately age and the disease got the upper hand in the end. You have a better starting point than Mom. You still have a chance! I think it's so inspiring to see the expression on your face in your pictures. You look worn out but you still have hope. Treasure every day! Appreciate the small moments! (I know you do already; you've proved that, time and time again.) While many of us would have given up, you still go to festivals. Small moments, Regine. To the people who even THINK about coming to this blog to criticize you for what you write, all I have to say is: What's wrong with you!!?? You're like me: You grimace as soon as you get a pebble in your shoe!! What do you know about being deathly ill at her age?! Get a clue!!! Damn it!! I don't know anything about it. I don't try either. I just know that you, Regine, you've got what it takes to survive. Use it! Your photos are fantastic! You see things in the world that other people just don't see. You capture a mood, and that's why your photos turn out so well! I'm still processing my impressions of some of the best ones. You have a talent that many photographers would envy. Use it. I'd like to write, "This will go well, Regine! Things go well for good girls. Be positive, and everything will be okay." But I can't make that guarantee. All I can say is that I hope with all my heart that you'll stay with us—as a photographer, or doing something else that you really love to do. I hope to see your happy face in the future. You deserve a full and happy life! You're a hero for me, Regine. Just like my mom.

—*Oystein*

Some better days
Sunday, August 23, 2009

Things have actually gone pretty well for me this weekend. It didn't start out very promising, but luckily things quickly turned around.

On Saturday, Karina and Silje came to visit. It's been a while since I've seen them, so that was really nice! We're able to chat about everything and nothing, but most of all we talked about our fear of Siv Jensen—she absolutely shouldn't win the election and come to power. We also wound up talking about the universe as a whole: because if we think about it, we're actually meaningless little creatures on a meaningless little planet. You could go crazy if you think about the infinite spaces of the cosmos, and about all the other things that are beyond our understanding. Anyway, in other news, we made plans to get together again next Friday. We're going to order food and watch a movie, so that will be nice.

Today Eli visited again, and we carried out our tried-and-true ritual: cake baking, Mario Kart, and *True Blood*. This time we made a foam cake. It turned out great, but it was really sweet and rich, so we couldn't eat a lot of it. It's so fun to bake, and *True Blood* is getting really exciting. There were a lot of people who asked about the recipe, so here it is.

Foam Cake

Ingredients:

Cake:

4 egg whites	6 sheets of gelatin
1¾ cups sugar	½ cup boiling water
4 tsp. vanilla sugar	

Frosting:

1 plate light cooking chocolate	3–4 tbsp. coconut to
3 tbsp. shortening	sprinkle on cake

Instructions:

1. Put the gelatin in cold water to soak.
2. Beat the egg whites until they're stiff, and carefully mix in the sugar and vanilla sugar.
3. Squeeze the water out of the gelatin and stir the gelatin in the boiling water.
4. Pour in the egg whites and mix for fifteen minutes in mix master.
5. Afterward, pour the dough in the pan and set in refrigerator for about one hour.
6. Melt the cooking chocolate and shortening together and spread on cake when it has set.
7. Sprinkle the coconut over the frosting.
8. Put the cake in the refrigerator when done.

Also, someone asked what kind of Smoothie Eli and I made here the other day.

Smoothie:

1 mango	5 cups Sprite
½ can peaches	

It was so, so simple. (We used much less of everything when we made it, by the way.)

We need more young men to donate bone marrow

Friday, August 28, 2009

I saw a news story on NRK today about how there are way too few young men acting as bone marrow donors. Of the 28,000 registered donors, only 2,300 are men under 36. Young men are the ones best suited to being a bone marrow donor, because you can always get the most cells from young men. They have a high cell production and it's easy to draw from them because they have good veins. Doctors are concerned about these statistics.

How you can become a bone marrow donor

First of all, you have to be a blood donor. To do that, contact your local blood bank. As a volunteer donor, your tissue type will be determined during a routine blood test. The results are saved in a bone marrow donor registry. Stem cells will only be harvested if you are chosen, and the chances of being chosen as a donor are very small. Still, it's incredibly important for people who are able to register to do so, so that people who need bone marrow have the possibility of finding a donor. Imagine if YOU could contribute to saving a life?

Donating stem cells is completely safe and is done by drawing blood or bone marrow. Everyone has ample bone marrow, and the small amount taken out is replaced by the body in a few days.

Imagine knowing that you might have saved a life—it must be a great feeling. Those are the things that give life meaning. Even if there's no guarantee that the bone marrow transplant will be successful, you'll still have given someone a chance at recovery. I wouldn't have had a chance without at least a transplant, and it felt amazing just to have the opportunity. The donor gave me hope, and I still have hope that I can manage to have another stem cell transplant in order to get well (even if things don't look too good right now).

This is an appeal to register, people.

N.B.: You must be over eighteen in order to act as either a blood or a bone marrow donor.

The Last Autumn, 2009

The Last Autumn, 2009

Over the mountains and through the . . . thorns

Tuesday, September 1, 2009

Just thought I'd post a quick update, even though there's not much to write about anymore. My motivation is basically gone. I'm consumed with dark thoughts. My strength has evaporated. I'm worn out. Life's a struggle. I've lived with this for a long time now—this uncertainty, this fight between life and death. It does something to you, psychically. Not being able to participate in life, not being able to pursue your dreams, and just not knowing . . . it kills the joy of being alive.

My blood tests have at least been stable, but blood tests aren't everything. On Monday, I'm going to Trondheim for a bone marrow biopsy. I haven't been over there for a while now. I don't have any idea what to expect, but I probably shouldn't be too optimistic. I've been through around four to five cycles of Vidaza now, and they say you need to have six before the medicine really takes effect. I'm really anxious about the results. I almost don't want to know what they are, just on the off chance that they'll signal the end. I need motivation, and if the test shows signs of improvement, it'll be easier to carry on. If it looks really bad, or if the numbers haven't improved at all . . . then I'll be crushed. I'm tired of the uncertainty though. Once I see the results, I'll have a better sense of whether or not it's worth continuing.

I just want to be myself again, but something is telling me it's never going to happen.

From bad to worse

Saturday, September 5, 2009

Things aren't going very well these days. I've gotten even worse. I don't know exactly what's going on though. It started with some stomach pains on Monday. Was examined by a doctor on Wednesday, but it's hard to give an accurate diagnosis when all you can do is just press on my stomach. My other pains have also gotten worse—especially in my muscles and my bones. I have trouble walking. It doesn't help that I get headaches either. No, it's just misery, you guys. I've probably gotten some kind of virus. I've also had a fever these last two days. In the evenings. But I haven't had the energy to go to the hospital. Hopefully it won't get too high, because then I'd have no choice: I'd have to go to the hospital.

Tonight I'm planning on watching the Norwegian national soccer team play. I've even bet money on the game. So despite everything, I'm pretty excited about that.

Yesterday I got a package from the Record Company. I got *Magnolia, 12 Monkeys, Spider, The Rules of Attraction, Naked Lunch,* and Tool's *Undertow.*

So at least I'll have something to do for the next few days. Can anyone recommend some other movies?

I found a picture of myself in London from last year. I want to go back! I miss just being able to do things like that. It's crazy to think that was only a year ago. Things sure can change fast.

Regine in London, Easter 2008

Arrival in Trondheim

Tuesday, September 8, 2009

We checked into Trondheim yesterday morning. They took a lot of blood tests and I went through several examinations. They also took an X-ray of my lungs and an ultrasound of my stomach. Everything looked fine there, so at least my organs are in good shape (amazingly enough). My spleen was bigger than it should be, but that's the way it is when you have leukemia.

Then this morning I had to be anesthetized so that the doctors could take a bone marrow biopsy and get some spinal fluid. (I had to lie flat for two hours after it was over.) I'm not sure if I'm supposed to get the results today or tomorrow though. They were going to take a long look at the marrow before planning our next move.

My marrow isn't in good shape—we all know that. The question is, has there been any improvement? Because about a third of my blood is made up of blasts right now, we also know that there are some cancer cells in my marrow, so we're trying to figure out if Vidaza will help. It's the next steps that I'm interested in, but I also understand that they're not going to provide a definitive answer now either.

In the eye of the storm (again)

Wednesday, September 9, 2009

I'm back home. My bone marrow has improved a little. Not many AML cells are left, but now I've got myelodysplastic cells instead. They're less aggressive, but I don't think the overall percentage has really decreased at all—the cells have just changed. On the other hand, I do have a few more healthy cells now. I'm going to keep taking the Vidaza. I'll probably be on it for quite a while longer. The doctor said I might need to keep taking it for a whole year.

I don't know what I think about the next steps. I want to get well, but I don't have the strength to sit here like this for twelve more months. I'd rather get well right away, of course, but it doesn't work that way. I don't even know if I'll ever be well again. It looks like I have a tough time ahead of me.

But my god, I'm so glad things have improved! I just have mixed feelings about the future. There's so much I still want to do.

I want to live normally again. I'm struggling with depression, and I don't know exactly how to motivate myself and hang in there.

9/15/09

Tuesday, September 15, 2009

Things aren't getting any better. I sort of thought I'd gotten rid of the fever, but it just refuses to go away; it comes back every other day or so now, and no one knows what's causing it. But anyway, after I got back from Trondheim, I thought I would try getting into better shape. The Vidaza is doing its job and keeping me from catching anything new, but it doesn't do any good if I have to just lie around here at home. So I thought I'd try to go on daily walks. But of course it wasn't that simple, and on Saturday I got this headache—which is literally the worst headache ever. I can't sleep very well because of it (or I guess now I should say because of *them*), and every time I wake up, I can barely manage to move my head it hurts so much. None of the pain-killers do any good either. It's even hard for me to stand up. I guess it's a little bit better today, and hopefully that will continue. This is all because of the spinal chemo.

On another note: You shouldn't take what I said about "one year" too literally. Nobody has given me a sell-by date, as some people thought. It was only a way of saying that maybe I'll be someone who needs to be on the drug for a long time—and that sometimes those people need to take it for up to a year. The malignant cells could still come back and ruin everything, or the Vidaza could lose some or all of its effectiveness in knocking out the cancer cells. The last time I checked, I was supposed to have two to three cycles, but they don't want to give it to me if it's not working, because it makes me so sick.

If I don't see any improvement soon, it will be hard to keep going.

I wish things would get better
Sunday, September 20, 2009

I've been sick ever since my last post. My energy is at a low point and the pain is wreaking havoc. I haven't been up to seeing any visitors.

I spend my days lying in bed and on the sofa. That's all I can handle. I have a fever almost every night now and no one knows why. It doesn't seem to be going away; it's hopeless.

Last weekend when I thought I was starting to get a little bit better, I planned a small "vacation" in Trondheim. The Cancer Society has an apartment they lend out, and I thought that maybe I could borrow it for the whole fall vacation week. By then the Trondheim culture festival (aka "The Week") will have started in Trondheim, and there are a ton of concerts to see. So yeah, I ordered three concert tickets and reserved the apartment. But it's only two weeks away now, and I'm really worried that it just won't work out. With the shape I'm in now, it's just not realistic.

I just wanted to take a break from all the misery and somehow enjoy myself a little in Trondheim. Go to the shops, cafes, and concerts, and just relax. We'll see what happens.

My appetite is totally gone, too. I eat just two meals a day, and that's nowhere near enough. After all, I don't want to totally waste away. So if anyone can suggest something simple and easy to eat, I would be really grateful.

I'm proud of myself
Tuesday, September 22, 2009

When I got up today, I was just as worn out and exhausted as ever (and didn't show many signs of improving, either). But I had to do something, I thought. I can't just wither away in here on the sofa. After all, I'd decided to exercise more to try to up build my strength. So even though I was weak and tired, I got myself dressed and went outside. I walked up the neighborhood hill and then back down again, and after that I walked a little behind the house, in the forest. When I got home, I was completely exhausted—but I was smiling anyway, because I'd done it.

This wouldn't be exercise for you healthy people, but for me it is, and it really helps. I felt so much better afterward. I took a bath and fixed myself up and rested. I haven't put on nice clothes and makeup in about a month. It felt good. I felt more upbeat. Then later on, Ida came to visit, and we chatted and ate raspberries. It's been a good day. Finally.

Regine's entry generated 232 responses, in which readers expressed their happiness about her progress. Here's a small selection:

So incredibly good to hear, Regine! That made me so happy! ☺ Stop by your blog about five times a day, and have been a regular reader for the past six months. Your writing is so inspirational!
　—Oda

I'm so proud of you that I don't even know what to say!!!! SO great that you managed to be proactive about your happiness and well-being—happiness can truly be found in the little things, and after a while you see that those so-called little things are actually the biggest things of all, because the simplest pleasures are the best. ♥ I actually

got dizzy just from reading this—I'm so happy for you, and so incredibly proud of you!
—*Rebella*

This is the best thing I've read in a long time—and I hope you'll continue to defy this horrible cancer!! I'm so proud of you—keep it up! ☺
—*Greetings and hugs from a grandmother in Nordmore*

Good evening. I'm a woman with a son who's almost seven and a fifteen-month-old daughter. My partner is in school and (as a result) only home on the weekends. My days are often stressful and exhausting. I first heard about you and your blog in April, but as soon as I started following your story, I was deeply moved by all you had to say. I've only written one comment, but it was probably from around the time that I started following you. I'm also fighting a daily battle as a recovering drug addict. Following your blog gives me something. It's simple: Your words help me to value life and try to get something positive out of each day. It's not always easy to be happy about your lot in life, but if you look hard enough you'll always find something . . . Most importantly: Face your fear. Accept your war. It is what it is . . .

What you managed to do today—taking this walk—was a victory in and of itself!! I admire you so much—you're a very special person!
—*Warm greetings from Linda*

GOD BLESS YOU, REGINE! Now I'm crying for you—with tears of joy. That you managed to dress up and take that kind of a walk says something about what you're made of. This mental strength of yours is what will get you through this. (And maybe some more short walks will help build up your appetite, too.) But be careful not to wear yourself out—you probably need a lot of rest now. I—along with thousands of other people out here—wish you the very best in the days ahead, and I pray that you get the strength you need to get through the hard parts as well.

—*Little old lady*

Regine, you should ALWAYS be proud of yourself. Do you know why? Because you're Regine—and you'll never be anything less. And that's a lot, isn't it! ☺

You're an inspiration!

—*Big hug from Linn Inger*

You go, girl! If it's any consolation, you're probably in better shape than I am. I get worn out just from walking up the stairs. Haha. No kidding.

No, really—I'm proud of you! Besides, you're the prettiest girl in the world. ☺ I totally agree with Linn Inger above: You should be proud because you're Regine, and no one else.

You're the coolest person in all of Norway!

—*Sofsen*

Read Linda's comment. You're a phenomenal inspiration for so many people. Running a marathon is peanuts compared to you just getting off the sofa and hiking around the neighborhood.

I hope that people understand what kind of strength and courage you actually have.

Good luck getting further up that hill.

—*GSC*

Really great to read about this experience. You should definitely be proud of yourself! I'm proud of you! Truly a medal-worthy performance!

—*Espen*

Hi! My heart aches for you, Regine. You're so young and you deserve the chance to enjoy your life. I really don't know how to express the way I feel about you and your situation. I'm a mother of three from Varmland in Sweden who's followed you for a long time, and although it's a thoroughly depressing situation that you're in, I don't feel sad after reading your blog; instead, I feel inspired. You should be proud of yourself, Regine. You're a real giant.

—*Hug from Maj-Liss*

Yes! I also take walks in the neighborhood . . . I suffer from arthritis and have to move around every single day, no matter how painful it is. ☹ A short daily walk with my cat makes a big difference for me, but it's not easy. (I'm pretty lazy by nature, so it's doubly hard, haha.) Even a short little walk can make a world of difference . . .

My dad had the same disease as you, and he was frequently feverish. On the other hand, he also had periods when he was just fine. He lost his taste for food when he felt the worst though. Have you lost your appetite, too?

I have to add that my dad didn't wind up dying from leukemia. The treatment worked for him, but then he suddenly had a heart attack—and that was that.

I'm wondering if you have the latest Dan Brown book? I have it on tape and can put a copy in the mail for you, if you like ☺ . . . so that you can listen to it when you want to. It's in English though, but that probably isn't an issue for an eighteen-year-old. (The original language version rocks.)

Feel better soon. You're really impressive. I'm crossing my fingers for you.

—*Knut, a neighbor (sort of)*

And the water takes hold

Friday, September 25, 2009

I took photos today. For the first time in forever. The fall weather isn't great, but I went outside anyway.

It felt good to feel the wind on my face. The air was refreshing, and it seemed like it gave new life to my thoughts.

Alone time

Sunday, September 27, 2009

It's raining outside and I'm all by myself, but feeling just fine. The house is empty, and that doesn't happen very often. I've always loved being by myself—always appreciated the chance to just sit down and watch a good, thought-provoking movie (or do something else like that). My privacy flew out the window when I got cancer. Suddenly everyone needed to know everything about everything. All the strangers in lab coats. When I was at the hospital, they never left me alone. They were in and out of my room all day. They dropped in even if they didn't need to. Being at home isn't the same as it used to be either. I used to be home alone more often. But that almost never happens anymore. Today I am though, at least for a few hours.

Later I'm going to watch *Roswell*. It's good entertainment. I'm thinking about starting the third Stieg Larsson book, too. Either way though, I'm going to see *The Girl Who Played with Fire* tomorrow, and I'm really looking forward to it.

Josefine attacked my foot in bed last night and I got a cut on my heel. Bad kitty.

Carry, by Isis*

Sunday, July 19, 2009

And the water takes hold

Fills his lungs and crushes his body

Dust floats through sun and water

As you draw close

Fall to me

He sees like he's never seen before

I will carry you

True and free

And the water carries him away

Now that you're here

You'll swim with me

Soon he ceases to be at all

I am clutching you

True

He sees like he's never seen before

He is light in the water

**Isis was a post-hard core/post-rock band
active in the late 1990s and the 2000s.
They announced their retirement in 2010.*

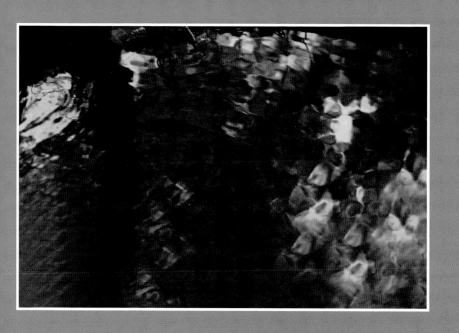

Erratic days

Friday, October 2, 2009

The last few days have been super erratic, if that makes any sense. One day I feel fine, but the next day I wind up with terrible pains and a fever. The blood tests weren't very encouraging earlier this week, and that made me even more anxious. I've been thinking the worst, but my thoughts haven't been too negative today. Everything changes so fast from one day to the next. It would be much easier if things didn't always change so much. But every day there are different answers and new questions. Maybe it's just me who gets hung up on this stuff. I don't know. I'm still hoping the trip to Trondheim next week will be nice, in spite of all my pain and discomfort.

By the way, *The Girl Who Played with Fire* was amazing. The book was better of course, but it's always like that. Thanks for the tickets, Caroline Movie Theaters!

I'm having a hard time answering all your emails lately. I get so many! But you'll get answers eventually.

Take me out

Sunday, October 4, 2009

I'm really looking forward to the Trondheim trip! I just hope I'll be in good enough shape to do everything I want to do. As I mentioned earlier, things are up and down these days. I still get fevers, and the pain is always there, but I'm hoping it'll get better next week. I'm wondering when I'll need to start the next cycle. The doctor's going to look at a blood smear tomorrow, and he'll make a decision after that. Hopefully I won't need to do it next week. That would be disappointing (not to mention boring). But if I have to, that's the way it is. My health comes first.

I don't know what to pack exactly. Painkillers and warm clothes, definitely. One of the concerts I'm going to will be outside. I'm a little worried about that performance, since it's insanely cold in Trondheim right now. On Thursday we're seeing the Eagles of Death Metal, and on Friday we get to see Franz Ferdinand. Really looking forward to it! When I get back, I'm also going to see Gåte.

It'll be good to get away for a while. I need this trip. I'm going to try to go shopping, go to cafes, and enjoy myself as much as possible.

Going with the flow
Tuesday, October 6, 2009

Eli and I are sitting in the Trondheim apartment, right in front of the TV. So far the trip has gone really well. It started out kind of rough yesterday, when I woke up with a fever of almost 104! I was worried that all of our plans would go down the drain, but luckily I'm in better shape today. I went to the hospital and it doesn't look like we'll be able to start the cycle this week. I'm trying not to think too much about the blood test results or anything else like that. I don't want to worry, so basically I decided that I didn't want to know the white blood cell count. The ultrasounds they took of my stomach were fine at least. I've been struggling with stomach pains for over a month now, but they gave me some antacids and I think they're helping. Finally.

After going to the hospital, Eli and I went shopping in town. I managed to spend way too much money at the first store. But I don't shop that often, so I guess I have an excuse. They had so much cute stuff. Eli bought a badass leather jacket that I was a little bit jealous of. ☺ Since I get tired so fast, we didn't shop for long, and after about an hour we went back to the apartment. By the way, the apartment is actually pretty nice! It's so great that the Cancer Society for Children has this kind of setup. I think it's important to have a place like this.

Later in the evening, it was time to eat. We went to Jonathan's Food & Wine Cellar, under the Britannia hotel. The food was incredible. It's expensive, but it's worth it! I really recommend it: awesome service, nice people, and such delicious food. What else can you ask for?

We're going to watch a movie now, and just relax and enjoy ourselves. I hope you all are doing well, too!

Another blow to the head

Thursday, October 8, 2009

Things haven't exactly turned out as planned. Today I got some really bad news. I went to the hospital for blood tests and the results were catastrophic. They confirmed that the Vidaza isn't working anymore. The aggressive cells have come back and I probably have one foot in the grave. They want to start me on a low-dose chemo cycle, but it's only helped one person get into remission before me. Most likely it will let me live on for a little longer than I otherwise would. I asked the doctor how long I could live while taking these pills. They told me anywhere from several weeks to several months. But they also said it was important to remember that there was still a tiny chance. I take that to mean there's no chance at all.

I've been crying nonstop since one o'clock today. My face is totally swollen. My eyes are sore. This wasn't supposed to happen. The last time I met with the doctors we discussed the future, and talked about when I could start taking classes again—and now all of a sudden, it looks like I'm going to die. Things changed so fast, and I don't understand anything. This is the worst thing I've ever experienced. Going through something like this is just absolutely brutal. No one deserves this.

I'm thinking about my family having to go through all of this. It's so awful to think about. It's not just my life that's being ruined. I really don't know how I'm going to get through the next few days. I really don't know.

In total, 1,165 readers sent Regine their encouragement after this entry. Here's a small selection:

Regine . . . This is so, so sad to hear! I've been reading your blog for so long now . . . through all the ups and downs . . . I feel so close to everything, as if I knew you. I often think of you. I'm a nursing student and I meet a lot of people with the same diagnosis as yours at the hospital, and so this seems especially real to me now. This is all so unfair!!!
    —*Anonymous*

Don't be afraid. Remember that you're unique, and totally one-of-a-kind. Special people like you, Regine, survive everything. You have to fight tooth and nail on your way to getting well. Hang in there; you're fantastic.
    You also take incredible photos. You're an artist, Regine, and you'll go far with your art. It's a subject you should consider pursuing when you start university. Your art and creativity are unique. With your amazing talent, you'll get far in life. Fight, Regine, FIGHT. We all love you very much. A big warm hug from everyone to you, Regine. ♥
    —*Anne Marie*

Dear Regine,
    You've made your way through your short life, and moved people all over the country in the process. You've changed people's attitudes, thoughts, and values—you've touched us with the stinging, painful, and profound stories from your life. Thank you so much! No one

knows where your path will lead next, but there are a lot of us who keep you, your family, and your friends in our thoughts. It's a small consolation, I realize that, but still . . .

—*Many warm thoughts from Hanna*

This is difficult stuff, Regine. With all the bad news you and your family have received lately, I hope that your doctors have offered you the option of professional counseling. Your entire family is tough, but what you're going though is brutal. The good thing is that you've been faced with similar issues before, and impressively enough you still found happiness afterward. I'm following the suggestion of the person who proposed that we think of you every morning and evening at eight o'clock. It can't hurt, anyway. Say hi to your parents.

—*Bengt E.*

I love you!

—*Sofsen*

Dear Regine,

You're the same age as my youngest daughter, and thinking about what you must be going through is just heartbreaking. I sympathize with you and your closest family and friends who probably feel so incredibly helpless right now. No matter what happens, you've accomplished so much more than most other people do in the course of a normal life span. You've moved the entire country. You've brought out empathy and emotions in total strangers, Regine. That's a huge accomplishment. There were 500 people who commented on your last post, and we don't know how many others also read the news and cried.

Don't underestimate your body's power to heal itself. You have to believe it's possible; you have to imagine that you're healthy and strong! I'm going to participate in the vigil for you, and I also light a candle each night at eight pm. It's been decided, Regine: You'll be the second person to go into remission from this treatment.

—*Ase*

It says "Face your fear" when we click on your blog, and you've shown the whole country that, true to your word, you're really staring down your biggest fear now that the chips are down. You need to know that there are thousands of people thinking about you, and that YOU'RE NOT alone!

Friends and strangers alike are impressed by you, and love what you've done (and who you've shown yourself to be) on your blog.

You're not going anywhere. Long live Regine Stokke—the girl who faced her fear.

—*Thea*

You've shared your words, thoughts, fears, and smiles with us all. And there are many, many people in this country who you have moved to tears. If only our thoughts could make you well . . .

You have, in any case, gotten me to think a lot about how lucky I am to be healthy, and you've made me think more about what I can do to help. Thanks to you, I'm now a blood and bone marrow donor. I'M THINKING OF YOU AND HOPING FOR THE BEST!!

—*Angelique*

I'm crying.

I don't know what I'm going to do. I can't do anything but hope.

My life hasn't been the same since I started reading your blog, close to a year ago now.

You're incredible!

—*Ida*

Regine!

You don't know how beautiful you are. You've melted the hearts of thousands of people out here, including me.

You've inspired a 37-year-old dad to become a blogger, and you've made a 37-year-old father shed real, honest tears.

Do you know what? I've got young children, and they've asked me why their dad never cries. I'm a father, and I cry. But I'm probably like most men: I can only cry when my children can't see me.

But now they've seen that their daddy *can* cry, and do you know why? They've seen me crying because I've read your whole blog . . . You have an amazing power to awaken feelings in other people, Regine.

I've told them about you and your disease. They want me to say hello from them. They're also thinking of you.

You've done so much with your blog—you have no idea.

You've made it easier for people to talk about serious diseases. You've made it easier to understand what life is like for seriously ill people.

One of my kids is often very sick, so I know what it's like to be in your family's shoes.

Take in all the love that people send to you, Regine. It's real, and we're really thinking about you.

You're probably scared to death. You're worn out and tired, but I have a belief burning inside me: Everything will work out in the end; everything will get better.

The fact that one person has made it before means that it's worth trying. It will be wonderful when the doctors can say that not one, but two people have now made it.

I believe in you, Regine. You're obviously stronger than most people. I have faith that this will work.

Regine . . . you're so important. You're courageous and persistent. You're an inspiration without equal, and you're such a beautiful human being.

You show the true fullness of life in your blog. You capture the vividness of the world in your photos. You're so vital, so full of life that I can't see how life could ever be taken away from you.

Take care of yourself, Regine, and do everything you can to keep your hope alive.

A warm greeting from someone who admires you, and will admire you forever.

—*A 37-year-old dad*

Regine's poem generated 200 comments. Most of them contained high praise and were filled with adjectives like beautiful, lovely, and powerful.

It's wonderful how much you have inside you, Regine. Just think of how much you've done, and how much you've provided for other people! The list includes:

1. your descriptive and (for us readers) informative blog posts,
2. artful, high-quality photographs, and
3. a fantastically compelling poem that I just had the honor of reading.

You've augmented your surroundings with intelligence, art, and inspiration. You've offered more than healthy people EVER give. It's incredible to think of how much you've done—even while fighting this battle.

Opium

Thursday, October 15, 2009

Give me sweet candy. Give me sweet dreams.

I don't want to feel anymore. I don't want to be where I am.

I want to swerve. I want to dance.

I want to smile. I want to laugh.

Let me avoid today. Just let me pretend.

Pretend that I'm another me. Let me escape the shadows, evade the fog.

I'd rather be under the starry sky, see the northern lights.

I don't want to think. Just for today. I want to be spared.

I want my body to sing inside.

Because this shadow dance in the dark isn't me.

Give me sweet candy. Give me sweet dreams.

It's only fair that you get back some of the magic that you've put out into the world. It's only fair that you achieve your goal (and our dream for you): a long life.

—*Bengt*

Hi there! Every day when I turn on my PC, the first thing that I do is check your blog. What's happening? Where is she? What's she doing, what's she thinking, what does she wish for, what's she feeling? And when you don't post anything, I get anxious.

Everyone is hoping you'll get good news soon! The poem you wrote is beautiful, Regine . . . You're so talented. Katrine, Camilla, Kristiina, and I talk about you often, and never stop thinking about you and wishing you well! We're with you!

I went to take tests to see if I could become a blood donor after you encouraged us, and do you know what? They need my blood type, so I'll get going with that on Tuesday. They said there were many people who registered here in Kristiansund after you asked them to give blood! THAT'S ALL THANKS TO YOU! Well, say hello to your family, and keep it up.

—*Hugs from Marianne*

A stranger to myself

Saturday, October 17, 2009

I've lived all I can.

I've done my best

To live.

But still, I don't get anything back.

Everything's been taken from me.

Soon, there will be nothing left.

Less and less every day.

Soon nothing will be left of me.

I want to exist, but this body can't carry me any longer.

I fall apart alone.

I'm the only one who's able to feel this pain.

Desperation.

Frustration.

There's nothing I can do.

It's not up to me.

Nothing is up to me.

Even my face feels strange to me.

I assume I died a year ago.

Something has taken hold of me, something I didn't want, and never asked for.

Something that will continue eating me until I'm gone.

I'll never be set free.

Regine's brutally honest description of her situation generated 415 comments. The psychologist's comment was representative of a large group of grateful readers. And Thea and Proben's comment represented a large group who were left speechless:

We're completely speechless. This is really hard to read. But we still hope that the tide will turn, and that things will start to get better soon.

Is there anything we can do . . . anything at all?

As we said, we're speechless, but we're thinking a lot about you and your family!!

—*Thea & Proben*

No, Regine. You didn't die a year ago. This fantastic and impressive blog isn't the work of someone who's died. It's the work of someone who's alive and very talented—someone with a strong will to live. And it's written by one of the strongest and most impressive people I know.

If best wishes, crossed fingers and toes, prayers, and hope could get rid of the disease that's taken up residence in you, the disease would have lost a long time ago. But unfortunately it doesn't work that way.

Regine, thank you for giving so much of yourself to those of us who are sitting on the sidelines, hoping and praying for a miracle.

With a big hug from me to you.

—*CSG*

Dear Regine,

I've been following your blog for a long time but never written any comments. I'm an aspiring psychologist and, of course, a fellow human being, and I've experienced some incredible happiness and some incredible sorrow in my life.

In my training and in my work, I've studied many aspects of the human brain in depth. Even though I've read several thousand pages of literature on the subject (and am currently working on my dissertation) nothing has given me as much insight into a young human mind as your blog has. In the course of my long career, I've never come across anyone else—young or old—who has marshaled all the intricacies of language and art in order to give full voice to their emotional lives, as you have. With your talents, your gifts, and your pain, you've taught me more than I ever could dream of learning from books or scientific articles. I'm deeply thankful to you, Regine.

From all the hundred or so entries that I've read here, I've also gotten a fantastic sense of the emotional potential that we share as human beings. By far, the majority of the comments show how much concern and consideration we long to give each other. There's an incredible range of life experiences for our young people, as always: Some have experienced life's dark side, while others have been fed with a silver spoon their entire lives. The sad truth is that we don't often get to decide how our lives will begin and where they will end. Young people who haven't had to endure any crisis moments don't really have the ability to put themselves in the complicated spectrum of feelings and thoughts that you show here on your blog, and some of the comments can seem clumsy and not well thought out to someone who's just struggling to keep her head above water. But still, I see that a lot of these people try as hard as they can to give you tools that can help you—they really want to contribute to your recovery. From your position, you can see that some of these tools won't help you, and rightly so. Your intelligent responses to them show self-assurance and calm.

Unfortunately, I've met way too many people—young and old—who've read and seen *The Secret*. As a psychologist, I work with people's feelings and thought patterns on a daily basis, and on the one hand, it's totally true that in some situations, it can be effective to think positively and see the possibilities, but in *The Secret*, that idea is expanded (not to say twisted) well beyond the point where it has real value.

If it were as simple as thinking positively, no one would ever die of cancer or any other miserable disease. When people uncritically accept the messages that show up in these types of books, I really believe that life's unhappy phases and experiences can lead to even more depression, and increased feelings of inadequacy. (Like I tell my students, "It's good to take your vitamins and nutritional supplements—but at the same time, you still need breakfast, lunch, and dinner too.")

In your blog, through your text and photos, you've shown, with amazing clarity, that you—Regine—have used all of the tools at your disposal. You've appreciated friendship and family. You've gone to concerts and festivals. You've taken photos—excellent photos. You've engaged with the media when and where it felt right. You've definitely increased the number of blood and bone marrow donors. And you've *definitely* had an effect on making people more aware of what cancer does (emotionally and physically) and what cancer patients go through—not least among us psychologists. On some of your very worst days, you still managed to haul yourself up, get dressed, fix yourself up, and go for a walk. And on top of that, you managed to think positively about what you accomplished that day. There aren't many of us who could have managed that, Regine—no matter how old they are.

You've done everything you could do, Regine. You've done more than anyone could imagine in a situation like yours. You've demonstrated a will to live and an energy to survive that few of us are capable of. You take my breath away.

I wish for days where you can push the pause button—moments where you can sit back and savor the sweetest candy in the world. Moments where you can just *be*.

With thanks and admiration. ☺

—*The Psychologist*

Where did I go?

Monday, October 19, 2009

The past few days have been harder and more challenging than anything I've ever experienced before (and trust me when I say that even that's an understatement). I've never been this worn out before. The stomachaches are wrenching; I can hardly stand the pain.

The painkillers haven't worked as well as I had hoped they would. The pain isn't constant, but when it starts, it's really bad. It's all so frustrating—you have no idea. All you can do is just sit there, totally helpless. I haven't had a fever for a few days, which means that the antibiotics are working, but nothing helps with these stomach pains. I've had two ultrasounds and a CT scan, but nothing shows up there. Luckily during the "healthy" moments, a lot of people have come and visited me. That makes me feel a lot better. The TV's like my best friend now. A lot of times, it's the only thing I can stand to do. Luckily though, my family doesn't mind watching with me, so I don't get too lonely. I'm fed up with just surviving, but in a way I'm proud to even be managing that much.

Wrong turn

Thursday, October 22, 2009

This pain is unbearable. I haven't been able to have any visitors, but it was really nice of the attending nurse to come out to the house yesterday to set up the pain pump. She had to put a needle in my stomach, which is really unpleasant. It hurt a lot, and I don't like dragging the big stand around with me either. My skin is so sensitive now that even pressing the button to get more of the pain medication made me cry out, it hurt so much. (And it didn't help anyway, so I decided to take it out.)

I've been in a lot of pain again today. I tried wearing the pain patch again. And I'm taking Oxynorms, which are morphine-like pills. My body is so accustomed to the painkillers that the normal dosage isn't enough for me. Frustrating. Right now it feels like I took too much; my head is spinning and I'm nauseous. But at least the pain is gone.

I'm not sure what to say about the blood tests. The white blood count is going up again, but the Trondheim doctors want me to continue taking the chemo for another week before they decide on next steps. I see where things are heading.

Waiting for the end

Thursday, October 29, 2009

Things aren't going well these days. My blood tests have gotten much worse, and the pills aren't working well either. I'm in such pain these days that I can hardly do anything. I just have to stuff myself with painkillers and just lie in bed. I can hardly eat anything. I had to start taking an antibiotic because my C-reative protein levels have gone up a lot these last days (which generally indicates that my body is experiencing a bit of inflammation). No one knows what's causing it.

I'm trying to focus on the fact that at least I've lived a good life, and enjoyed everything as much as I possibly could. I've had tons of great experiences. I had a great childhood, and lots of great times out with family and friends. I've always enjoyed life, which makes it hard to think about all the things I'm going to miss out on now. I don't want to miss out on the future with my family and friends. I want to study. I want to have a family. I want to live a good life. I want to do *everything*. But I'm not the one in control. That's just the way it is. It's so depressing and sad. I could have had such a wonderful life, if it hadn't been for this evil disease.

A lot of people are complaining that the support group on Facebook isn't being updated. I'm not in contact with any of the administrators and don't have any control over the group, but I hope people still want to join up and show support. ☺

. . .

Thursday, November 5, 2009

Things are getting worse and worse every day. This is the worst my blood tests have ever been. My leukocytes are at 40. I've been off chemo for a week now, but the chemo wasn't working anyway. The doctors in Trondheim want me to continue taking the pills even if they're not working. I'm going to take a few more of them, but still . . . I was surprised by their decision. But they may not have anything else to offer. The pain has been a bit better lately, but that may change now that I'm going to start the chemo again. The infection I had has at least calmed down.

My worst fear has come true. A cure is now completely impossible for me. It won't be long before I die. All I want is to live, but I can't. I've fought and fought; I've done everything possible, and at this point there's nothing left to do. If the disease doesn't loosen its grip, it won't be long before it sucks me down. I'm scared to death, and sad.

People shouldn't think that I've handled this well, because I haven't. I'm human after all. A lot of times it seems like people don't

see me that way. I'm handling this like anybody else would. I have no choice *but* to deal with this. A lot of people have said they couldn't have done it. But what would they have done instead?

No one can say I've given up. I hate it when people say that. I've done everything I possibly could. But this is something I have zero control over.

You wouldn't think that life in 2009 would be so dangerous, but it is. If you get a serious disease, you're out of luck. Of course, a lot of people do get well, but there are so many others who don't. You're the future, so I encourage you to try doing something to help. Support medical research, become researchers yourselves—there's a lot you can do, if you put your mind to it.

Sentences like "All I want is to live, but I can't" moved more people than ever. Regine's two previous entries resulted in 1,699 comments. Here's a small selection:

"Life is like a box of chocolates"—you never know what you'll get . . . Cancer is a monster that chooses its victims randomly, and it could just as well have been me. There aren't any guarantees in life, and even if you don't get cancer, you could die in a car accident tomorrow! Who knows, Regine, maybe Norway will be annihilated by an atom bomb in two years, and we'll all die. Maybe there's going to be a killer virus that kills all mankind . . . and maybe not . . . One thing that's certain is that nothing is certain; nothing lasts forever. Some people live to be 87 without having truly lived a day in their lives. I'm a nurse and I want you to know that I see many people who die alone, with no one at their side, with no one to mourn for them . . . . Yes they've lived, but without making tracks. You have truly made your mark, Regine, and there are thousands of people who have followed your story who will keep it with them for the rest of their lives. I understand that death is difficult, and maybe even impossible to come to terms with. But who knows what happens after this . . . I believe that *something* does, and I believe that it's only then that we'll get the answers to all of life's big questions. Things will work out for you, Regine, I just know it.

Big hug,

—*Anonymous*

I watch the snow falling slowly from the sky, and it reminds me of my tears. Every snowflake is like a life in miniature: It's ephemeral, and it rushes toward its end. More than anything, I wish you peaceful and happy days with your loved ones—days without fear or pain.

I don't know why people write, "Don't give up." It's obvious to me at least that you'd never give up. You're doing the exact opposite of giving up. You're seeing the situation for what it is, you're realistic about the outcome, and you're handling it all as best you can. And you're doing it bravely and with dignity.

I'm thinking of you and will light a candle for you tonight, my dear Regine. Please take a break from your sorrowful thoughts—however understandable they may be—and let a wave of loving thoughts and feelings (from so very many people) wash over you. Can you feel the warmth?

—*Frances*

You're not inhuman; you're proof that there's hope for everyone. You give people something to believe in—and you're hanging in there like nobody's business. You're strong. And it's profoundly generous of you to share your experiences with us all. It's sad to read about your daily reality. I could easily fill pages of this comment board with my reactions, but I doubt that my words would make you feel any better. But there are a lot of us out here who've learned valuable lessons from you, simply due to your incredibly insightful nature. We've learned to appreciate every day, because cancer can hit anyone, anywhere.

Regine, I admire you so much. You're such a good example. Not just for me, but for so many others as well! If only there were more people like you. I'm crossing my fingers for you!

—*Hugs from Anne-Bente*

Hi Regine,

I'm a leukemia patient who's receiving life-extending treatment, and I just wanted to say that your blog has been a rare bright spot for me. What you've put into words—your feelings, your experiences, and your responses to the comments—have given me a new strength, a new sense of meaning, and a new way of understanding. I admire the courage you show in displaying your rawest human side. I've wished with my whole heart for your recovery. I know you won't give up!

—*Tore*

Dear Regine!

You're handling things in your own way. It's not necessary to analyze it or wonder how someone else would do it. You're obviously handling it in the best possible way. (Or anyway, that's what I think.) Among other things, you've decided to work through your reactions in this blog. You've found your own way to deal with everything. And you've been extremely successful. Maybe this blog is one of the key things that's enabled you to hang in there. That, and your irrepressible will to live; your love of your friends and family; your passion for art and for creation—even in the face of all of this pain. That's what you're accomplishing now, Regine: You're advocating for art in an amazingly visceral way. You capture what is light and colorful, and what is heavy, dark, and painful. That range of emotions is what makes your art so much more alive than a lot of other art I've seen.

Your last self-portrait in black and white is one of the most powerful photos I've ever seen. I've been to several workshops with the photographer Morten Krogvold, but your last self-portrait is way better than what I saw there.

You've done so much, Regine!!!

You're built to last, and that's good. Not everyone is. I had a friend who wasn't, and he ended things suddenly and brutally.

The ones who give up don't have the slightest chance of getting well. Your courage and your will to live give you the best chance of survival.

You should be proud of the will and the endurance that you've shown in this fight.

You're not inhuman, Regine. You're extremely human. You're real, honest, down to earth, and extremely alive. You live in the here and now as few can.

Your eloquence shines through both your words and your photos, and that's really impressive. I take photographs, too, and I can honestly say that I use your photos (and your creative spirit!) for inspiration. I bet I'm not the only one. Based on the response you got from Morton Krogvold, it's clear that you're blessed with a special gift. Your art and your message are a true inspiration for thousands of people. (Myself included.)

I know you'll never give up, because you've shown such strength and courage.

Even if you have to close your eyes one day, even then, you won't have given up.

I think it's safe to say that you've already won in life. You've really shown what it is to live.

No matter how weak you may become in the future, I'll always believe that things will turn around for you. It's strange to say, but my own daughter's death has made me realize that anything is possible—

for both good and for ill. My belief is unyielding because I've seen the impossible happen with my own eyes.

I'm holding out hope for you, I'm praying for you, and believing in you—along with everyone else.

And I hope you don't have to suffer. You really don't deserve that kind of pain.

I know you've managed to touch a lot of people with your blog. And out there . . .

If I'd been twenty years younger, I really believe you would have convinced me to go into medical research. But it's a bit late for me, and so I'll leave it to the younger generation. The rest of us will do what we can in other ways.

Regine . . . you're living in the here and now. Even if it's tough.

Do the best you can; find happiness and pleasure wherever you can. Your family is lucky to have such an amazing daughter. I'm sure they know that. ☺

I still believe things can turn around, Regine. I do.

—*Warm thoughts, from a 37-year-old dad*

Hi Regine,

I've read your blog for a while now, but I've never left any comments before. I've lost a lot of close friends to cancer, and I also have a serious diagnosis myself (not cancer). I recognize myself in what you say about "handling it": "You're handling it so well" and "I could never handle it"—like you say: What choice is there?! Give up without trying? It's not in our nature! You have to do what you can; you hope and hope, but at the end of the day, hope won't change reality. It doesn't mean you have to give up, but in the end you just have to realize that there's nothing more for you to do. You've fought long and hard, and you and I and everyone else who reads your blog will continue to hope for a miracle. Someone came up with this "miracle" word, right?! And that means it's something that *could* happen! If it doesn't, I want you to know that you've touched a lot of lives; you've shown that it's pos-

sible to live a good life even despite medications, pain, and the terror of the end.

You're in my thoughts, Regine—I'll light a candle for you tonight. —*Julie*

Here it comes again . . .
Sunday, November 8, 2009

As soon as I started taking the chemo pills again, the pain came back in full force. We immediately realized that it wasn't going to work. We called the doctors in Trondheim to ask about other options. After a while, the doctor decided I could get it intravenously instead. Thank God. I was going to take it for three days; today was the last day. I'm worried about how this will affect my blood values. It's important to find the right balance. Not too powerful, because then all the healthy cells will be killed, but not too weak either. I'm also really scared that it won't do anything at all. I want to live as long as possible. I really want to celebrate Christmas Eve this year, too, but it doesn't look good. Maybe we can celebrate Christmas early this year?

I've been slightly more energetic for the past few days. Silje and Karina visited me, and so did Eli. Eli and I even made chocolate fondue here one day. It turned out perfect (yummm). Otherwise I just try to make the most out of every day, even if I don't have energy to do too much. Yesterday I had a nice time with Mom, Dad, and Elise. We watched *P.S. I Love You,* which was really good. Sad but also enjoyable. We had a cake today and we gave Dad a gift for Father's Day. I'm really glad that I have my family with me. They're so great. I couldn't have handled this without them. I think about everything they've done for me since I got sick. They've really been there for me. They're also worn out from all of this. It's good that we get to be at home.

My ultimate dream for this blog is that it will be published as a book after my death. I know that a lot of people like this blog, so I think it would be a good idea. I know that my family will do anything they can to help. It would be so great.

I think about everything that I've been through since the relapse. Despite everything, I've really been able to enjoy the time I've had. I sincerely don't regret that I've kept trying. If it hadn't been for the doctors in Trondheim, I would have died in May. They did everything they possibly could. They tried all kinds of medications, and researched my options really carefully. I'm so happy they never gave up.

A girl emailed me a few days ago and told me she's started a project. If you send her a photo of yourself, a professional photographer will arrange all the photos on a large poster, and send it to me. I thought it was a great project, and it really made me happy. Check out her stuff over at her blog.

Soon it will all be over

Monday, November 16, 2009

I'm so worn out and tired of this. Everything's going wrong. I'm suffering and suffering. We had a shock today. The blood tests were insanely bad. We already knew that I would die—that it would come to this in the end. But that it's gone so quickly is really surprising. If things continue like this, it will all be over soon. It's pretty hard to think about everything that will be taken away from me, and everyone I'll leave behind. I'm in miserable shape during the day. It feels like I'm being tortured. I'm so sick that a lot of times I'm scared I'm dying. Luckily I'm on painkillers. But since I need such heavy doses, I've become dependent on them, too. If I wait too long between doses, I have withdrawal symptoms. I'm also taking antibiotics because my infections have flared up again. I'm changing chemo medications tomorrow, but it's not guaranteed that they'll stop the cancer. I'm so scared . . . so scared. I don't want to die. Sometimes I think that it might be an escape, but I just wish I could get well. Get to live life. I miss my life so much.

My family spends a lot of time just crying together these days, and we have a lot of hard talks about serious things. I'm really lucky that I can talk to them about everything.

We're good at making the most of the time when I feel more or less okay. We've gotten so close!

. . .

Thursday, November 26, 2009

I thought I'd post a quick update: The chemo knocked me out completely and I've been in bed ever since. I've never felt so terrible before. I was sure I would die. The worst part is that it didn't even help: It just killed my healthy cells—the ones I need so badly right now. I took a small break from the chemo, and I've managed to spend some quality time with my family in the evenings—some, but not enough (to put it mildly).

On November 24, we celebrated Christmas at home, since I probably won't be alive at Christmas. As we usually do, we invited Grandma and Grandpa. I was in good shape and we had a nice evening, luckily. We had a delicious Christmas dinner, and dressed up and decorated the house for the occasion. I'm so glad I was in good shape for everything. The only thing missing was presents, but that's not really what Christmas is about anyway.

There was a candlelit vigil for me today. I don't know how many people were standing in front of my house holding candles, but it was a lot. My whole family stood on the verandah taking it all in. It was really touching, and we all really appreciated it. It's so nice to see how many people care. There were people I knew and people I didn't all mixed together in the crowd.

I started chemo again yesterday. I'm totally miserable, and I'm so tired of it. It will probably be my last chemo because my body can't tolerate it anymore. My stomach is shot since my spleen and liver are both so swollen. I'm still struggling with stomach pain, so I need big doses of painkillers. I don't think anyone can understand how exhausted I am, and how much pain I'm in.

Regine is in continual contact with Eli Ann. The best friends exchanged these text messages on November 28:

I just have to say that it's been such a powerful experience seeing you go through all of this. You've never let the cancer define who you are. The whole time you've been the same Regine as ever—the same

Celebrating Christmas early on November 24, 2009. From left: Regine's mother Julianne, grandmother and grandfather, sister Elise, father Lasse, and Regine.

Regine that everyone loves so much. I have so much admiration for you. I hope we get to see each other soon!

—*Eli*

Things are just getting worse and worse. I can barely move. It hurts so much to even breathe. I have to start taking the sleeping pills that I mentioned before. But they won't knock me out for sure. They'll probably mess with my head, but . . . I really want to see you before it's too late. Maybe we can find a way, even though I'm usually out cold in bed. Just want to say that you have to take good care of yourself after I'm gone. Believe in yourself and follow your dreams. Look forward to graduating from high school. Then you can do what you want. And you'll definitely make new friends. Promise me that you'll have a good life. That's the best gift that you can give to me.

—*Regine*

My condition is getting worse

Tuesday, December 1, 2009

Things are going really badly these days. Today I probably sat up for a total of two hours. Otherwise I've just been lying in bed. The pain in my spleen is excruciating. If feels like it did last fall when I had a spleen infarct. But I don't really know what it is—we haven't done any tests since there's nothing we could do about the results anyway. I couldn't complete the chemo cycle. My body just couldn't tolerate it, and absolutely no chemo medications were attacking the cancer cells. The white blood cells (the leukocytes) have risen to 200, so it's a miracle I'm still alive. I could die at any minute now, and I can feel it in my body, too. I've never been so sick before, and it's an absurdly terrifying feeling. But at least right now I'm not as afraid of dying as I was before. Maybe because I'm so worn out and exhausted and in such pain. I'm still scared, but not as much as before. I'm more worried about the people around me, the ones who have to stay behind and grieve. I'm so grateful for all the support I've gotten during this time—from family, from friends, and from my blog readers. You have no idea how much you mean to me.

By the way, a few days ago I received the poster you readers put together for me. It turned out so well—and it's so giant! Special thanks to all who spent their free time putting it together. Also want to announce that we earned 106,000 crowns from the clothes sold on Beltespenner. Altogether we've collected about 300,000 crowns—all of which will be donated to fighting cancer. Thank you so much to everyone who contributed.

Regine's last four entries resulted in 6,698 reader comments. Here's a small selection:

Dear Regine! It's so painful for me to read about your declining health. No one deserves to go through what you've gone through. I've never been as adamant in my belief in an afterlife as I am right now. I know in my heart that there must be something good out there waiting for you. You've been so strong—no one could have been stronger—and you've shown such an amazing will to live the life that's suddenly being taken away from you. I wish you all the best, Regine, and I hope that there's something better out there that can give you the happiness you deserve. You've given so much of yourself in your too-brief life. You've lived life to the fullest, and that's as much as we can ask from anyone. You've inspired everyone you've come into contact with, and your soul will shine like a star, forever. (But in the meantime, in my heart, I still hope that a miracle will give you back your life.)

My thoughts are with you, dear Regine!
—*Anonymous*

I'm crying for you, Regine. My thoughts go out to you and your family.
—*Karina*

Dear beautiful you. It's a miracle that you can even pull yourself together enough to write to us out here. I bow to you, stunning, wise, brilliant Regine. Do you know what? This Christmas will be special for me. Your blog taught me something. I've learned to value being healthy, having a good life, and I've learned to appreciate how important it is to enjoy every day. Every single day. Everything else is just secondary.

At the same time, it's so hard for me to see you suffering—if we blog readers could just take SOME of your pain. It's unfair. You're the most valiant, courageous girl out there.

I'll light some candles for you.

I wish you all the best—no matter what happens.
—*Marte*

Dear Regine!

This is so hard to read. I can't believe you're suffering like this.

I hope more than anything that your suffering will end, and that you'll get better.

I hope that this terror will release its grip on you. You said that you're not as scared as you were before. It makes sense to be scared. But if some of the terror can go away, that would be good.

Your loved ones will carry the sorrow. It will be a lot to bear. But if things go badly, they'll be proud to carry it, because they're mourning *you*, Regine. (That is, if this really is the end.) Remember that if the worst really happens, they'll support each other in their sorrow. Your family's very strong.

Another thing, Regine. If the worst happens, we'll all be following after you. Me, your parents, the rest of your family, your friends, and all of your blog readers. We'll all arrive at the final chapter of life one day, and we're all going to join you in the end. We and your loved ones will follow you.

Keep hoping for a miracle. I'm still hoping for that. And I'm not the only one. Not by a long shot!

We're all still hoping for a miracle. You deserve a better fate.

But there's no doubt that you're incredibly sick right now, so if hope doesn't change anything, try not to be scared. Try as hard as you can.

I don't think there's anything to be scared of, in the end. I really don't.

I'm not religious either, but I'm praying in my own way to my own strange powers, gods, or whatever you want to call them: I'm asking for a miracle. I'm hoping that things will change. That you get well. I'm praying and hoping for that.

If that doesn't happen, then I hope you can feel all the love and admiration that's coming your way. Take in all of the incredible positive energy. The support coming your way is enormous, because you've given so insanely much of yourself.

... Thank you for all the texts, thoughts, and photos you've given us. It means a lot!

With wishes for a pain-free, peaceful night,

—*A 37-year-old dad*

You know me, Regine. I've always had too much to say. But I've been struggling to find the words to say to you now, and I just can't seem to find them. There's nothing I can say. I'm just not taking this very well. It shouldn't be this way.

This can't happen! I'm dumbstruck by all of this. I just don't understand it. I love you. I love you a lot.

—*Sofsen*

Hi! I am a thirteen-year-old girl who almost had cancer too, but the doctors removed the tumor before I was diagnosed. Your blog makes me realize more and more how lucky I was, and still am. I sympathize with you, and hope with all my heart that a miracle can still happen. I know that you give hope to a lot of people out there. It's incredible that you can blog, despite your situation. When I was at the hospital after my operation, I couldn't do anything. Things are probably worse for you than they were for me, and still you post regular updates. I'm thinking of you.

—*Andrea*

Dear Regine,

Life is full of happiness, and life is full of despair. I've been following your blog and I've read about your happiest and most despairing moments. Dear Regine, I'm the mother of a 22-year-old girl. She's my greatest joy and my profoundest happiness—just like you are for your mother. I send warm thoughts your way all day, every day. Thousands of us are praying for you and yours, and sending all of you our love. Take care of each other.

—*Beathe*

Dear, dear Regine: I have no idea how many tears I've shed since I started reading your blog. It's been a true privilege to participate in your life and your pain.

Dear Regine: I just want to say thank you again from the bottom of my heart.

Thank you for letting me share in your life.

Thank you for everything you've meant to so many people.

Thank you for your spark, and for your courage.

Thank you for being such a good role model for so many people—however old they may be.

Thank you for being so honest about life—and about death.

And most of all: Thank you for being the fantastic person that you are.

You've earned a place in so many people's hearts.

I'm hoping and praying that you have a peaceful night, without fear and pain. I think a lot of us would do anything possible to ease your pain if we could.

—*Warm thoughts from Wenche*

I think about you all the time, Regine. You're the strongest person I've ever come across. I cry when I read your story; it makes me realize how unjust life can be. You must be one of God's sweetest angels, since he's calling you back so soon.

If I have a daughter one day, I'm going to name her after you, and I'll tell her what a strong and amazing person her namesake was—you: Regine Stokke.

—*Linda*

Dear Regine!

You've made the world a better place. You've contributed a complete and unique life's work just since you got sick! You've done it with your blog, and with your art, and just by being who you are.

We're able to see things more clearly because of you; we're more grateful—less egotistical, less self-centered—and wiser, more generous.

Your life has touched so many people—you've made a huge impact. Thank you so much, Regine!

I'm so glad you're less scared than you were before. Even though we're all wishing you'd had a longer life, it's not hard to see that the end is near. So, realistically, the best I can hope for now is that you can leave this life with peace in your heart.

Peace be with you! Warm thoughts to you and your family.

—*Ingrid*

Dear, beautiful Regine: I've never written to you before, but I've been following your blog for almost a year now, and hoping and hoping that you'd hear some good news from the doctors. But right now I just have to say that I'm angry. I'm furious, because it's crazy that such a beautiful, smart, positive, and lovely person, who's only eighteen, has to experience such torments! It's absurd. No matter what happens, Regine, I hope that your pain is at an end. Hopefully you'll have some quiet and pain-free days ahead of you, with your fantastic family and friends. I think of you night and day. "How's Regine doing today?" is the first thing I think about when I wake up. I've never met you before, but I've gotten to like you so much!!

—*Hug from a concerned grandmother in Frederikstad*

I'm thinking of you, Regine!

You've made me more aware of my life. You've changed me. I took life for granted before, and didn't consider how incredibly lucky I am just to be alive. Now I feel like a criminal, sitting here in comfort, knowing that I don't have a life-threatening disease—while you have to live with the knowledge that you might die at any moment.

But you've changed my life. I'm not as superficial as I was before. I'm not a girl who just thinks about boys, makeup, and clothes.

Instead I'm thinking about how I can make a difference with the time I have on this earth.

This will be an entry without a smiley face, hearts, or a "lol." And that's because I'm thinking of you, and your incredibly harsh destiny.

I'm not a Christian, but I know that something good is waiting for you, Regine. I just know it!

Farewell!

—*Oda, thirteen years old*

You're an amazing person, Regine!

You've won a gold medal, you've earned the applause: You're an extreme sports athlete.

Unfortunately, right now, you're probably at the end of the road, with no strength left, and in the middle of all this, the sound of applause just sounds like so much noise. I want you to know that you've made a huge difference: You've gotten people to donate bone marrow; you've made people change their outlook about what's important in life; you've made them stop and think. You've given readers of your blog—young and old—a lot of insights into what it's like to live with terminal cancer.

You've enlightened us, inspired us, informed us, and increased our understanding. You've made a lasting impression. A huge impression. You won't be forgotten. I hope that this means something to you now. I want to thank you for how much you've given of yourself. I want you to know this, even though of course I want you to stay on this earth for a good while longer. You're an important person. I admire you.

Most of all, I'm hoping for a miracle. I hope you get relief from all this pain, and can soon find some peace in this overwhelming chaos.

I hope that you'll feel surrounded by warmth from all the people who care about you. I think of you and cheer you on. Always.
—*Ashild*

Oh no. Don't leave us. ☹
—*Kaddy*

I'm thinking of an incredibly strong girl: I'm thinking of you, Regine . . . You've been fighting for so long now, and you've won so many battles, even if the disease seems to have the upper hand right now.

The pain passes, but the beauty remains. ~Pierre Auguste Renoir (1841–1919)
—*Heidi*

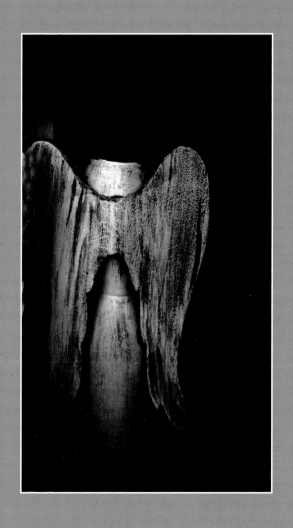

After Regine

After Regine

Dear beautiful sister
Thursday, December 3, 2009

Dear beautiful sister,

After fifteen long months of fighting, you've finally found peace. These were probably the longest and toughest months of your life. They were for us, too. We endured a lot together, but we had a lot of good times, too.

After a while, I suppose we all realized that things were nearing the end, and that you were suffering. You needed a lot of painkillers, and you were exhausted.

On Thursday, December 3, 2009, at 2:02 pm, our beloved Regine passed away peacefully with mom, dad, little sister, and kitty cat at her side.

The photo that's included here was taken in Rome, right before her diagnosis.

—*Hugs, from your little sister Elise*

Almost 9,000 readers sent a last goodbye to Regine. Here's a small selection:

Two beautiful brown eyes
    A brilliant smile
    An enormous heart
    And a life that was much too short
    You won the hearts of everyone
    You gave all of yourself

Even with all the pain
That awaited you
Sleep sweetly, little angel
You will never be forgotten
You can sleep safely now
Your soul at rest
My deepest condolences to Regine's family and friends in this
time of sadness.

—*Tutta*

Many kind thoughts to you in this difficult time.
Regine will never be forgotten.
She's touched so many people.

—*A fellow human being*

Regine inspired so many people to reflect on their lives. We all grew to
love her through her blog—which was beautiful even when it was sad.
Condolences to the family.
Sleep well, Regine. And thank you so much for everything you
gave to us.

—*Frida Petrine*

*Condolences—in the form of visits, phone calls, text messages, Facebook
messages, and countless blog posts—kept pouring in from the friends
and family that Regine left behind. Regine's childhood friend Marte
Steffensen wrote the following on her own blog:*

I can't find the words. I'm just overwhelmed with emotion. I can't
breathe, and everything is confused and mixed up. I've checked your
name on MSN at least a hundred times today just to see if you're

logged on. When I found out that you'd left us, the whole world stood still. I couldn't hear anything, and time seemed to stop.

We had such a great childhood together! I swear, no one had more fun than we did when we were kids. We did so much. We made tree houses, recorded Smurf music videos, and made the world's best horror movies. (And yes, I also remember the time we found a skull out in the woods. An animal skull—which we promptly placed on top of a stick so that we could pretend it was a horse.) You, me, Malin, and Therese—we did everything together. We even brought the same imaginary friend home from school every winter! (Actually, we alternated who was going to have to take "Ank" home every week.) We were both obsessed with photography, and I remember like it was yesterday the time when we went to the *Nordic Lights* photography festival together, and met those famous artists. The high point was probably meeting Matt Mahurin. We both loved Metallica, and Matt had recorded a video with the guys, and knew Metallica personally. We stood there talking to him for a *while*, now that I think about it. Oh my God, we were so happy then.

We spent ten years together as classmates. And every year, on the first day of school, we would walk to school together. It was the same every year, from first grade through tenth grade . . .

I miss you already, Regine. We've shared so many incredible memories! I'm proud to have known you for so long, and I'm proud to have been your friend. I hope you're doing well now, and that you get some peace after all the pain you've been through over the last fifteen months. You deserve the best.

You've just gone on a very long holiday, and before too long we'll be on holiday together again. Our group will definitely get together one last time.

Rest in peace, dear Regine Stokke.

I love you so much.

—*Marte*

Time stands still

Tuesday, December 8, 2009

Things have been tough since Regine passed away. Everyone in the family shares a profound sense of emptiness, I think, especially when we're at home. Something's missing. That's not so strange really, since Regine was so important to us. She got to lie at home in her bed all the way until Sunday. We were all really happy for that. It felt good to have her nearby. I'm pretty sure that she would have wanted to be at home for as long as possible, too. As pretty as she was, she lay in her bed looking like the world's most beautiful porcelain doll. It was really tough for us when the funeral home came to get her.

The past few days have been spent planning for Regine's funeral. There's a ton of stuff we have to organize, but it's actually kind of nice to have to think about something else sometimes. Any distraction is welcome. The funeral, which is open to the public, will be held at Festiviteten on Wednesday at 12:00 pm. Since Regine wasn't a Christian, we struggled a bit with deciding where to have it. She herself thought Festiviteten would be a good idea, and that's probably why we chose it. It will be a special funeral, for a very special girl.

—Elise

On December 15 Sofie Frøysaa (Sofsen) wrote a goodbye to her friend on her blog, and titled it "I find some peace when I see you in my dreams."

Dear Regine,

It's been twelve days now since you left us. Twelve long days of sadness, emptiness, anger, and frustration. Twelve long days spent missing you.

I sent you a message on the same day that you died. I wrote: "Love you. Always. I know you can't read this. And I know that we don't believe in heaven. But right now, more than anything else, I want to know that there's a better place out there for you. I just want the chance to see you again. I think of your beautiful family. Imagine all of the people who are missing you right now. Thank you for everything, Regine. Thank you!"

I'm never going to erase your phone number. I'm never going to take your blog off my list of favorites. I'm never going to take you off my list of contacts. I'm probably not going to be able to stop myself from thinking, "I hope Regine logs on soon! I need a dose of Regine-and-Sofsen humor!" Ever since I met you, that's been one of my first thoughts after logging on. And that's one of the things I'm going to miss the most, Regine: your sense of humor. We always laughed at the same things, and laughing together was always so much fun. Even though we were miles apart, it felt like we were in the same room. Like you were right there. Everything seemed so close by.

I talked to your little sister Elise tonight on Facebook. It was so great. Elise, you, your mom, and your dad make for one pretty great family. When I visited you in Kristiansund, I noticed a rare closeness and warmth among you all. It was special to see. But things will never be the same without you, Regine. I'm so concerned about your family, now that you're gone. Your parents have experienced the worst thing of all. They've lost the most irreplaceable and precious thing they have. Your sister has lost her only older sister. Your grandparents have lost their little girl. Your family, your friends—even your cat has lost a fantastic fellow being. Strong, beautiful, wise, honest, bright, talented, fun, warm, creative, engaged, open, and wise Regine. The little girl with the big heart.

In your big, brown, and beautiful eyes, I could see honesty, curiosity, and a sincere delight in life. I saw hope, strength, and endless love. You never did anything halfheartedly, Regine. You threw

yourself into so many things. Photography, writing, politics, and even in your contributions to the cancer cause through your media appearances. What you've done will go down in history. You had a rare talent for moving and motivating other people. Your story has gotten a lot of new people involved in the fight against cancer, and it's also gotten so many people to appreciate their lives more—to live life for its own sake. I'm always going to be so incredibly proud of you!

Forever grateful for our friendship. Love you forever.

Martin Hilstad took countless photos of and with Regine. He remembered her like this:

Regine and I watched a lot of movies together. *A lot*—either from her hospital bed, or in her loft, or even once at the movie theater I rented so that she could see *Max Manus*. We often had to look to the extraordinary to make Regine's existence seem even a little bit normal by comparison. Movies (in particular David Lynch's bizarre small-town scenes) also helped us to escape the everyday. But when Regine's condition and the weather permitted, photography was the thing that made us happy. Seeing the world through a lens also gives you some distance from it.

Before her relapse, Regine and I had made a lot of plans for the near and not-so-near future. Maybe we made too many plans, but at the time everything seemed to be going so well. We were going to "live life now," as she put it. One of the first things we were going to do was to take her photos to *Nordic Light* for the photography competition. But then everything was turned on its head again, before we'd even found our feet in the first place! It was April 4, and I'd just come home for the Easter holidays. I was just waiting for the all-clear to go visit, but when the phone rang and I picked up, all I heard was silence. Then, after some time had passed, I heard a low and trembling voice say, "I have bad news . . . " Things never go as planned.

Near the end of Easter, it must have been April 13, we went out on a small photo excursion. I remember it perfectly. We went down behind Regine's house. Followed small trails that she had probably made herself. She walked in front with a combination of care and determination— just like she used to, actually. At that moment she seemed healthy, and it was so strange to think about what was happening inside her body. She took a lot of breaks, but it wasn't just to rest; it was also, maybe just as often, to look at something interesting (e.g., a small leaf on her shoe). We walked down along a marshy area where Regine used to go on camping trips. She photographed all kinds of things, while for the most part I ended up taking photos of her—a kind of "behind the scenes" documentation of the photos she took. Even though *Nordic Light* didn't seem

© Martin Hilstad

like a realistic possibility at the time, a lot of her photos from this trip ended up in her exhibit a few weeks later.

One particular moment really stuck with me. I'm not sure if it was that day, or another day around then, but Regine said something simple like, "The best flowers get plucked first" (something she'd heard Svein Kåre say at Riksen), but then she added, "so you need to start preparing yourself." At the time, it was kind of awkward to hear her say that, because I didn't like the idea that she was already resigned to what was happening, but in hindsight, when you come right down to it, it's almost reassuring.

We'll talk, Regine.

Eli Ann described the sense of loss and sorrow that she felt for her best friend like this:

My dearest friend,

I remember the day you got the awful news like it was yesterday. We were looking forward to a Friday night filled with laughs and good friends. There's no one who could have predicted that we would end up sitting at the hospital, sobbing.

Thinking about what lay in store for you was really scary. I didn't want to accept the idea that things might not work out in the end. It wasn't a viable alternative in my mind.

Every other weekend, a couple of us—your concerned and worried girlfriends—would come to visit you at the hospital in Trondheim. It was so hard to see you getting worse and worse, but it was always good to be with you.

Not having you close by was really hard on us. Sometimes at night we'd have long phone conversations about how you were doing. We'd talk about the pain and despair, but we'd talk about the good times that we'd shared, too. In the middle of the most difficult times, there was also a lot of laughing. I think it did us both good.

I admire you so much for how you tackled this cruel disease—and I know I'm not the only one. You felt that you had to keep fighting, that you didn't have a choice—even when it was hard for you to find the strength. But not many people could have done it with so much courage, almost in spite of the fear you had to feel. Not many people could have done it with so much strength, even though your body was weak. Or with so much compassion for the other people with cancer—even though you had more than enough to worry about already.

I'm so glad that you got to celebrate your eighteenth birthday, a day they didn't think you'd get to experience. It was so great to celebrate with you, our dear friend, just like old times. Everyone loved

Regine and Eli Ann during their helicopter ride to RaumaRock, August 2009

it. The evening was unforgettable for all of us, and it was great for everyone to see you so happy and content. Leukemia devastated your body, but it couldn't break your will to live. And in spite of how limited you were by the disease, you still got to experience so much. You always knew how to appreciate the little things—even as you dealt with the big things. Things like picnicking in the forest (with strawberries), and eating out of a picnic basket surrounded by ants; baking (with enthusiasm—and with varied results); and all those rounds of Mario Kart in the beanbag chair in the attic living room. I remember one time in particular when you finished the course and smiled that big smile of yours, and said, "Eli, you're terrible!" because I still had a whole other lap to go. I miss this all so much that it hurts; I miss our talks about the hard realities of life, about the small pleasures, and about the big mysteries, too.

It was an intense fifteen months, and it went quickly from total happiness to an almost incomprehensible sadness. It hurt so much when they told you that you didn't have much time left. But even though you were suffering, you managed to pull yourself together so that I could come and visit. I know it took a lot out of you.

I'll never forget the last evening you were alive. You were so exhausted, but still so brave. You managed to get out of bed and sit in the living room, but it wasn't long before you couldn't handle it anymore. We probably both knew that this was the last time we'd see each other. Even at the very end of your life, you were thinking of other people. The friendship necklace you gave me that night is the best gift I've ever gotten. It brings back so many memories; it reminds me of all the years we had together: all the great times, sad times, and close times. I'll carry them with me, and when I miss you, I'll think of them.

It was hard to see you get taken back to bed, and to hear you say that you felt like you were dying. Your pain was so visible. I gave you a hug and told you I loved you, painfully aware that this would be the last time I would see you alive.

You lay quietly in your bed, like I saw you doing the night before. But the pain had eased and the fear was gone. Finally you were getting some rest. We got to say things that needed to be said while you were still alive, and that conversation has helped me to deal with my sadness—although nothing could compensate for the loss of such a beautiful person and friend.

I love you so much, Regine. You'll always be my best friend, and you'll always have a totally special place in my heart! Whatever I do, I'll think of you, and I'll never stop wishing you were here. But we'll meet again one day, in a better place, without pain and sorrow. I could talk for hours about how much you mean to me, Regine, but the inscription on the jewelry puts it best. Thank you, Regine.

Elise had lost her big sister. This is how she described missing her:

Dear Sister,

I was just thinking about everything that a sister means, everything that a sister gives to you. A sister offers support, love, understanding, and laughs; she's someone to argue with, someone you can lend clothes to, and someone to just hang out with. Those aren't things you can get from everyone, and no one can give you all of those things at once like a sister can. You gave a lot to me, Regine, and I gave back to you as well. We shared everything. Everything. It was us two. Big sister and little sister. Regine and Elise. And now that's gone forever. The word "never" is difficult to get your head around. I've tried. I've tested it out for a while now, but I've never managed to really understand it.

It's impossible to think that I'll never get to see you again. I would do anything to see your smile one last time, hear your happy laughter, or see your fed-up expression when I make a mess or when I just don't get something. You weren't supposed to leave me. Not yet. We were supposed to travel together. You were going to move to a big city after high school, and I was going to come and visit whenever I wanted. We were going to have kids at the same time, so that they also could be best friends. We were supposed to fight about the front seat in the car, and about who would get to have the attic room. We were supposed to get old together, and live next to each other in the nursing home. We were going to plan Mom's and Dad's funerals when that time came. Now I'll have to do it all myself. No more Regine. Ever. Still there were a lot of things you wanted me to experience, accomplish, and achieve. I made a lot of promises to you and you told me secrets that you didn't tell anyone else. It's a big thing for me to be the one carry-

Regine and Elise

ing your deepest secrets. Not even your best friends, just me. I'll keep my promises, and your secrets are so well hidden that no one will ever find them. Trust me.

I have a crystal clear memory of the day when the funeral home came to get you. It was late Sunday evening, and Mom and Dad had gone to bed a while ago. I was sitting in the living room with my computer on my lap, just like we used to do together. Before Dad went to bed, he turned off the TV and put the TV controller at the edge of the table. Of course I was so lazy that I didn't want to reach for it, so the TV was still off. Then with no warning it suddenly turned on, all by itself. MTV was on—your go-to channel. Not only that, but they were airing a show about Metallica—one of your favorite bands. I felt like it was you reaching out to me, so I kept the show on. Just like you to be a little smart-ass just like that—crossing the divide, via Metallica.

I pray to whomever's out there that there's a place where we can meet again. A place where we can laugh and be happy and just be together. I hope things are good where you are now. I want you to be happy. I want things to be good for you. I'm scared that place doesn't exist, and that you're totally gone. Where are you? Come back, come home again. We miss you; everyone misses you; I miss you. You'll always be my big sister, no matter what.

Love you forever, Regine.

With profound love and gratitude, Julianne wrote this to her beloved daughter Regine:

Some words from Mom—a declaration of love

I'm sitting on Regine's bed with a cup of hot chocolate right now. Lasse and I just went on our daily visit to the grave site and lit some candles for her there. It's below freezing outside and there's a lot of snow. I hope Regine doesn't feel this cold wherever she is now. She should be here with me, drinking hot chocolate, and working on her book release herself. Instead, I'm going to try to write a few words on my own. Publishing her blog as a book was one of her big dreams, and we promised we'd make it happen for her.

I've spent a lot of time in Regine's bed since she died. I cry out my sorrow, my loss, and my despair here. We've lost our dear daughter Regine, who was only eighteen years old. Sometimes our cat Josefine joins me here. I think she's sad, too. Josefine was a big part of Regine's life for eleven years, and they meant a lot to each other. Josefine was a real consolation to Regine during her illness, always faithfully rambling after her. The week before she died, Regine said that when Josefine died she wanted her to be buried alongside her at the grave site. We'll see when the time comes—but if I know her father, he'll make it happen. I think back on when Regine was born. She smiled for the first time when she was only a day old, and it wasn't because of colic if that's what some people are thinking. She was so beautiful that I couldn't stop looking at her. With big brown eyes and long curly eyelashes. Oh how I miss looking into those beautiful, wise, and warm eyes of hers. I look into them, in her picture by the bed, and feel my throat tighten before the tears come. It's so unbearable. A few days ago, I dreamt that I looked into her eyes and stroked her lovingly on the cheek before she laid her head next to mine. It was so vivid and comforting. It didn't last long, and I didn't dream anything before or after that; it was as if she came home to comfort me in that dream.

All her life, Regine continued smiling at the world. We even called her Sunshine! She was a quick learner and could count to ten when she was only twenty months old. Bubbly and full of life, Regine loved to work on dances, plays, and miming songs. I remember how hyper she would get when she had something to tell us; she couldn't stand still, and would stand there shifting from one foot to another and hopping on the floor. And, being the monkey that she was, she was also prone to climbing up between the door frames with her feet planted on either side. I also remember now the presentation she made when we were in the country: Regine, with her incredible imagination, was going to impersonate the newscaster Traula. She dressed up in an oversized down jacket, with glasses that were way too big, and a green hat, and read the weather report. The forecast was for buckets of beer, and all the men were racing outside with their mouths wide open toward the sky (there was also soda rain and candy hail for the kids). And when she was seven years old, she sang along to the Bon Jovi song "It's My Life"—complete with the refrain "It's now or never. I ain't gonna live forever. I just wanna live while I'm alive." I'm relieved now that we took videos and photos of those performances.

It wouldn't be hard for me to fill whole notebooks with more stories like this, with Regine always in the starring role. When she was around eleven or twelve, she became somewhat shy, and started to move behind the camera instead. She became interested in taking photos and making movies. She and her friends were particularly fond of making horror movies. They used to head to the forest, and with Regine behind the camera, they made such classics as *The City Witch Elvira*. Regine got help from her dad and edited it and added sound effects, and it turned out to be a really well-done movie.

Regine had just turned three when her little sister, Elise, was born, and I remember her first visit to the newborn unit. She was glowing with happiness when she held Elise in her arms and sang children's songs to her. My belly was still a bit big, and Regine wondered if there was another baby in there . . . Regine was never jealous of Elise and was a kind and caring big sister. Regine said that one of the worst things about dying was that she wouldn't be able to support Elise while she was a teenager, and that really says something about how much her sister meant to her.

I think I can honestly say that Regine was a truly *good* child. She was always happy, kind, full of understanding, fair, agreeable, and hardworking. But we got a surprise two days before Regine was due to start high school. She was out with her friends Eli Ann and Anne Marthe, and it was eleven at night. Her father called to find out where they were. Regine told him that they were out by the lake grilling fishcakes. Regine had trouble pronouncing the word "fishcakes," and we realized they were drinking. We were shocked. Not in our wildest dreams could we imagine that our "angel," who (we thought) could never do anything bad, could be out drinking with her friends. It turned into a big to-do, and we made it very clear how we felt. We could safely say that the "good child" period was over . . . Later, Regine told me that she'd been to a lot of parties after this, and that we never

Playing in door frame

*Regine's newscaster impersonation—
ready to read the weather report*

noticed anything. I only believed good things about Regine, and that probably blinded me a bit.

After she'd been in high school for a while, she got a boyfriend, and we weren't very happy about that either. He was handsome—it didn't have anything to do with that—but he was also a bit older than she was, and he lived in a studio by himself. It probably lasted five months, and I was relieved when it was over.

After Regine got sick and died, though, I began to see things differently. Now I'm glad that she had the experience of being in love, going to parties, and having fun. She went on a language trip, and got to go to concerts and festivals with Eli Ann and Anne Marthe. She got to experience a lot before she got sick, and for that I'm glad; it was a consolation for Regine when she realized where things were heading. Regine talked about these memories a lot when she was sick.

Regine loved shopping for clothes, and she was right in her element when we took a girls trip to London during Easter 2008 with Aunt Anne, cousin Fride, and Elise. Oxford Street was like heaven on Earth for her. She could check out the new offerings at Top Shop and go to other stores that we just don't have at home. It was a lot of fun. She decided where she wanted to shop before we left and took the lead and got the rest of us to come along. She liked leading the way and getting clothes that nobody else was wearing yet. She had her own way of putting together outfits that really worked. We went to see the musicals *We Will Rock You* (with music by Queen) and *Les Miserables*. We especially liked *We Will Rock You* and it was a fun experience for all of us. You aren't allowed to take photos at the show, but Regine couldn't restrain herself and clicked away anyway. To my embarrassment a guard even wound up reprimanding her. We strolled around beautiful Notting Hill and looked for the bookstore from the movie, which we eventually found. We really enjoyed ourselves with good food, good conversation, and a lot of laughs. After three days of going almost nonstop day and night, Aunt Anne and I were totally exhausted. Nonetheless, we'd had such a great time together that we started planning our next trip, either to Barcelona or New York, almost immediately. But things didn't turn out that way. That was the last trip Elise and I took with Regine while she was healthy, and it's a precious memory for us.

Regine wrote in a blog entry that it would have been better for her family if she had never been born at all; that way, we could have avoided the sorrow. I was so sad when I saw that, because how could she ever think that? I could never imagine life without her. I still can't! She and Elise are the two best things that ever happened to us. Think of all the great years we've had! Think of all the love, happiness, warmth, and pride she gave us—nothing can compare to that. These memories are stored away in our hearts like priceless treasures. I told her before that it would be unbelievably painful for us to keep on going after she's gone, and that we'll grieve and miss her so much. But this is something we've got to learn to live with, and that over time the pain will get less intense. Eventually I think we'll only feel joy and be grateful for all the great memories we've had together. But we're always going to miss our precious darling.

When Regine was sick, it was a tumultuous time, filled with highs and lows, laughter and tears. Powerful feelings for Regine flared up in me, and in some ways it was similar to when she was little—when we had a basic and profound dependence on each other. The only real difference was that I wasn't nursing anymore.

After her relapse, we knew it would be difficult for Regine to ever get better. But as long as the doctors were willing to try new treatments, we had some small rays of hope, and we managed to be positive and encouraging. After Regine got sick, we saw new qualities in her that we didn't know she had. She went from being a typical, self-absorbed youth who thought friends were more important than parents to a person who really cared about others and showed a lot of concern for everyone around her. She wanted to encourage and help other sick people, even while she was busy fighting her own battle. She also had courage and a strength in her that I didn't realize was even possible. It turned out that she was the strongest one of us right until the end. We knew that she was a good writer, but we never could have dreamed that she would be able to give so much of herself through her writing. It all seemed to come out of her so honestly and sincerely, and I think that's why her words resonated with so many other people. But still, her fame is still kind of unbelievable even today.

In the same way, her photos developed a particular expression that reflect her feelings about the situation she was in; they're so naked and sensitive. I think that she wanted to create something lasting so that she would be noticed, and so that when she was gone she wouldn't disappear completely. I think that's also why she agreed to talk to the media, and worked so hard to recruit blood and bone marrow donors, and help other sick people of course. And the reason that she really wanted her blog to become a book—so that she would be somebody, both a photographer and a writer.

Regine also liked to help when the doctor in charge at Children-4 in Trondheim visited on Thursdays with new medical students. She told them about all the symptoms she'd had before her diagnosis and answered questions frequently. The doctor in charge bragged about how good she was at mediating for him and providing instructive insights for so many future doctors. Regine was really bright and taught herself a lot about the disease, blood values, medications, and other technical terms used by doctors. Sometimes she could sound like a fully trained doctor, and she herself claimed that she knew more than certain doctors she met along the way.

My solace in the sorrow I feel is the strong bond that developed between us. Regine and I developed a closeness that I think would be difficult to experience with another person without being in a situation like ours. I'm so grateful to Regine for letting me get so close to her. It was a closeness that was so full of warmth and love for each other. It's hard to describe in words what this means to me; it means so infinitely much. She showed so much confidence in and openness with me when we stayed up late at night talking, often while I massaged or stroked her back, feet, and arms. (She liked that so much.) It was obvious that she needed to talk about everything: politics, family, her disease, death, and even the most personal things she experienced at parties and with friends and boyfriends. But as she said before she died (with a clever grin on her face), she had kept *some* of her secrets . . .

And we had such a great time watching *One Tree Hill*! Both of us were hooked, and watched all the episodes twice. On her worst days, it was comforting for her to escape reality and watch an episode or two. Two days before she died, we watched Episode eleven of the seventh season for the last time together. In early January I watched Episode twelve alone, and sobbed and cried for forty minutes. It was awful to watch it without Regine. I could see Regine in front of me where she used to sit on the sofa and it felt like I could almost touch her. It sounds dumb, but I felt that I had to keep watching the series in case Regine is still with us in some way, so that she can also see the rest of it.

Closer to the end

During the last month, Regine's stomachaches just got worse and worse. The only thing that helped was getting big doses of painkillers directly from the Hickman line (intravenously). To solve this without having to admit Regine to the hospital, we asked her doctor at the Kristiansund hospital if we could learn how to do it ourselves, so that we could give her the necessary painkillers at home. And after we were skillfully trained by Regine's cancer nurse, we were allowed to do it. From then on I slept with Regine at night. She was calmer and more relaxed now that she knew she had painkillers on hand that would work immediately. After a while she had to have painkillers more often and in stronger and stronger doses. Since we knew how to administer the painkillers, we were also able to give her antibiotics and manage her blood transfusions as well. This wouldn't have been possible without the amazing kindness of the Cancer Polyclinic doctors and nurses. They provided the help we needed, and were available around the clock if we ran into any difficulties. We wanted to do all of this for Regine to make her as comfortable as possible. We were so exhausted in so many ways, but we put all we had into making life as pleasant as possible for her. As Aunt Anne said, she'll never forget the atmosphere of security, calm, and quiet at our house over the last weeks of her life.

During the last week, she had two pumps attached to the Hickman catheter, one with painkillers and the other with sleeping medication, and those lines worked nonstop around the clock. That way she could push a button every time she needed an extra dose of painkillers, and it made things easier for all of us. Even though she was on high doses of painkillers, her pain never went away completely and Regine got more and more exhausted. Every day during the last week she would say that she could feel it in her body that she was going to die. During the last two or three days, she mostly lay in her bed and we noticed that she started breathed heavily and that it became tiring for her to talk. That's when we understood that it was almost over. Regine managed to talk with Elise and gave her her Dolce & Gabbana watch. She wanted Elise to engrave the back so that it said: "To the world's best sister, from Regine."

The last evening she was alive, her breath was even shorter than usual. She got so much worse in such a short period of time that when Grandma and Grandpa came to visit, it was painful for them to see her (even though they'd only just left three days before). We all cried. Earlier in the week, at Regine's instructions, I'd bought a piece of friendship jewelry with a white gold chain engraved with "Thank you, Regine" on it. Regine really wanted to give the piece to her best friend Eli Ann, and surprised us all when at around seven, she said she wanted to try getting up. Regine called Eli Ann, who didn't hesitate and came over right away. It was always like that with Eli Ann. As soon as Regine called and was up for company, Eli Ann would come over. Regine used all her strength and went into the living room to give the piece to Eli Ann. They sat talking for a while, but after half an hour, Regine was totally worn out and had to go lie down again. I heard Eli Ann say to Regine, "Maybe I won't see you again," and they hugged each other and said goodbye for the last time. It was so sad.

After Eli Ann left, I asked Regine if she wanted me to give her a bath since she hadn't been able to take a shower for a few days. She said yes, and I washed her from top to bottom. Regine smelled like lavender soap all over. Again she showed me the greatest trust she could give me. I know Regine is naturally shy, and her body was the most private thing for her. She was so content, happy, and also calm and relaxed before going to bed, and then she told me she would probably sleep for the rest of her life. As her doctor had advised, we increased the painkiller dose so that she could sleep at night. I lay listening to her breathing and couldn't sleep. Regine slept well, but her body worked hard to breathe. Her chest rose and fell, and at the same time there was a wheezing sound. At seven in the morning, she suddenly got up and needed to use the bathroom. She was really drugged and didn't remember the pumps she was attached to. So I had to rush to carry the pumps and support her at the same time. She got to the bathroom, but couldn't hold herself up. "Hold me, Mom, I'm dying now," she said. I supported her back into bed and decided I would read the advent messages to her.

I'd made an advent calendar for Regine with heart-shaped cards filled with beautiful verses for her and lots of comments about how much she's meant to us. I really wanted her to hear all of the hearts before she died. When I started reading the eighth heart, she said her last words to me: "Stop fussing." She was tired and wanted to sleep. She didn't wake up after that, and died quietly and calmly several hours later. When she passed away, she was in my arms with Dad, Elise, and Josefine by her side. I had my hand on her heart, and I felt her heartbeat getting weaker and weaker until it finally stopped. Then Regine calmly inhaled twice, and with that the life was gone from her body. It happened so easily and just like Regine wanted, totally without pain. Regine's long hard fight was over; the worst had really happened. It was so unreal, and we just sat by her bed for a long time, crying and crying. For those who have read *Ida's Dance*, Ida's last words to her mother were, "You're pretty"—whereas Regine's last words to me were, "Stop fussing." But I think it's funny, and I laugh inside when I think about it. It was so typical of Regine, to be a little harsh without meaning any harm.

The family members who lived nearby came to our house as soon as they found out. Aunt Anne helped me take care of Regine and change her clothes. We put on her favorite everyday clothes. A lilac-colored T-shirt, gray sweatpants, a black knit hat, and the wool socks that Martin's mother had knitted, with Regine's name on them. My father laid a rose between her hands, and she was so beautiful lying there with a knowing smile still on her lips. A flickering light on the table cast a beautiful light over her face.

Just like when she was born, I couldn't look at her enough. I didn't know it was possible for a dead person to look so beautiful and happy. She lay in her bed for three days, and it was so good to have her there, to be with her, talk to her, and touch her. The funeral home put her in the coffin with her lilac pillow under her head, and her blanket over her. We put things in the coffin that meant a lot to Regine, as well as photos of the family, a photo of Josefine, and some teddy bears. Then it was time for them to close the coffin and take her away. It was so agonizing, so painful for all of us—and my reaction was so much worse than on the day she died. Now she was gone physically too and we would never see our lovely daughter again. I couldn't stop crying.

Once, as a joke, Regine asked me if we could get Wardruna to play at her funeral. We laughed and didn't think about it much after that. Lasse and I played the CD and listened to what Regine had picked out. What if we could get them to come here, just like Regine had joked about, I said. Lasse took me seriously and called Einar Kvitrafn Sevik from Wardruna in Bergen. The funeral was in three days, but they managed to gather the troops, and the only thing we had to pay for were the plane tickets. It didn't seem real, and we were so happy. It meant so much to us to be able to fulfill this dream of Regine's. We found out that Wardruna was actually going to play for Regine at the Fosse concert in Valsoybotn last summer, but it didn't happen because Regine was sick at the time. So it felt right for them to come, even if they usually didn't play at funerals. If only Regine knew that her favorite band came to play for her, or maybe she found out—who knows?

The funeral service in the big living room at Kristiansund's Festiviteten on December 9 was moving, beautiful, and special. The coffin was gorgeously decorated. This is where Regine had done so many dance performances over the years, and this is where Regine's dance instructor, Anett Hjelkrem, had a full house sing happy birthday for her in English—a big moment for Regine, Lasse, and me. Now Wardruna was on stage next to her coffin. The performance opened with the powerful sounds of cascading water and birds from the song

"Laukr." It has the lyrics: "Laukr is water, tears from your eyes, mountain waterfalls, drops from ice, waves on the water."

Afterward, there was a remembrance by Berit Jorgenvag, a moving dance by Marte, Vilde, Maren, and Nathalie from the Kristiansund Dance Studio, and the song "You Are the Best" by Hanna Malm Erdtman. Then Bengt Eidem gave a speech, and we closed with Wardruna singing "Dagr"—which features the words, "I salute the sun. Rise up from the dark, rise up today." It turned into a beautiful, moving, almost mystical goodbye for us and the 400 to 500 people who came. It was a powerful experience that suited Regine perfectly; it turned out to be exactly what she would have wanted. Gunnhild Corwin (who wrote *Ida's Dance*) sent us a poem[1] that she was given many years ago, and that she felt suited Regine really well. It was read near the grave:

Lasse decided not to have a reception after the funeral; he said he couldn't handle it. I objected, because it's something that you just do—people would expect it. But I'm glad he got his way, because I couldn't have managed it either. We were completely exhausted after the funeral and it was good to come home and just be alone together, just us three. Luckily Grandma had made bacalao and took care of visitors and everyone else in the family.

A thank you (from Regine and from us)

First of all, we want to thank Children 4, the cancer and blood disease unit at St. Olav's Hospital. The nurses and doctors there are a fantastic group. They took such good care of us and followed up and were responsible for Regine from beginning to end. They didn't give up and wanted to try new medications even after Riksen told her she didn't

---

1 Poem appears on the facing page.

Gone From My Sight

I am standing upon the seashore
A ship at my side spreads her white
sails to the morning breeze and starts
for the blue ocean
She is an object of beauty and strength
I stand and watch her until at length
she hangs like a speck of white cloud
just where the sea and sky come
to mingle with each other
Then, someone at my side says:
"There, she is gone!"
"Gone where?"
Gone from my sight. That is all
She is just as large in mast and hull
and spar as she was when she left my side
and she is just as able to bear her
load of living freight to her destined port
Her diminished size is in me, not in her
And just at the moment when someone
at my side says, "There, she is gone!"
There are other eyes watching her coming,
and other voices ready to take up the glad
shout:
"Here she comes!"
And that is dying.

—*Henry Van Dyke*

have long to live. Because of that, Regine found new hope, and had a great summer with wonderful experiences. Thanks to their cooperation with the Kristiansund hospital and thanks to their almost daily phone calls with Lasse, Regine was able to be at home most of the time since February 2009. I didn't think it was possible to live with the blood values that Regine had for such a long time, and I think it's a miracle that Regine lived as long as she did. A big thank you to the bone marrow transplant unit at the National Hospital, who did everything they could to cure Regine. Thank you so much to the nurses and doctors at the Cancer Polyclinic and Palliative Care team at the Kristiansund hospital who took us in so completely and did everything possible to make Regine comfortable. They even came to our home on evenings and weekends when they were actually off work. Thank you for all the help that made it possible for us to care for Regine during the last three or four weeks of her life. You have no idea how much it means to us. I'm also glad we live fifteen minutes away from the hospital, since being at home allowed for Regine to have a much better quality of life during her last ten months. In addition to the fact that we were at the hospital almost every day for blood tests, Regine occasionally needed antibiotics three times a day over a several day period. If we'd been far from the hospital, it wouldn't have been possible for Regine to live at home.

At times from August 2008 to February 2009, Regine was so ill that she needed both Lasse and me to be at the hospital with her. Elise was invited to stay with us and take classes at the hospital.

But she didn't want to. She wanted to be at home where she had friends, dance classes, and school. We always worried about Elise who was at home and had to manage a lot of things on her own. Luckily we've had a lot of help from Grandma, Grandpa, Aunt Anne, and Uncle Arild who watched out for and took care of Elise. I don't know how we would have managed without their help and support.

Thank you so much to Regine's friends for all the visits and support you gave Regine. She was so happy and content on the days she had visits. She came alive and we saw that it did her good. Special thanks to Anne Marthe, Martin, Silje, Karina, and last but not least, dear Eli Ann, who's been her closest and best friend and who was there when Regine needed her most. Eli Ann was the one who understood what Regine was going through, and this understanding meant a lot to Regine; she said so herself.

Thank you to the people who contributed with experiences that made Regine so happy, like the Quart festival, the helicopter trip to RaumaRock, the Ulver concert in Lillehammer, the Caroline movie center, and photo exhibits at *Nordic Light* and in Surnadal. Thank you also to participants in the benefit concerts for Regine, and in the torch light parade on November 26. Thank you to Jan Erik Haglund from Norway, Inc., for everything you did in regards to the Metallica concert (which unfortunately she wasn't able to attend). And thank you to *Dagbladet* and its readers for selecting Regine as the 2009 person of the year.

And then there are all the blog friends. All of you amazing people out there who didn't even know Regine, but still showed her so much care and warmth. You should know what important support you were to Regine. It was a great comfort to her on her worst days to read all your comments. Thank you to those who set up the Facebook pages to help Regine to overcome the disease and to achieve her dream of making a book. Thank you as well to all those who supported these pages.

Thank you to those who set up the support fund and to everyone who contributed monetarily, both individually and as businesses. A special thank you to Ann Olaug Slatlem, who's updated Regine's photos and who made it possible for her to set up and sell her photos at the *Nordic Lights* photo festival. All the proceeds went into the benefit account. Also a special thank you to Beltespenner who made a clothing line with Anne Marthe and Regine after being urged to do so by Line Victoria, and who donated the sales profits to the benefit account. For so long we were hoping that Regine would improve from the treatment and could use the money for a new transplant, but that didn't happen. At Regine's request, 240,000 crowns were donated to blood cancer research at the Radium Hospital; flatscreen TVs were also provided to the bone marrow transplant unit at the National Hospital; and 20,000 crowns were given to fellow cancer patient Espen Steen, who has to buy his own medications. So all the contributions were put to good use or donated to a good cause.

Thank you to the Gyldendal publishing company and editor Bjorn Olav Jahr for all his help with Regine's book.

Lastly we want to thank everyone for all their concern and supportive phone calls, emails, letters, gifts, flowers, and greetings both to us and Regine. They warmed us all. Thank you also to understanding employers and to everyone else who we know thought a lot about us.

We've been through some really intense times and there's more still ahead, but the days come and go whether we want them to or not, and you just have to try to participate in regular life again, even though it's not easy. Elise, Lasse, and I need to remember what we promised Regine before she died: that we'll take care of ourselves. Her biggest worry when she died was that the family would be torn apart. Regine recorded a voice message on my cell phone that she wanted us to listen to after she died. She said that she loved us, that we were the world's best parents, and that she couldn't have had a better childhood. She had so many great memories, and she regretted that there wouldn't be more of them. But she hoped we'd manage to enjoy life together—because that's what's important: to take care of the days you have on earth. And then she said we had to take good care of Josefine. We all have to try as hard as we can to do what she wanted. We have to be thankful for our good health, and use it to do the things we enjoy in our lives—things that aren't possible for a lot of people.

My thoughts go out to all of those struggling with serious illnesses. I really sympathize with you and know the fight you are fighting and really hope you'll win in the end; you all deserve it.

It's so sad that the most beautiful flowers are picked first, but I'm incredibly proud of having been the mother of one of them.

Julianne, Regine, and Lasse

After Regine's death, Lasse and Julianne found this poem (undated) on Regine's computer:

My path has only one direction

There are no signs

And there is no map

It's impossible to go to the left or the right

It's impossible to turn

I can only go straight ahead

But the road is crooked

It's neither light nor dark in front of me

There's fog

And no one knows what

Will be found on the other side

About the Translator

Henriette Larsen grew up in Switzerland and the U.S. speaking Norwegian at home. She has fond memories of beautiful summers (but no winters) in Norway. She earned a Bachelor's degree in French Literature from Pomona College and completed graduate coursework in French and Comparative Literature at San Francisco State University. She lives in San Francisco.

More True Stories from Zest Books

Zoo Station [A Memoir]
The Story of Christiane F.

by Christiane F.

Dear Teen Me
Authors Write Letters to Their Teen Selves

Edited by E. Kristin Anderson and Miranda Kenneally

How to Lose Everything

by Philipp Mattheis

Little Fish
A Memoir from a Different Kind of Year

by Ramsey Beyer